Rebels and Revolutionaries in North China, 1845-1945

D0932143

Rebels and Revolutionaries in North China, 1845-1945

Elizabeth J. Perry

Stanford University Press
Stanford, California

Stanford University Press
Stanford, California
© 1980 by the Board of Trustees of the
Leland Stanford Junior University
Printed in the United States of America

Cloth ISBN 0-8047-1055-4
Paper ISBN 0-8047-1175-5

Original edition 1980
Last figure below indicates year of this printing:
92   91   90   89   88   87   86   85   84   83

Original edition published with the assistance of the
National Endowment for the Humanities

For my parents, Charles E. Perry and Carey Coles Perry

Preface

As a doctoral candidate in search of a dissertation, I set out some years ago with the immodest ambition of discovering the origins of the Chinese revolution. Though scholars had focused on peasant nationalism, land reform, or the mass line to explain the success of the Communists, it seemed to me that still another factor—the age-old heritage of Chinese peasant rebellion—should also be taken into account. To be sure, elements of this theme were evident in the writings of a number of authors, but the precise linkage between traditional protest and modern revolution was as yet unspecified. Argument for a connection usually proceeded by analogy: one identified those features considered "revolutionary" in the Communist movement and then demonstrated that these had precedents in rebel uprisings some hundreds or thousands of years before. Although suggestive, such an approach seemed unsatisfactory. After all, showing that certain ideas and practices were part of a repertoire of Chinese peasant protest did not establish that revolutionaries learned from or built upon these precedents in any direct fashion. To demonstrate conscious continuity called for another method.

I decided to pursue the relationship between rebels and revolutionaries by means of a local area study. The design was to concentrate on a geographical region which had been the home both of a well-established tradition of peasant insurrection and of a Communist base prior to 1949. By looking at a single coherent region over time, I expected to be able to identify actual links between one uprising and the next. The area selected was Huai-pei, habitat of inveterate rebels as well as a Communist

border region during the War of Resistance. Even more promising, Huai-pei was reputedly a center for the White Lotus Society, a loose network of religious sects credited with inspiring
many an insurrection in the area. Surely, I reasoned, the local
secret society must have constituted the critical nexus between
rebellion and revolution. To test this assumption, I decided to
conduct case studies of two "traditional" Huai-pei rebellions—
the Nien and the Red Spears—and of the Communist movement in the area. Buttressed by a sizable secondary literature
which argued that the rebellions were properly understood as
White Lotus insurgencies, I was prepared to reinforce and extend this interpretation to see whether the Communists had
managed to penetrate the sectarian network and convert it to
new revolutionary ends. As I departed for field work in East
Asia, I felt confident that I had laid all the groundwork for what
political scientists are wont to term a "theory-confirming"
study—that is, the analysis of one's own case within a framework of established generalizations.

Unfortunately for these neatly laid plans, however, the primary sources encountered in Taiwan and Japan proved considerably less tractable than anticipated. Research began at the
Bureaus of Investigation and Intelligence in Taipei. Over several
months of reading through inner-party journals and reports by
Communist cadres working in Huai-pei, I grew dismayed by
repeated accounts of the tremendous *difficulties* created by the
activities of recalcitrant bandits and sectarians in the area. Persistence of a rebel tradition, it now seemed, presented more of a
barrier than a boon to modern revolutionaries. Armed with this
unsettling information, I proceeded to the National Palace
Museum, to plumb its Ch'ing archives in pursuit of the Nien.
Scores of memorials and record books later, it was painfully evident that the Nien were bandits who were remarkably free of
any religious coloration. In desperation, I turned to the Red
Spears. Happily, the newspapers, Mantetsu reports, Kuomintang archives, and eyewitness informants consulted in Tokyo
and Taipei confirmed the influence of White Lotus traditions on

Red Spear practices. Less reassuring, however, was the realization that this religious inspiration was not so significant as the simple fact that the Red Spears were a form of village self-defense, promoted and led by the rural elite. Far from a heterodox sect aiming to topple the state, the movement was essentially a conservative enterprise on the part of local notables struggling to preserve their threatened privileges.

This series of discoveries meant, of course, that my understanding both of the dynamic behind traditional rebellions and of the relationship between these and modern revolution would have to be drastically revised. My initial reaction was despair, coupled with a strong temptation to resign myself to the uniqueness of historical events. But after the depression had subsided, I began to see a certain order in the data after all, albeit not the one of my original presuppositions. Peasants were indeed mobilizing in similar ways over time, but this continuity, it now seemed, was due less to a radical White Lotus Society than to persisting realities of everyday life in the Huai-pei countryside.

Theorists of collective action argue convincingly that rebellion is constructed from ongoing patterns of group behavior. Logically then we should seek the roots of peasant mobilization in more mundane rural activities. It was with this thought in mind that I began to sift through local gazetteers and Chinese and Japanese socioeconomic surveys of the Huai-pei area. Only after developing a clearer picture of the context and configuration of peasant life could I expect to explain either the recurrence of traditional rebellion or its peculiar resistance to revolutionary transformation.

The book that follows is my answer to these puzzles—an answer quite different from the set of assumptions with which the dissertation research began. My work has retreated from the "theory-confirming" study I had anticipated to what is known in the discipline as a "hypothesis-generating" study—or, in plain English, a study that raises as many questions as it answers. Most notably, perhaps, the book raises questions about the form of peasant behavior in other settings. How, for example, might different environments have engendered distinct patterns of peasant action, bearing a relationship to the revolution quite unlike that of Huai-pei? Regrettably, ecological variation is not a part of this particular research design; quite frankly, I failed to recognize the critical importance of such considerations until the final stages of work. My hope is that other scholars will step in to provide the necessary comparisons, so that one day we may truly understand the origins of the Chinese revolution—in all its wondrous complexity.

It is a pleasure to acknowledge the many individuals and institutions that have contributed to this study. The members of my doctoral committee—Michel Oksenberg, Norma Diamond, Albert Feuerwerker, and Allen Whiting—provided encouragement at all stages of the project. Others who merit special thanks for a critical reading of the manuscript in various forms of revision include Ch'en Yung-fa, Bruce Cumings, Jack Dull, Robert Entenmann, Fritz Gaenslen, Thomas Gottschang, Roy Hofheinz, Philip Huang, Harry Lamley, K. C. Liu, Ramon Myers, Susan Naquin, Robert Netting, James Palais, Carey Perry, Andrea Sankar, Charles Tilly, Robert Weiss, Ernest Young, and especially Kathleen Durham, William Durham, Joseph Esherick, Robert Somers, and Andrew Walder. Although probably none of these individuals would agree entirely with all of the arguments of this book, their thoughtful suggestions have helped immensely in improving the presentation.

In seeking to understand an extremely complicated time and place in the Chinese experience, I am greatly indebted to the wisdom of numerous persons much closer to that experience than I. Sincere thanks are due to the former residents of Huai-pei who gave freely of their time and memories to recollect the traditions of their native locale. I also owe a major debt to the many Chinese scholars who provided research direction and who discussed (and criticized) aspects of this study. Special acknowledgment is due to Ch'en Hua for long and informative exchanges on the Nien, to Liu Shih-chi for aid in the use of local gazetteers, and to Hu Ying-fen for help in deciphering palace memorials and other primary sources.

In many of my sources it is not clear whether such place names as I-hsien and Feng-yang refer to counties or their county seats, and there is the further complication that when a county seat is also a prefectural seat it is known in the first context as, say, Shouhsien and in the second as Shou-chou. At the risk of puzzling readers with a strong English or American sense of the difference between counties and towns, I have made no particular effort to distinguish between counties and their county seats except where this distinction is both clear in my source and useful to make. At the further risk of violating a long-established Western idiom, I have carried this amalgamation of town and county names to the point of permitting one-syllable town names. Thus "Shou" in my text may stand for either the county sometimes rendered as Shou Hsien or the town normally rendered on Western maps as Shouhsien and sometimes referred to by the Chinese as Shou-chou. On my map of the Huai-pei area, where dots clearly stand for towns and not counties, I have used the conventional Shouhsien.

The directors and staffs of the following institutions contributed crucial research assistance: Academia Sinica (Nankang), Bureau of Intelligence (Taipei), Bureau of Investigation (Taipei), Institute of International Relations (Taipei), Kuomintang Archives (Taichung and Taipei), National Palace Museum (Taipei), Tōyō Bunka Kenkyūjo (Tokyo), and Tōyō Bunko (Tokyo).

Financial support was provided by a foreign area fellowship of the Social Science Research Council, a Rackham predoctoral fellowship from the University of Michigan, and a grant from the Graduate School Research Fund of the University of Washington.

E. J. P.

Contents

Rebels and Revolutionaries in North China, 1845-1945

1. Introduction

Why do some peasants rebel?* Scholars have argued at length over issues of peasant personality, class identity, social organization, and political proclivities. Yet any search for universal answers must bow before the undeniable fact that only *some* peasants rebel. Furthermore, only in certain geographical areas does rebellion seem to recur frequently and persistently. Students of China have long recognized the importance of regional differences in rebel behavior. Although China lays claim to an exceptionally ancient and colorful history of rural insurgency, the turmoil tended to cluster in particular geographical pockets. The bandits of the Shantung marshes, the pirates off the Fukien Coast, the brigands of the Shensi hinterland—all are local figures of long-standing fame. Yet despite widespread recognition of the existence of local traditions, very little scholarship has been directed at solving the mystery of why particular regions tended consistently to produce such patterns.

This book seeks to answer the question of why peasants rebelled for one key area of China: Huai-pei, site of the first recorded popular uprising in Chinese history and of countless subsequent rebellions down through the ages. By examining a century of rural violence in one notably rebellious region, the

*The term *peasant* here refers to a rural cultivator living within a state system, the fruits of whose labor go primarily for family consumption, rather than for marketing. Since the household is the basic accounting unit in a peasant society, members of a household whose basic livelihood is derived from agricultural work are referred to as peasants, even though many of these individuals engage regularly in nonfarming occupations to augment household incomes. (Numeral superscripts refer to the Notes, pp. 274–93, used primarily for source citations.)

study is designed to explore the long-term causes of recurring peasant insurrection.

To date, most theories of peasant revolt have addressed themselves primarily to one question: how has it happened that traditionally isolated and impotent peasants—the "sack of potatoes" as Marx so vividly characterized them—have in recent years managed to take center stage in the making of revolution? Starting from a view of the traditional peasant as weak and disorganized, the theories have naturally tended to emphasize the role of outside persons and forces in permitting revolutionary breakthrough. Although the argument may help considerably to explain the emergence of modern revolution, it does not shed much light on the causes of earlier rebellions, tending to dismiss traditional peasant protest as "spontaneous, anomic, irrational," and the like.* This book takes issue with such a view of rural rebellion and proposes an alternative interpretation of traditional peasant insurrection as a sustained, structured, and sensible form of collective action. The analysis focuses upon the rural inhabitants themselves, emphasizing the adaptive value of peasant violence for coping with the local environment they inhabit.

Anthropological conceptions of the peasantry, though varying in detail, virtually all agree that peasants must be defined relationally with respect to (1) the wider sociopolitical world and (2) the particular natural base on which they make their living. As Eric Wolf has pointed out, "The existence of a peasantry involves not merely a relation between peasant and non-peasant, but a type of adaptation, a combination of attitudes and activities designed to sustain the cultivator in his effort to maintain himself and his kind."[1] Most theories of peasant rebellion have centered their attention on the first relation—the links between peasant and overlord—relegating the ecological question to a

*The term *revolution* will be used here to refer to a violent process that both envisions and achieves rapid political, social, economic, and cultural transformation. *Rebellion*, by contrast, refers to the much more common phenomenon of organized protest against the government—without any stipulation as to ideology, class consciousness, or political success.

distant second place. When we recall, however, that rebellion tends to be concentrated in certain geographical areas, the importance of the natural setting is immediately apparent.

In certain environments, the most adaptive strategy for survival may well be collective violence. The functional significance of human aggression has been noted by several anthropologists and human ecologists who point out that, under conditions of scarcity, violence against fellow competitors is often a rational strategy.* Environments where resources are in short and unpredictable supply may breed conflict as a way of life. Denial of essentials to others is seen as contributing directly to one's own chances for survival.†

Huai-pei, as Chapter 2 will document, was an exceptionally harsh habitat. Repeated ravages of flood and drought created a difficult and insecure milieu in which aggressive survival strategies flourished. For the most part, these forms of collective violence can, I propose, be categorized into two modal types. The first method of survival, termed the *predatory strategy*, entailed illegally expanding the resources of some members of the community at the expense of others. It ranged from theft, smuggling, and banditry to organized feuds. The reaction against such assaults, the *protective strategy*, was an effort to preserve

---

*Durham, 1976; Harris, 1975, 1977; Rappaport, 1968; Vayda, 1976. For the purposes of this book, *survival* is defined as the maintenance of oneself and one's family at a minimum level of food and shelter. *Adaptive behaviors* are those which enhance one's ability to survive in a particular environment. *Resources* are material goods that further survival capacity (such as land, tools, crops, money, and guns). *Competition* is an attempt to seize or withhold resources in such a way as to reduce their availability to others.

†The unpredictable environment must usually be coupled with a certain level of population size and stability to induce violent competition. In hunting-gathering societies where game and vegetable foods are scattered, the scant population is mobile and often quite free from conflict. Only when the environment allows the build-up of a larger and more settled population is competition common.

Much of the ecological thinking on this question has unfortunately been heavily colored by a stress on system stability in which warfare is explained as a homeostatic device to maintain a favorable equilibrium between population and resources. Although collective violence may in fact have this end result, its origins are best explained at the level of individuals and groups, rather than the ecosystem as a whole.

one's belongings in the face of predatory threat. Under this rubric were included crop-watching, private vigilantes, village militia, and the construction of fortified communities.

As Chapter 3 will explain, both the predatory and protective strategies were adaptive solutions to the problem of attaining and retaining hold over precarious resources. These were rational means that villagers used to maximize gain and minimize risk in a situation where alternative opportunities were extremely limited. Since these were essentially strategies for enhancing and ensuring a livelihood, they were adopted differentially according to one's access to resources. The predatory strategy was typically undertaken by people with few material possessions, who had less to forfeit and more to gain by this high-risk behavior. Predators used their one asset—surplus labor—to seize a livelihood from more affluent neighbors. The protective response, by contrast, was generally led by those who had both something to lose and the wherewithal to defend it. Surplus resources were put to use by protectors to safeguard their possessions against the threat of predatory plunder.

A very rough notion of social class—or relation to the means of production—helps to account for reliance on one as opposed to the other of these two modal strategies. In the context of a peasant society, where land constitutes the most prized resource, we would expect predatory behavior to be more common among the landless and protective measures to be more typical of landowners. Historical reality is, however, a good deal more complex than such a hypothesis might suggest. In the first place, peasants do not adopt collective strategies as individuals, but rather as families, clans, villages, and so forth. Then, to complicate matters further, these larger units do not act as simple sums of the individuals involved. Their behavior is shaped by considerations of leadership, group cohesion, past experience, and outside intervention. Such factors have a decisive impact on the extent to which different social groups are actually willing and able to mount an effective predatory or protective strategy.

Thus, although the model begins with a picture of individual peasants competing for scarce resources, it admits the importance of kinship, patron-client ties, and other communal allegiances in determining the degree and manner in which the struggle was conducted. Social structure exerted a critical and complex impact on the pattern of collective violence. Not all poor tenants were predatory bandits, just as not all landlords were protective militiamen. Higher-order collectivities defined the membership, and often the ideological justification, of group survival strategies.

Although the predatory-protective dichotomy is intended to focus attention on the fundamental issue of resource competition, it is important to note that the struggle was pursued with varying degrees of ideological awareness and concern for justice. Some predatory outfits were "social bandits," robbing the rich to assist the poor; others plundered indiscriminately and demonstrated no social conscience in distributing their loot. Likewise, some protective activities were conducted in an egalitarian manner and justified by appeals to traditional community rights, whereas others were organized in an authoritarian fashion to serve the interests of a single powerful landlord. These differences were of course a major factor in deciding the fates of particular predatory and protective movements. Still, such variation should not obscure the underlying connection of all these movements to the ongoing struggle for survival in a formidable environment.

While, during the century under consideration, some level of organized violence was a constant feature of the Huai-pei scene, at certain critical times the fighting intensified dramatically. Natural catastrophe was a major stimulus to increased predation and protective response. Invasion by outside forces—whether rebels, warlords, or foreign armies—also gave rise to heightened local competition. Although government concern for Huai-pei was ordinarily minimal, when violence reached an unacceptable level it would elicit state repression. Government intervention, if matched by recalcitrant local leadership, was a catalyst for rebellion, turning endemic forms of collective action into vehicles for antistate revolt.

Chapters 4 and 5 present case studies of two massive insurrections that developed in the confluence of ecological and political crisis in Huai-pei: the Nien Rebellion of the mid-nineteenth century and the Red Spears of the early Republican period. The movements are interpreted as outgrowths of the two modal strategies of peasant survival in the area. The Nien are shown to have emerged from the predatory behavior—smuggling, banditry, feuds—endemic to this unruly border region. By contrast, the Red Spears illustrate the protective reaction against just such activities. Led for the most part by rich peasants and landlords, and based on the concept of village defense, the Red Spears developed as the conservative antithesis to predatory aggression.

An ecological approach offers a new perspective on the study of Chinese peasant rebellion. Although informative monographs have been written on several specific Chinese uprisings, we lack a useful body of theory to integrate these various cases. Rich in empirical detail as the monographs are, the many idiosyncrasies of any particular rebellion have tended to inhibit efforts at formulating general hypotheses on the causes of peasant involvement. Conventional wisdom has held simply that it was the presence of secret societies—the White Lotus in the North, the Triads in the South—that contributed to any enduring patterns of insurgency. In keeping with this view, the two movements chosen here as examples of traditional revolt in Huai-pei, the Nien and Red Spears, are commonly interpreted as White Lotus–inspired insurgencies.[2] Chapters 4 and 5 will, however, raise questions about this interpretation, asking whether secret-society influence may not have been less significant than the fact that the two movements represented contrary solutions to fundamental dilemmas of peasant survival. By locating the origins of rebellion in ecological circumstances, one is encouraged to bridge the gap between "event studies" of unique uprisings and "local area studies" of enduring socioeconomic conditions.

The ecological approach should by no means be construed as

environmental determinism; the natural setting simply provides certain limits and parameters to human activity. Peasants are often characterized as an intermediate type of rural cultivator, distinct both from primitives living in a simple exchange economy, and from farmers fully integrated into the market system.[3] On the one hand, like primitives, they are extremely influenced by the exigencies of the particular ecosystem they inhabit. On the other hand, peasants are not pure primitives unencumbered by outside forces. By definition, the peasant is a member of a state society. Although peasants may not be business entrepreneurs in the same sense as farmers, they share with the farmer a stratified political world. For this reason, the explanation of their collective violence calls for attention to this larger context. Tied into a complex social, economic, and political network, peasants may rebel not only against immediate threats to livelihood, but against perceived injustices in the wider system. And, precisely because they are members of class societies, peasants may participate not only in rebellion, but in revolution as well. They may act, in other words, not merely to replace individual politicians, but to restructure an entire social system—to transfer state control from one social class to another.

To the extent that this book succeeds in explaining why peasants rebel, it may also suggest some insights into the related question of why some peasants engage in revolution. Although traditional rebellion is often treated as an anomic phenomenon, the notion of a positive connection between a long tradition of rebellion and the potential for modern revolution is a familiar theme in general theories of peasant revolt. The structural weaknesses that facilitated endemic insurrection in premodern times are said to have enabled revolutionary breakthrough as well.[4] Scholars in the China field have also suggested that the legacy of peasant rebellion was an important ingredient in the Communists' rural success, serving both as a source of inspiration to the early revolutionaries and as a familiar frame of reference for peasants who joined the movement.[5]

Huai-pei was the home not only of countless traditional rebellions, but also of a Communist base area prior to the victory of the revolution in 1949. Chapter 6 looks at Communist mobilization in Huai-pei in an effort to assess whether the rebel tradition furthered the cause of modern revolution. The revolutionaries, we will see, elicited distinct receptions from predators and protectors—reactions which changed over time as the Communist movement itself underwent transformation.

In the case of Huai-pei, we will question whether tenacious survival strategies actually constituted the sort of rebel tradition that modern revolutionaries could easily adapt to new purposes. But the verdict on Huai-pei will by no means settle the issue. If it is recognized that peasant insurgency originated and persisted more as a response to local conditions than as a direct challenge to state authority, regional variations assume central importance. For the argument is that any lasting pattern of collective violence was quite likely an adaptation to the parochial setting—one which could be variously hostile or hospitable to revolution depending upon its particular content.

We would expect in peasant societies, with livelihood so immediately dependent upon soil and climate, that natural conditions would assume a greater importance than may be true in other contexts. As Chapter 7 will note, a stress on the environmental background invites comparison with other similar areas, both within the diverse Chinese empire and beyond. Nevertheless, the contention here is not that a given environment leads automatically to a certain form of rebellion or revolution. Subsequent chapters deal with the complex and contingent intermediate links involved in adaptive survival strategies. Although many of the particulars described may be unique to the Huai-pei area, it is hoped that the theory and method of analysis will be more generally applicable to peasant societies elsewhere.

In sum, the main contribution of an ecological approach lies in its ability to account for enduring *traditions* in certain geographical areas. The perspective is a long-term one that stresses the continuity over time of broad patterns of peasant violence. As such, the approach does have inherent limitations which should be identified at the outset. On the question of the timing of a particular revolt, an ecological perspective is of little predictive value. Still less can it account for the idiosyncrasies of individual rebellions, the very stuff of which colorful history is written.* Thus the approach is no substitute either for additional efforts at generalization or for detailed histories. It is admittedly a supplement, but one that promises to bring new understanding to the problems of peasant rebellion and revolution.

*One of these idiosyncrasies was the propensity of uprisings, once they developed into large-scale movements, to overstep the neat geographical boundaries drawn by the local area specialist. The lack of perfect congruence between geographical region and actual rebel movements has required that, in this study, reference sometimes be made to events outside the Huai-pei area when these were of critical importance to the evolution of a particular rebellion.

2. Prelude to Protest:
The Huai-pei Environment

Few areas of China can claim a legacy of collective violence more ancient or continuous than that of Huai-pei. Occupying the lowland territory between the Huai and Yellow rivers, Huai-pei is in the heart of China's so-called flood and famine region, an area noted for the harshness of both its geography and its people.

As early as the Chou dynasty, inhabitants of this area were known as "Huai barbarians" because of their recalcitrance in the face of repeated pacification attempts by Chou rulers. During the spring and autumn period (772–484 B.C.), the Huai River valley was the home of the states of Wu and Ch'u, regarded by members of the more northern states as bastions of belligerence. With such a reputation, it is not surprising that the area was the site of the first great popular revolt in Chinese history, the uprising of Ch'en She in 209 B.C. The rebellion, which helped to topple the mighty Ch'in empire, was directed almost entirely by men from the Huai region. Rebel leader Liu Pang, a peasant from what is now northwest Kiangsu, founded the Han dynasty, which persisted for some four hundred years. Repeated disturbances throughout the Han (209 B.C.–A.D. 219) led the historian Ssu-ma Ch'ien to characterize the people of this area as "proud, unruly and fond of making trouble."[1]

This well-known propensity for violent resistance was demonstrated in the antiforeign struggles of the early Chin (265–316) and Southern Sung (1127–1279), when the Huai valley area played a key role in repulsing outside invasion. Significantly, opposition to Mongol rule (1277–1367) was also centered in this region. Northern Anhwei provided hundreds of thousands of recruits to form the Red Turban Army which brought down the Yüan dynasty. Chu Yüan-chang, leader of this peasant army and founder of the Ming (1386–1644), was himself a native of northern Anhwei. Thus, in the closing years of the dynasty, the Huai valley was where Ming loyalists chose to make their last stand against the Manchu invaders. Throughout the Ch'ing (1644–1911) and Republican (1912–49) periods, the area continued to be a staging ground for countless rural upheavals.

How does one explain this impressive record of protest? What was it about Huai-pei that sent generation after generation of peasants down the path of rebellion and resistance? Behavior that endures for centuries is not easily dismissed as sporadic or ephemeral. Rather, endemic peasant violence may well represent an extension of activities designed to permit and promote survival in a given environment. That environment is, of course, a product of both natural features and human action. Indeed, it is the relationship between physical setting and human modification that defines the ecology of particular areas.

In the case of Huai-pei, certainly part of the explanation for the persisting violence lies in the strategic geopolitical situation of the region. Forming a demarcation between South and North China, Huai-pei constituted a natural battlefield for contenders to national power. Thus it is hardly surprising that over the centuries the area should have been the site of many a military confrontation. The destruction wrought by repeated battles in turn undermined the possibility of sustained economic development, leaving the inhabitants of Huai-pei to the mercy of the unbridled natural elements.

Situated amid the raging Huai and Yellow rivers, the area demanded an effective system of water control as the sine qua non of agricultural security. Actually, northern Anhwei was the site of the earliest known large-scale irrigation project in China, the Shao Reservoir, apparently constructed in the sixth century B.C. The reservoir is said to have regulated water for some forty thousand hectares of land in its time. But the strategic military importance of the Huai valley, which provided the impetus for the remarkable project, also prevented its endurance.[2]

After the fall of the Northern Sung in 1126, the area suffered a long-term economic decline. Huai-pei's irrigation works were reduced to ruins by conflicts between Chinese and invading Jurcheds, and the region was converted into a desolate, floodprone plain.[3] The warfare destroyed the restraining dikes of the Yellow River, an event that had major consequences for the fate of the Huai River as well. Originally the Huai had flowed across Kiangsu and into the sea. When in the twelfth century the Yellow River burst its banks, it usurped this ocean route, forcing the Huai to empty instead into Lake Hung-tse on the Anhwei-Kiangsu border. Together with its tributaries, the Huai must carry off rainfall from a catchment of approximately seventy thousand square miles. The limited holding capacity of Lake Hung-tse meant that heavy rainfall produced severe flooding for the entire Huai-pei area.[4] As one observer put it, "When the snowy waters from Tibet come down in July, the result is precisely the same as when a pitcher of cream is suddenly emptied into a cup of coffee. . . . The great wheat fields of North Anhwei are converted into a veritable wilderness of water."[5]

For nearly eight centuries, the turbulent Huai and Yellow rivers were to pose enormous difficulties for agricultural development in Huai-pei.*[6] Within that long span of time, however, there were notable fluctuations in the degree of human control. Indeed, one can perceive the outlines of a "hydraulic cycle" of natural and social interaction, as rivers and people vied for the upper hand.† During much of the Ming dynasty, the rivers seem

---

*Although the twelfth century seems to mark a period of economic decline, ecological instability was an age-old problem in Huai-pei, as the table in note 6 suggests. Recent centuries have seen an increase in frequency of natural disasters.

†This idea is inspired by Pierre-Etienne Will, "Un Cycle hydraulique en Chine: La Province du Hubei du 16ème au 19ème siècles," paper presented to the Symposium on Oriental Ecological History, Paris, 1976. Will makes the interesting point that as people diked the rivers, they inadvertently created the potential for progressively more destructive floods by blocking river outlets. Since the dike-building was limited by the state of technology and finance, the rising rivers would eventually reach a breaking point.

to have been reasonably restrained. As the Korean traveler Ch'oe Pu was informed on his tour of the Huai in 1488, "There is a god . . . [who] looks like a Macacus monkey; he has a turned-up nose, high forehead, blue body, and white head. His eyes flash like lightning. The legend is that when the Great Yü channeled the waters, he bound that creature with a great rope and ordered him to live there and make the Huai flow quietly."[7] For a time, the monkey-god seems to have fulfilled his duty. However, by the seventeenth century, the waters were once again out of control. Silting had caused a dramatic rise in the height of the rivers, which then overflowed their banks in devastating floods. The bandit-rebels who stormed across Huai-pei in the closing days of the Ming dynasty were a direct reflection of the ecological disasters of the time.[8] The warfare occasioned by these rebellions, in turn, destroyed dike works and severely depopulated the area. In 1680, for example, a major Huai River flood inundated the whole of Ssu-chou city west of Hung-tse and permanently drowned it at the bottom of the lake.[9]

After the founding of the Ch'ing dynasty, a new phase in the "hydraulic cycle" was initiated. Dike repair and population resettlement began anew. To encourage land reclamation, local officials were instructed to welcome rootless persons to the Huai-pei area, without regard to their previous background. Any immigrant who registered in the *pao-chia* security system could be granted permanent rights to cultivate unclaimed lands. To survivors of the floods and fighting who already owned land in the area, the government offered seeds and draft animals as an inducement to resume production. Furthermore, lands in the hardest-hit regions were declared tax-exempt for several years.[10]

For more than a century, the people of Huai-pei fared relatively well under the changed conditions. The rivers having unburdened their excess silt in the enormous inundations of the late Ming, floods were now less disastrous in scale.* Over time,

* Although floods apparently wrought less devastation at this time, they were hardly less frequent. In the first 170 years of the Ch'ing dynasty, the Yellow River

however, the situation that had induced the late Ming catastrophes was re-created: land reclamation and a galloping demographic explosion were accompanied by extensive dike construction and the inevitable rise in the height of the rivers. By the early nineteenth century, massive flooding once again posed a major hazard for Huai-pei residents.

As water control disintegrated in the face of devastating floods and inadequate government response, inhabitants were once again exposed to the full brunt of nature's tyranny.

The major reason for the frequent floods was the heavy load of silt that the Yellow and Huai rivers carried in relation to their volume. Swollen by their burden of loess soil* from the western highlands, both rivers stood considerably higher than the surrounding countryside through which they flowed. During the late Ch'ing, with government administration on the decline, silt steadily accumulated in the river beds while officials ignored the necessary maintenance. In 1841, floods swept away dikes on the Yellow River's northern bank west of Lake Wei-shan in Kiangsu. Finally, in 1853, the river broke loose from the channel it had occupied for more than five hundred years and commenced a disastrous move north. Whereas previously the Yellow River had entered the sea from the coast of Kiangsu Province, its new outlet was at a point in Shantung some 250 miles to the north.[11] Widespread flooding left millions of victims in its wake.

For the next century, Huai-pei inhabitants lived literally at the mercy of the restless rivers. As a poem of the late Ch'ing period recorded:

> Pitiful Huai people—victims of flood.
> Our temples have been inundated and our ancestral
> tombs deluged.

---

alone had thirty-nine major inundations, thereby averaging a flood once in nearly every four years (Shen Ping, 1960, pp. 31–34).

*Loess is a yellowish gray soil composed of very fine-grained and loosely compacted loam. Cliffs formed by loess deposits are highly susceptible to erosion.

Our houses are like fish swimming in a stewpot.
The old peasant planning a dike shoulders his bamboo
   baskets of dirt.
His feet torn, his hands blistered, he ceases not his labor.
Muddy waters reach his waist; grass covers his stomach.
He draws water, yet the waters refuse to subside,
Rising, in a single night, four to five feet.
Good fortune brings abundant green seedlings.
But suddenly the fields become white waves.
Alas, why is the river god so unkind?
Raise high your head and cry to heaven.
But heaven answers not.
We cannot wait for the rivers to clear;
We pray only that the dikes will hold.
The merit of those who control the rivers will be engraved
   upon tablets of jade.[12]

The Republican period saw a continuation of the calamities. In 1911 the American Red Cross estimated that Huai-pei was subject to some form of natural catastrophe at least once every three or four years.[13] For the next two decades, the Huai River regularly exploded in enormous floods. The magnitude of the disasters wrought by these inundations is shown in Table 1.

The mid-nineteenth-century change in the Yellow River's course was actually the eighth time in recorded history that the river had undergone a major shift. In 1938, the river moved south again—this time by human design. Chiang Kai-shek had ordered the blasting of the dikes in a futile attempt to prevent the Japanese forces from advancing south. Once more the Yellow River reclaimed its former Huai-pei route, and in the process flooded at least forty-four counties, killing 900,000 people and turning some 3.9 million others into homeless refugees.*

The return of the Yellow River also had the effect of raising Lake Hung-tse by more than a meter. In the expanded marshy

---

*Frederic Wakeman, Jr., *The Fall of Imperial China* (New York, 1975), p. 18. Ch'en Ch'iao-i (1952, p. 36) gives the following casualty statistics for the 1938 flood: 17 million *mou* of inundated land; 1.5 million destroyed houses; 500,000 drowned animals; 470,000 human deaths; 6.1 million refugees. Hu Huan-hung (1952, p. vi) presents the following figures: 64 flooded counties with 14 million *mou*; 500,000 human deaths; 5 million refugees.

Table 1. Casualties Caused by the Huai River, 1916–31

Year	No. of victims	Amount of flooded land (mou)	Damage (silver yüan)
1916	3,009,456	21,774,120	93,499,345
1921	7,693,415	49,729,680	215,163,074
1926	3,129,573	18,157,693	92,097,730
1931	20,024,508	77,741,208	564,261,330

Source: Ch'en Ch'iao-i, 1952, p. 31.

swampland along the shores of the overflowing lake, dense grasses soon sprouted. The grassy areas then became a breeding ground for locusts, adding yet another scourge to the life of the Huai-pei peasantry.*

In sum, interactions between people and nature rendered Huai-pei a highly precarious ecosystem. During the century under consideration (1845–1945), nature wielded the upper hand. It was in the context of this harsh and fickle environment that age-old strategies of adaptive behavior assumed renewed importance.

GEOGRAPHY

Huai-pei, broadly defined, is the region north of the Huai River, from its source in central Honan to the Yellow Sea, some 650 miles away (see Map 1). Comprising about 40 percent of the Huai River delta, the area includes approximately 100,000 square kilometers of eastern Honan, southwestern Shantung, northern Anhwei, and northern Kiangsu.[14] More narrowly conceived, Huai-pei is often defined as limited to the northernmost parts of Anhwei and Kiangsu provinces, or simply north Anhwei alone. Whether broadly or narrowly conceived, Huai-pei is a sizable geographical area. This naturally implies a certain diversity

*Ch'en Ch'iao-i, 1952, pp. 36–37. Locust plagues often followed on the heels of flooding. As an adaptive mechanism, when locust nymphs mature in a crowded environment, they develop into the swarming, rather than sedentary, form. By reducing breeding areas, floods apparently gave rise to hordes of swarming locusts.

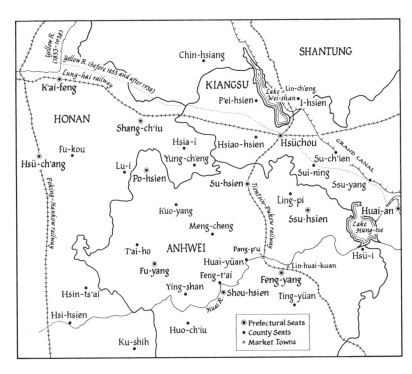

Map 1. Huai-pei

within the region as a whole. Even so, there are cogent reasons for treating the entire area as a coherent socioeconomic unit. The terrain is basically similar, a common language is spoken, and the same crops are generally grown throughout the region.

Huai-pei is a part of the loess region of China, which stretches from Shansi in the west, across Honan, western Shantung, and northern Anhwei and Kiangsu provinces. Loess soil, gradually being removed from the eroding highlands south of the Great Wall, was carried along by the Huai and Yellow rivers to its final destination in the sea. The North China Plain formed a way station for this transient soil. In ancient times, Huai-pei was apparently one great lake on which alluvium and loess were subsequently deposited by the Yellow and Huai rivers.[15] Today most of the surface layer of the Huai-pei plain is loessic alluvium—silt from the highlands brought down to the plain by the rivers and here deposited together with coarser sand and pebbles. Although loess soil has a capillary capacity that enables soluble minerals hidden deep within to rise to the top, this property of self-fertilization operates only when matched by an adequate water supply.

In good years, loess could enable agriculture to support a surprisingly large number of people on the North China Plain. As Ho Ping-ti has stated, "In retrospect, it was largely nature, specifically loess, that from the very beginning shaped the self-sustaining character of the northern Chinese agricultural system."[16] Yet a price was paid for this soil: the frequent flooding of the rivers, swelled by their heavy loads of highland silt.

Popular jingles from the area abound with ironic references to the frequency of natural calamity. In the words of one flower drumsong from Feng-yang County, sung by flood victims as they traveled to other places to beg for a living:

> Speaking of Feng-yang,
> Boasting of Feng-yang;
> Basically Feng-yang's a fine old place.
> Ever since the glorious Ming emperor,
> Ten years have brought nine of famine![17]

These famines, according to the gazetteer of Kuo-yang County, birthplace of the Nien Rebellion, were caused 30 percent of the time by drought and 70 percent by floods.[18] Built up by successive layers of alluvium deposits, the terrain of all the North China Plain is virtually level. Huai-pei itself has an elevation of less than 50 meters—"flat as a billiard table," as one missionary described it.[19] The gradient to the sea is so gentle that large areas, even in the recent past, were seasonally covered with water. Inundations meant prolonged hardship because water could not easily be drained off the plain. One geographer wrote, "A bizarre though not exceptional scene . . . was to see a walled city that rose out of a broad sheet of water, and to see farmers fishing in their flooded fields outside the city walls."[20] Although in some years the plain was brown and dusty, the summer rainfall proving barely enough for its dry crops, in the late nineteenth and early twentieth centuries flooding was the principal danger.

Floods might replenish the soil with their gift of alluvial silt, but they could also cause severe damage by depositing coarse sand. Such a possibility grew increasingly likely as the eroding highlands began to lose their cover of loess and to shed underlying clay, bedrock, and sand instead.[21] As an engineer who observed a Yellow River flood in 1898 reported:

I estimated that at least one hundred square miles were turned into a sandy waste of almost absolute sterility, while over an area of two hundred square miles a deposit of more or less sterility was laid. . . . At the few places where actual examination was possible the depth (of the deposit) was from six to ten feet. . . . The river *Taotai* (officer in charge) concerned considers the average depth to have been about five feet. Now, if we adopt the figure of five feet, it is seen that the sand which was poured out of the river in a single flood was about one-fifth cubic mile (twenty-eight billion cubic feet)![22]

Although careful dike maintenance and adequate irrigation were necessary to preserve the fertility of the land, in the late Ch'ing and Republican periods the region lacked an efficient system to control its uncertain water supply. Heavy seasonal rainfall was exacerbated by land overuse to create a severe leaching problem. Soil sample experiments conducted across Huai-pei in the 1930s revealed the area as uniformly deficient in both nitrogen and phosphates, in contrast to the more northern parts of the North China Plain, where soil was considerably less depleted.[23] In the absence of regulation, topography and climate combined to produce a forbidding natural environment.

POPULATION DENSITY

The harsh geographical setting was reflected in the level of population, whose distribution paralleled topographical patterns. Although the early years of the Ch'ing brought considerable expansion to Huai-pei, by the second half of the nineteenth century a combination of warfare and natural catastrophe had notably depleted the population.

The depressed level of population persisted through the Republican period. In 1934, a survey of Anhwei found that the Huai-pei portion of the province averaged 150 to 200 people per square kilometer, in contrast to the Yangtze valley portion, with 250 to 300 people per square kilometer. Although density was quite uniform throughout Huai-pei, most of the variation that did occur could be attributed to differences in ecological security. In the area bordering Lake Hung-tse, where water works were in a state of disrepair and disasters frequent, population density was correspondingly low. Similarly, because of the continued flooding of the Huai River, settlement along its shores was sparse—a striking contrast to the situation along the more stable Yangtze. Despite the relatively moderate density of population in Huai-pei, the author of the 1934 survey noted that this was, judging from the extreme poverty, the one part of the province where population had exceeded productivity.[24]

A parallel situation existed in neighboring Kiangsu. The northern section included some three-fourths of the total land area of the province, but it supported a mere one-third of the population. Yet in spite of this low density, peasants from the north migrated south in search of seasonal or permanent employment.[25] A similar discovery for the winter wheat–kaoliang region as a whole was made by John L. Buck. Population density, when computed as a function of cultivated land, was shown to be lower in this area than in any other region in the country. Despite this apparently favorable population-land ratio, however, Buck noted that, in relation to high-quality *resources* (defined by agricultural productivity), the density was extremely great. Consequently the people of the region were forced to migrate en masse or leave as individual bandits and soldiers.[26]

Although the population of Huai-pei was sparsely distributed by national standards, such dispersion was the result of ecological insecurity and did not imply prosperity for the inhabitants of the area. Low density in turn depressed the potential for agricultural growth. As Ester Boserup has pointed out, cultivation systems are largely a reflection of population density. Where density is low, intensification of agriculture is unlikely.*

CROPPING PATTERNS

The combination of natural and social handicaps limited the form of Huai-pei agriculture. To begin with, the severity of soil and weather restricted the types of crops that could be successfully cultivated in the region. Only the hardiest plants could flourish in the sandy deposits left by floods. Likewise, only the sturdiest of crops could withstand the harsh climate. Temperatures in the area dropped from the 90s during summer to 10 degrees Fahrenheit in winter, with frost covering the ground about half the year.[27]

Like the rest of the North China Plain, Huai-pei topography was marked by depressions of varying sizes which became lakes in the summer, and were therefore popularly known as "lake-

*Ester Boserup, *The Conditions of Agricultural Growth* (Chicago, 1965), p. 41. Boserup (p. 117) argues that cultivation systems are best explained not as adaptations to natural conditions, but as a result of population density. In Huai-pei, where density was itself a reflection of natural circumstances, this distinction is difficult to draw.

lands," but which generally dried up early enough in the fall to permit the sowing of winter wheat. Wheat was planted just after the recession of floods and harvested before the onset of the heavy summer rains. It was supplemented by other durable crops. Kaoliang, or sorghum, was the major spring crop in Huai-pei, favored for its resistance to drought and flood. Soybean, another sturdy plant, was the chief summer crop.[28]

In 1939 about 65 percent of the total cultivated land in north Anhwei was planted in winter wheat. Since crop rotation was prevalent, soybeans were also grown on 51 percent of the farmland. Sorghum was planted on nearly one-quarter of the cultivated area.[29] The total output of the three principal crops fluctuated widely from year to year in response to weather conditions. Despite these variations, however, a roughly similar pattern of production obtained over time.[30] Wheat consistently provided the most output, soybean was second, and kaoliang third. This ranking of crop output, judging from the general descriptions of local gazetteers, may be said to have held for the nineteenth century as well. Naturally, the exact proportions varied over time and from place to place. Counties with relatively low population density, and commensurately low market demand, tended to grow less wheat and more sorghum, for instance. Places adjacent to rivers and lakes also cultivated more sorghum because of its resistance to flooding.[31]

Village cropping patterns are illustrated by the case of Yang-chia-kang, a fifty-three-household village in Anhwei's Feng-yang County. The community's main crop was wheat, of which 500 piculs were grown in 1940. Soybean was the next major crop, with 450 piculs of annual yield. However, since sorghum production was very low (only 50 piculs), about 70 percent of the soybean harvested was sold in order to purchase kaoliang. Normally the village would acquire 100 piculs of sorghum annually in this manner, although when the wheat crop was poor such purchases might soar to over 300 piculs. For home consumption, the village also grew in an average year 50 piculs of barley, 30 of green beans, 8 of rice, 6 of sesame, and 5 of peas.[32]

Table 2. Agricultural Seasons in Huai-pei

Crop	Plowing	Planting	Mid-plowing	Harvest
Wheat	September	September	—	May
Soybean	May	May	June	August–October
Sorghum	late February	March	March	July

Sources: *Chiang-su-sheng nung-yeh*, 1925, p. 147; Ida Saburo, 1940, p. 203.

For the region as a whole, a general pattern of crop rotation prevailed. Each year after autumn harvest about 60 to 70 percent of the land was planted with wheat. The remainder lay fallow until the next spring, when it would be planted in sorghum. Sorghum is an economically inefficient crop, with a low weight yield, long in stalk and short on edible grain. In Huai-pei, however, sorghum stalk provided the major source of fuel. For this reason, some 20 to 30 percent of the area was planted with the crop. On land where wheat was grown, after harvest nearly 90 percent was replanted in soybean. The rest grew maize, sweet potatoes, legumes, millet, sesame, and other assorted crops.[33]

The dry-cropping that prevailed in Huai-pei was an extensive form of agriculture. Whereas the intensive wet rice cultivation of South China required an average of 192.7 days of human labor per hectare, the wheat crop of Huai-pei necessitated only from 31.1 to 34.1 days of human labor.[34] Again, unlike the South's growing season Huai-pei's was short. The annual schedule for the three principal crops was generally as shown in Table 2.

Agricultural work was thus concentrated in the fall, spring, and summer. Then from November until late February, peasants were basically free of farm work. Although at planting and harvest time able-bodied people could find ample employment, for a full one-third of the year no farming to speak of was carried out. The labor surplus that resulted from this four-month period of agricultural slack had critical consequences for the shape of collective action in Huai-pei. Faced with a dearth of alternative means for augmenting their agricultural income, idle peasants often resorted to violence to gain needed resources.

AGRICULTURAL OUTPUT

The necessity for a supplemental income was to some extent a function of agricultural productivity during the remainder of the year. If ordinary output was high, then the need for additional resources was of course less pressing. The information is sketchy, yet evidence points to a rather low level of agricultural productivity. According to a 1940 study of northern Anhwei, which notes that the year reported (1939) was a bountiful harvest, yields averaged 0.78 piculs per *mou* for wheat, 0.39 piculs per *mou* for sorghum, and 0.66 piculs per *mou* for soybean.[35] This is considerably below the averages cited by John L. Buck for the winter wheat–kaoliang region as a whole between the years 1929 and 1933. When Buck's figures are converted from bushels and acres into piculs and *mou*, a sizable discrepancy is found between northern Anhwei and the wider region. Average yield per *mou* of wheat in the winter wheat–kaoliang region is said by Buck to be 0.9 piculs, for kaoliang it is 1.2 piculs, and for soybeans 0.9 piculs[36] (see Table 3).

A major cause of depressed productivity in Huai-pei was the absence of effective irrigation. Without a means of controlling the naturally variable water supply, Huai-pei peasants could not count on high or stable yields. Buck's survey shows that in the winter wheat–kaoliang region, irrigated land had wheat yields of 1.0 picul per *mou*, in contrast to the 0.7 average on nonirrigated fields.[37] In addition to raising the output of existing crops by blunting the effects of flood and drought, a functioning system of water works would have permitted a greater diversity of crops.

A number of Huai-pei gazetteers mention the existence of wet rice cultivation in the distant past and its disappearance with the subsequent breakdown of the irrigation system. The gazetteer of I County in south Shantung records that in ancient times the local inhabitants had an effective canal system for watering the fields, garnering a sizable rice harvest each year. By the twentieth century, however, not a single fragment of this once exten-

Table 3. Yield of Major Crops, North China
and Northern Anhwei, 1929–39
(piculs per mou)

Crop	Winter wheat–kaoliang region, 1929–33	Northern Anhwei, 1939
Wheat	0.9	0.78
Sorghum	1.2	0.39
Soybeans	0.9	0.66

Sources: J. L. Buck, 1964a, pp. 224–25; Kōain, 1940, pp. 14–17.

sive irrigation network remained.[38] T'ung-shan County in the Hsüchou district of Kiangsu was apparently famous for nonglutenous rice during the Han and Northern Wei dynasties (third century b.c. to third century a.d.). The decline of irrigation works, however, led to the abandonment of this high-yield crop. By Ming times a censor visiting the region reported that the people had all shifted to planting wheat.[39]

Evidence that Huai-pei may once have been a well-irrigated marginal rice region cautions against interpreting nineteenth- and twentieth-century agricultural patterns as permanent features, reflecting an immutable natural environment. Nevertheless, in recent centuries the Huai River has formed the demarcation line between rice-producing South China and the wheat-growing North. Lacking adequate water control, peasants turned to the cultivation of dry crops more capable of surviving obstacles of untamed soil and climate, but which yielded reduced outputs in return.

LANDHOLDING

Though the dryland farming of Huai-pei was less labor-intensive than irrigated farming, it also required more land in order to maintain a family. The normal family of five in Huai-pei needed at least thirty *mou* to support its livelihood.* Depending upon

*This calculation is based on Ramon Myers's figures for ten villages in Hopei and Shantung. There Myers found an average of twenty-five to thirty *mou* was necessary to sustain a five-person household (1970, pp. 150, 299). The basic crops

Table 4. Size of Landholdings in Northern Anhwei, 1936

Land size (mou)	Feng-t'ai County		Po County	
	Pct. of families	Pct. of land	Pct. of families	Pct. of land
0–29	84.77%	53.08%	72.26%	34.94%
30–99	14.14	38.31	24.60	46.51
100–199	1.06	8.01	2.66	13.33
200+	0.03	0.60	0.48	5.22

Source: Kuo Han-ming and Hung Jui-chien, 1936, pp. 28–29.

soil fertility, anywhere from thirty to one hundred *mou* might be necessary to sustain a household through several successive bad years of natural disaster and crop failure. The great majority of households in this area had, however, less than enough to weather the normal years, let alone the luxury of storing for future hardship. Table 4 illustrates the situation for two representative north Anhwei counties in 1936.

As these figures demonstrate, most peasant families suffered from an insufficiency of land to till. More than 84 percent of households in Feng-t'ai and 72 percent of households in Po County lacked the minimum necessary to ensure survival. Land scarcity was, however, not absolute, but socially differentiated. In Po County, for example, although less than one-third had enough land, their holdings composed nearly two-thirds of the total arable land in the county.

In some Huai-pei villages, land concentration was even more pronounced. Table 5 illustrates the discrepancy in holdings for the village of Chang-lao-chia, home of Chang Lo-hsing, leader of the Nien Rebellion. Ascertained through interviews with contemporary inhabitants of the village, the figures refer to the situation that obtained in the mid-nineteenth century. According to this retrospective survey, more than 70 percent of the village

grown in these villages were very similar to those of Huai-pei, although soil was apparently more fertile in the Yellow River region and lucrative cash cropping more common. Thus an estimate of at least thirty *mou* for Huai-pei seems reasonable.

Table 5. Landholdings in Chang-lao-chia, 1850

Land size (mou)	Families	Pct. of families	Combined landholdings (mou)	Pct. of land
0–29	19	38.8%	71	1.5%
30–99	15	30.6	717	14.5
100–199	6	12.2	670	13.5
200–700	9	18.4	3,480	70.5
TOTAL	49	100.0%	4,938	100.0%

Source: Hsiao Liu, 1959, p. 4.

land was in the hands of less than 20 percent of the families. Had land been parceled out equally to each household, every family would have had a sizable farm of a hundred *mou*. As it was, nearly 40 percent of the families had too little land to make ends meet.

In the Huai-pei portion of Kiangsu Province, every county had at least one or two households owning over 10,000 *mou* in 1933.* Such unequal distribution was particularly acute in certain villages where relatively stable ecological conditions had permitted the accumulation of surplus over time. An example of such land concentration was the village of Tuan-chuang, located south of Hsüchou in northwest Kiangsu. A 1930 survey showed that one family in the village owned 4,000 *mou*, 2 families had 2,000 *mou*, 10 owned from 40 to 80 *mou*, and the remaining 204 households had less than the minimum 30 *mou*, 10 of them owning no land at all.[40]

Landlordism was, of course, common in villages with extremely concentrated holdings. Nevertheless, on the whole, Huai-pei had a relatively low rate of tenancy. A government investigation in 1935 found that in Honan's Yung-ch'eng County only 6 or 7 percent of the peasants were tenants; in Ssu-yang,

*Chung-kuo nung-ts'un, 1971, p. 3. A similar situation existed in northern Anhwei in 1937. In Meng-ch'eng County, four households owned 100,000 *mou*; in Kuo-yang, four households owned 5,000 to 10,000 *mou*; in Po, seven households owned 1,000 to 4,000 *mou*; and in Fu-yang, sixteen households owned 3,000 to 10,000 *mou*. See Amano Monosuke, *Shina nōgyō keizai ron* [On the Chinese farm economy] (Tokyo, 1940), vol. 1, pp. 156, 167–68.

Table 6. Forms of Landholding in Northern Anhwei, 1936

Form	Pct. of families	
	Feng-t'ai County	Po County
Pure owner-cultivation	87.66%	82.01%
Combined owner-cultivation and tenancy	10.68	11.54
Pure landlordism	1.06	4.99
Combined landlordism and owner-cultivation	0.64	1.46

Source: Kuo Han-ming and Hung Jui-chien, 1936, pp. 23–24.

Kiangsu, tenants composed 15 percent of the rural population.[41] John L. Buck's survey of the greater winter wheat–kaoliang region concluded that only 1 percent of the peasants were pure tenants, although 19 percent combined tenancy with the cultivation of their own small lands. In the three Huai-pei counties of Fu-yang, Feng-yang, and Su, Buck found no pure tenants.[42] A similar absence of pure tenancy is reflected in Kuo Han-ming's survey of two north Anhwei counties, as shown in Table 6. As Kuo's findings demonstrate, the overwhelming majority of families were pure owner-cultivators who farmed only their own lands to make a living. Landless tenants were nonexistent, and those who rented lands to supplement their holdings composed only about 10 percent of the peasantry.

Low tenancy in Huai-pei was due both to the uncertain quality of the unirrigated soil and to the absence of a well-developed market system. If land was so poor that it could only maintain the cultivators on a subsistence level and no rent could be extracted, there would obviously be little incentive for prospective landlords to purchase it. Furthermore, even if the land were capable of producing some surplus, in areas where inefficient transport restricted the marketing opportunities, additional land was of limited value to landlords who had no use for the excess grain themselves and could not afford to ship it elsewhere because of high transport costs.

Low tenancy did not, however, mean economic prosperity for the peasantry of Huai-pei. As we have seen, most independent farmers owned parcels of land too small to support their families with ease. Since the opportunity to rent supplemental land was limited, these owner-cultivators were often in dire economic straits. The dilemma is illustrated by a 1940 study of a village in Feng-yang County, Anhwei. Although 84 percent of the families surveyed were found to be owner-cultivators, they averaged a mere 12.1 *mou* per household, a precarious land base for dry-cropping. Independent peasants who were also able to rent supplemental plots managed far larger amounts of land than did pure owner-cultivators. These part owner–part tenants farmed an average of 19.6 *mou* of their own land, plus 11.8 *mou* of rented land, a total of more than two and one-half times that managed by the pure owner-cultivators. However, these more fortunate peasants composed a mere 10 percent of the households surveyed.[43]

The fact that most Huai-pei peasants were not subject to rent payments thus did not imply financial security. The independent farmers were, on the whole, far from affluent. However, a relatively small number of landlords and rich peasants did have enough land to permit the use of tenants or hired workers. During the busy wheat and autumn harvests, additional labor was required by households with large holdings. Some rich peasants were able to hire one or two laborers on a yearly basis. Such workers—a kind of "rural proletariat"—were typically single males with wages barely sufficient to support one person. More commonly, laborers were employed seasonally and were seldom retained through the winter months. A holding of one hundred *mou* could usually support three hired workers during the busiest periods. The calendar for hired laborers in Huai-pei was divided into two seasons. The first hiring period was from the fifteenth day of the first lunar month to the fifteenth day of the seventh lunar month. The second hiring period ran from the end of the seventh month until the start of winter.* During the

---

*Chang Chieh-hou, 1927, pp. 72–73; Tsou Wan-chi, 1934, p. 88. In one northern Anhwei village, annual laborers in 1939 received yearly wages of 19 yüan plus meals. A temporary laborer hired during wheat harvest or soybean planting received for a week's work one yüan in wages, plus meals (Ida Saburo, 1940, p. 210).

period of agricultural slack there was thus a dearth of employment opportunities for most poor peasants.

Although tenancy was generally low in Huai-pei, there was considerable variation from village to village. Places with superior land or within easy reach of transportation tended toward more concentrated landholdings and greater numbers of tenant farmers. In Fu-yang County, Anhwei, for example, 84 percent of the peasantry were found to be owner-cultivators, and 16 percent to be tenants in 1935. Field investigations of certain villages within the county revealed a sharply contrasting picture, however. Professor Kuo Han-ming of the Nanking Central Political Institute studied several ecologically fortunate villages in southeastern Fu-yang where he discovered that tenants composed well over half the population.[44]

Tenancy, to the extent it existed in Huai-pei, was a system with little built-in security—a reflection of the uncertainty of the agricultural enterprise in this area. Contracts were usually nonexistent or of short duration. There were few formalities, most contracts being oral agreements between tenant and landlord. A deposit was seldom required and no clear limits were placed on the time period, which was left to the discretion of the landlord.[45] The contrast with the ecologically more stable South China is instructive. In the rice-growing South, where long-term security permitted planting schedules conducive to higher productivity, permanent tenure was common. In Huai-pei, by contrast, yields were less improved by such changes. Furthermore, fixed capital inputs (such as irrigation works) were less prevalent in the wheat lands. Thus long tenure, which was a means of guaranteeing such assets, was probably viewed as unnecessary by landlords in this area.

Rent arrangements also differed in the wheat and rice regions. In wet rice culture, additional increments of labor offer more payoff than is true in the cultivation of dry grains. Intensive individual effort is essential for high rice yields. As a result, rents in South China were usually defined in set quantities rather than as a percentage of the harvest. In this way, the peasant was motivated to take good care of the fields so as to increase his own incremental income. In the wheat-growing North, share renting—in which landlord and tenant jointly accept the risk of a poor harvest—was more typical.

There were four main rental arrangements in Huai-pei prior to land reform. The first, very prevalent, method was one in which the tenants who tilled the land possessed no means of production. Tools, draft animals, seeds, and even the house in which the tenant lived were all the property of the landlord. Under this arrangement, the landlord collected 60 to 70 percent of the harvest. In the second method, the tenant borrowed money from the landlord to purchase a draft animal. The tenant paid no interest on the loan but was not permitted to break tenancy before the debt was settled. From these tenants the landlord demanded 50 to 60 percent of the harvest. In the third type of arrangement, rents were paid in labor. The landlord lent the peasant four or five *mou* of land, on which he was not asked to pay rent. However, the tenant and his family were required to serve as guards for the landlord and as servants at feasts and other special occasions. This system was employed only by relatively wealthy landlords. Finally, and least common in this area, was a fixed-rent system as in South China. Because of the uncertainty of the harvest due to flood and drought, a set amount was unrealistic and was rare in Huai-pei.*

In addition to the rent paid to landlords, tenants were required to pay an annual commission to the landlord's manager. Usually a blood relation of the landlord's, the manager was responsible for deciding who would be permitted to rent the avail-

---

*Hsiao Liu, 1959, pp. 4–6. This information is based on field investigations by scholars at the Anhwei Institute of Modern History. The gazetteer of Lu-i County, Honan, provides a similar description of tenancy arrangements. It notes that when the landlord provided the tenant's house, while the tenant furnished his own animals, seeds, and tools, the harvest was divided equally between them. If the landlord supplied seeds, the tenant was allowed to keep only 40 percent of the harvest. When the landlord also furnished a draft animal, the tenant was left with 30 percent of the yield. Were the tenant to contribute nothing but his labor, he received a mere 20 percent of the harvest (*Lu-i-hsien chih*, 1896, 9/2–3).

able lands. Since land for rent was in scarce supply, the manager exerted considerable control. Tenants thus had little choice but to tender the extra fee so as to ingratiate themselves with this powerful go-between.[46]

The surplus garnered from rents provided the landlord with capital for loans to owner-cultivators in difficult straits. Often the loans were made directly in grain, rather than money. After wheat harvest, the debt would have to be repaid at the highest price of grain that year. With their small landholdings and frequent exposure to natural catastrophe, many Huai-pei peasants fell deeply in debt to local landlords.[47]

In places where land was highly concentrated, landlords who controlled enormous tracts of land were, moreover, sometimes able to maintain their prominent position for generations. Crop failure in one place could be offset by bountiful harvests in another, providing the large landowner with a wider margin of insurance against bad times than the typical owner-cultivator enjoyed. Nevertheless, there were always strong pressures working to undermine the maintenance of stable family holdings from one generation to the next. Partible inheritance, by which a family's assets were to be divided equally among all sons, tended to fragment landholdings over time. Equally important, natural disaster could reduce any but the most affluent households to sudden destitution. A few successive years of drought or flood in one locale would compel many of the victims to sell their lands to more fortunate neighbors who had escaped that particular calamity. Floods could also transform the quality of the land itself. As explained earlier, some floods replenished the soil, converting once barren plots into fertile, silted terrain. Others, however, turned formerly rich areas to sandy wasteland. The sudden ecological changes generated rapid vertical mobility among the resident peasant population.

Thus, although the basic pattern of small farms, widespread owner-cultivation, and low tenancy remained constant, the fortunes of particular households were subject to considerable flux.

Uncertain natural conditions created a general picture of rural poverty, yet the opportunities for sudden shifts in status were far greater than in ecologically more stable areas.

COMMERCIALIZATION

Commercial life in Huai-pei was, not surprisingly, quite undeveloped. To begin with, the low population density was not conducive to the growth of markets. Population dispersion increases delivery costs and thereby discourages functional specialization. Second, as economic historians have often pointed out, the key to commercialization lies in access to inexpensive and efficient transportation. Traditional Huai-pei was not noted for its transport technology. Roads were almost entirely earthen, turning into muddy ruts with the seasonal rains. Because of the poor roads, a unique kind of sledge pulled by an ox flanked by two horses was the main mode of land transport in the area. Villages located near rivers could, of course, rely on water transport to import and export commodities. Periodic flooding, however, undermined the development of stable commercial patterns.[48]

The construction of railroads in the 1920s did initiate certain changes in the patterns of Huai-pei trade. During the Ch'ing dynasty, the town of Lin-huai-kuan had served as the main market in northern Anhwei, thanks to its strategic location on the Huai River. Products were shipped in small boats along the river through Lin-huai-kuan across to Kiangsu. From there the goods were transported south via the Grand Canal. After the opening of the Tientsin-Pukow Railroad, by contrast, wheat was sent along the Huai to the market town of Pang-p'u, from where it could be transported by rail directly to the flour mills of Shanghai. Pang-p'u was thus transformed from a desolate village into a central Huai-pei market. The town saw a rapid growth of inns, warehouses, transport companies, and the like during the early Republican period. Agricultural produce from

Honan had previously also been sent by water route to Kiangsu. With the completion of the Lung-hai Railroad in 1925, most goods went by train straight from K'ai-feng to Hsüchou.[49]

The locus of long-distance trade shifted with transportation developments, but the actual volume of commercial activities in Huai-pei was low both before and after the railways. In 1928, the *Central Daily* described this area as still operating under a form of "medieval self-sufficiency." Except for streets near railroad stations, the roads were extremely primitive. Peddlers on foot and scattered roadside stands were the main mode of trade.[50] As one observer reported on a trip to Kiangsu's P'ei County in 1930:

Entering the city of P'ei is like walking into a rural village. The people are all farming. If there is someone hawking by the roadside from a cart on which is loaded some coarse material, that constitutes the clothing store. The only shops we could find were on the order of what would be considered tiny stands in the South. . . . In all of P'ei County, only some thirty stores had capital investments of more than 1,000 yüan. Adding all this capital together, one would attain the level of only a small firm in Shanghai—despite the fact that in territory P'ei is thrice the area of Wu-hsi County.[51]

Thus the trade scene had progressed little since imperial days.

Local gazetteers from the nineteenth century concur on the low level of commerce in the area. Merchants are typically described as "few, and all of them outsiders who live in the towns and are distrusted by the native peasants."[52] In Hsü-i County in northern Anhwei, stores were also said to be operated entirely by people from outside the area. Furthermore, no special local products were sold.[53] The reluctance of local inhabitants to engage in business activities continued into the twentieth century. In 1940, although only 9 percent of the population of Pang-p'u came from outside Anhwei Province, for example, these outsiders completely monopolized commerce in the city.[54]

Although commercial growth might, theoretically, have alleviated the problem of scarcity, environmental uncertainty made production for the market a risky venture. Threatened by perennial flood and drought, Huai-pei peasants were understandably reluctant to move into the world of business. Those few with sufficient capital to invest in enterprise tended to use their money to safeguard their precarious assets rather than experiment with risky innovations. Social disasters—war and banditry—were further deterrents to the growth of business. By way of illustration, take the case of the glass factory in Su-ch'ien, Kiangsu, which was started in 1910. Just a few miles outside the county, good-quality quartz was discovered. Since the town was located right on the Grand Canal, transportation seemed to pose no problem. The glass company was established with an initial outlay of 2 million taels, an unprecedented investment for Huai-pei. Capital was furnished jointly by the government and local gentry. The project appeared destined for a bright future indeed. Before long, however, serious difficulties developed. Rampant banditry in the area forced the factory to divert a considerable amount of money for a self-defense corps to provide protection. Then, with the rise of warlordism, factory buildings were converted into temporary barracks for passing troops. Ships intended to carry manufactured glass were used to transport soldiers instead. Soon the company was compelled to cease operations altogether.[55]

Lack of public security was a major impediment to commercial growth. In Po County, Anhwei, some thirty banks were in operation prior to 1925. That year, however, a major incursion of bandits from neighboring Honan Province extracted a severe toll from the local economy. By 1926, only five or six banks had resumed business.[56] Warfare was another barrier to economic development. A Japanese report noted that by 1940 annual trade in the central market town of Pang-p'u had declined 80 to 90 percent from prewar levels.[57]

This is not to say that no commercial activities were conducted in rural Huai-pei. Peddlers sold matches, oil, salt, and other daily necessities. Merchants acted as middlemen for the sale of crops, often garnering considerable profit in the process. In addition, periodic markets offered cotton, cattle, chickens, don-

keys, vegetables, firewood, and assorted sundries.[58] Cash cropping, although not nearly so developed as in other parts of
China, occurred on a small scale.

Silk and cotton were two types of commercial agriculture suitable to Huai-pei terrain and climate. Feng-yang and Feng-t'ai
counties in ancient times had been centers for silkworm cultivation. By the twentieth century, however, the area was bare of
mulberry trees, and few looms were to be found.[59] In Kiangsu's
Huai-an County, cotton had apparently been grown on a large
scale in early Ch'ing, but the endeavor had gradually declined
over time. Local officials attempted to convince the people to
resume cotton cultivation and to raise silkworms as well. They
hired teachers and provided the necessary tools to encourage
the development of a spinning industry. According to the gazetteer account, local inhabitants were, however, loath to take up
the trade.[60] Reports on the Huai-pei economy in the mid-
twentieth century also noted that little cotton was grown in the
region despite the crop's suitability to weather and terrain.[61]
This was in contrast to the Yellow River area of the North China
Plain, where cotton, tobacco, and other cash crops were rapidly
adopted after the turn of the century.[62]

Certainly success or failure in diversifying crop patterns was
to some extent a function of individual county conditions. In
Sui-ning, Kiangsu, for example, the local magistrate did manage
to promote textile production in the 1850s. A few decades later
both cotton cloth and silk were produced at considerable profit
to the local inhabitants.[63] Peanuts were also cultivated in a few
places. The crop was first introduced to Huai-an County around
1750, when farmers from Fukien and Kwangtung were hired to
instruct the Huai-an people in planting. One hundred years
later the county grew peanuts on a large scale.[64] Not until 1905
was the crop introduced to Feng-t'ai County, some two hundred
miles up the Huai River. There cultivation of peanuts brought
a good deal of profit to peasants living in disaster areas along the
river.[65] Opium was another cash crop. In Sui-ning County the
opium poppy was first planted on a large scale during the 1860s.

Although subsequently declared illegal, cultivation continued surreptitiously.[66] During the early Republican period, opium was cultivated in many parts of Huai-pei, as warlords demanded that the crop be planted and heavily taxed.

On the whole, however, cash cropping was not prevalent in this region. Under private subsistence farming, peasants are strongly predisposed toward growing enough food grains to ensure family survival, even though the land might be suitable for producing some more profitable crop. Were they to give up subsistence farming, peasants would become entirely dependent upon a market over which they could exert no control. Few are anxious to specialize in cash cropping unless the market is stable and well developed and the promised income significantly above the subsistence level.

With manufacturing virtually unknown, Huai-pei's commercial potential went unrealized. The gazetteer of Kuo-yang notes that the county had wheat which could be ground into flour, sesame and peanuts which could be crushed into oil, cotton which could be made into cloth, indigo which could be used for dye, mulberries to raise silkworms, and fruits for candies. None of these commercial possibilities was a reality, however. The only item the county exported on any significant scale was raw soybeans, transported out along the Kuo River.[67] As late as 1936, peasants in Ssu County, Anhwei, are said to have been almost entirely subsistence farmers, their very limited exports consisting only of surplus wheat, soybeans, and sorghum.[68]

Handicrafts were similarly undeveloped, owing to lack of both capital and demand. Huai-pei gazetteers describe local crafts as crude, unoriginal, or altogether nonexistent.[69] Products were for the most part limited to the coarse pottery and tools used in everyday life. Although simple and unsightly, such items as were made were durable and inexpensive. Handicraft production was not a lucrative profession, and artisans usually had also to cultivate the land in order to make a living.[70]

In short, the Huai-pei economic picture in late Ch'ing and Republican days was far from prosperous. Peasants stuck closely to the cultivation of staple grains, demonstrating little appetite for cash cropping or rural industry. With basic agriculture operating at a low level of productivity, it was only natural that commercial life should have been similarly depressed.

GOVERNMENT AND TAXES

The Huai-pei economic scene being less than prosperous, government interest in the region was commensurately slight. Lack of agricultural or commercial development meant that the area could not be expected to produce a steady surplus. An unreliable source of revenue, it attracted little attention from the state. To be sure, the government was well aware of the strategic military importance of the Huai-pei plain. Thus, during the Ch'ing dynasty, both Feng-yang and Shou counties in northern Anhwei housed government army units.[71] Such military forces could be called up in time of rebellion or invasion to protect state interests in this critical way station between North and South China. Nevertheless, this military presence did not provide security for local inhabitants. Police protection was notoriously lax, and the *pao-chia* system of household registration was poorly enforced. Huai-pei was clearly a low-priority area as far as the extension of administrative services was concerned. Government indifference toward the region was exacerbated by the fact that this was a highly fluid society in which the imposition of state control was objectively extremely difficult.

Reflecting the impoverished state of the economy, education was similarly undeveloped. Few families could afford to educate their offspring, and those with sufficient financial means usually ended up allocating the lion's share of their resources to purchase the protective services the government failed to provide. Since little money went toward education, Huai-pei produced only a small number of people capable of passing the state examinations and attaining official degrees. The dearth of gentry, in turn, reduced the informal contacts between officials and local residents that were so essential for attracting government services and ensuring peacekeeping efforts.

By national standards, land taxes in Huai-pei were light during both the late imperial and Republican periods. There were
several reasons for this state of affairs. First, of course, was the
limited productivity of the land. Even in the best of years, the
poorly irrigated fields of Huai-pei did not yield the amount of
agricultural surplus common to other regions. Second, the
founder of the Ming dynasty, Chu Yüan-chang, was a native of
the Huai-pei area. After his rise to power on the waves of peasant rebellion, Chu decreed a special tax dispensation for his
homeland. The practice of withholding taxes persisted for centuries, so that even as late as 1935 many Huai-pei counties
continued to remit at reduced rates. Finally, successive natural
disasters had also evoked periodic tax relief measures that
continued long after the immediate catastrophes were past. In
Anhwei's Shou County, for example, during the 1840s, taxes
were waived for thirty-six villages in response to severe floods.
Although the inundated lands were subsequently reclaimed, the
once stricken areas refused to resume payment.[72] Similarly,
Huai River floods in the 1850s and 1860s elicited special tax re-
ductions for lands in the most vulnerable sections along the
river. Decades later, these areas continued to remit taxes at the
reduced rate.[73] It was not easy to keep tax registers up to date
with the swift pace of ecological change. In 1855, a shift in the
course of the Huai River permitted the reclamation of some
three to four hundred thousand *mou* of land bordering Lake
Hung-tse. The new territory escaped registration, remaining entirely tax-free through the mid-twentieth century.[74]

Despite the generally modest rate of land tax, in certain
periods the burden on the peasantry was considerable. This was
certainly true in the mid-nineteenth century, when a rise in the
price of silver greatly increased the real cost of taxes.* The government required that land taxes be paid in silver, whereas any
cash the peasant received from the sale of crops was generally in

---

*In Feng-yang Prefecture, in early 1854, 2,000 *wen* of copper were exchanged
for one tael of silver, the value of silver having about doubled compared to
twenty years earlier. See Yang Tuan-liu, *Ch'ing-tai huo-pi-ping shih-kao* [A history
of currency circulation during the Ch'ing] (Peking, 1962), p. 189.

copper. Thus it was necessary to exchange the copper for silver, a transaction that worked greatly to the peasant's disadvantage as the value of silver soared with the depletion of the national treasury in the aftermath of the Opium Wars. In Huai-pei, where the great majority of peasants owned some land, an increase in taxes was an important stimulus to joint protest by landlords and freeholders alike. There is evidence that the Nien Rebellion of 1851–68 involved some antitax activity.[75]

The Republican period saw yet another major increase in the tax burden on the Huai-pei peasantry, as warlords competed with the Kuomintang regime to extract the greatest possible revenue from the countryside. Numerous surcharges were added to the land tax, pressing landlords and owner-cultivators to the point of resistance.[76] The Red Spears of the 1920s through the 1940s were in large part inspired by opposition to the exorbitant tax demands of the day.

The fact that the government presence in Huai-pei was normally rather weak fostered the development of indigenous predatory and protective strategies of survival. Banditry was feasible only because of the lack of state control, just as self-defense measures against banditry were necessitated by the absence of government protection. Nevertheless, in periods when the state endeavored to enlarge its presence by imposing higher taxes or mobilizing troops, these ongoing strategies could be activated for joint resistance struggles. In this way, government intervention played a critical role in converting preexisting forms of collective action into open rebellion.

STANDARD OF LIVING

Over the long run, the constantly changing Huai-pei terrain was what continued to attract peasants to the area. As river changes opened additional lands for cultivation and loess deposits replenished depleted soil, new economic opportunities were created. Nevertheless, although individual households might strike it rich in this roulette game with nature, for the great majority of residents the stakes were high and the winnings meager.

Most Huai-pei villages presented a picture of penury. Houses were constructed of earthen walls, the roofs consisting of several timbers over which wheat stalks were laid and then smeared with mud. In heavy rains, the mud on the roof would disintegrate, allowing water to leak through the wheat stalks and into the walls. Since peasants could seldom afford lime to mix into their earthen walls, in dry weather the walls would crack and begin to crumble. A house might have two or three rooms, one for cooking and eating and the other(s) for sleeping. Each room was lighted by a tiny window about one foot square, which faced south and was covered with paper. The houses were very dark and ventilation poor, although the lack of large windows helped insulate against weather changes. The life span of a house was about thirty years, after which the old walls and roof would be converted to fertilizer.[77] Even the houses of landlords were usually constructed of earth and thatching, although they were much more spacious, sometimes including several dozen rooms.[78] Peasants slept on beds of woven sorghum stalks. Since few households owned more than one or two quilts, on cold winter nights family members huddled together to keep warm. Less than 1 percent of the peasants could afford coal or oil for fuel; most simply burned sorghum or wheat stalks to take away the chill.[79]

Clothing was almost entirely made of cotton. Although a very few of the wealthy could afford linens in summer and furs in winter, the rest dressed in cotton trousers, jackets, and shoes.[80] Since cotton was generally neither grown nor spun in the area, a large part of the wheat harvest was exchanged to obtain the cloth. Thus, although wheat was the primary crop of the area, most peasants got a taste of it but once or twice a year.[81]

The staple foods were sorghum and soybeans, supplemented by sweet potatoes and a few other vegetables. In warm weather peasants ate their frugal meals squatting outdoors; on cold or rainy days they sat indoors on piles of sorghum stalks. Three meals were prepared on work days; during periods of agricultural slack, one or two meals a day sufficed. Only the well-to-do consumed wheat noodles as a staple food throughout the year, supplementing this with regular meat and fish dishes. For the majority of peasants the diet was bland and restricted, dwindling to almost nothing in years of natural disaster.[82]

The combination of poor diet and lack of sanitation contributed to widespread health problems. Latrines were simply large open pits covered with a plank and walled in by sorghum stalks. Well water was often polluted. Eye and skin diseases were chronic, and seasonal epidemics of smallpox, cholera, influenza, and malaria were common. In one northern Kiangsu village, incomplete statistics reveal that in 1942 at least 16 percent of the population was suffering from a serious illness. Little in the way of medicines, and almost no trained doctors, were available to provide relief. In the case of acute sickness, the local shaman might be summoned to exorcise the demon believed responsible for the ailment.[83]

Although belief in the power of the other world was strong, regular religious ceremonies were seldom elaborate. Not surprisingly, the river and earth gods were major objects of worship, but festivals were usually marked simply by the burning of paper money. Temple fairs generally took place just after the lunar new year and before the start of the new agricultural cycle, and were as much an opportunity to buy and sell animals and tools as an occasion for religious worship.[84]

The standard of living was barely above minimal subsistence for most Huai-pei inhabitants.* Although a small minority of residents managed to end the agricultural year with a respectable surplus, little of this extra wherewithal was invested in cultural activities or productive enterprises. Fearful that natural

---

*A 1935 government investigation concluded that in Huai-pei even a well-off family with 50 mou would have had a hard time making ends meet. In a normal year, income would be about 225 yüan, whereas expenditures would amount to 256 yüan: 117 for food, 57 for clothing, 20 for weddings and funerals, 15 for fertilizer, 10 for house rent or repairs, 10 for education, 9 for taxes, 3 for medical costs, and 15 for miscellaneous expenses (Nung-ts'un shih-k'uang pao-kao).

calamity or human competitors might do away with their margin of safety, the affluent put much of their surplus capital into the development of defensive measures. By contrast, those whom a disastrous harvest plunged below the threshold of subsistence set their sights on the grain stores of the well-to-do as a strategy for survival.

HUAI-PEI PEASANT MENTALITY

Theories of personality have constituted a common theme in much of the anthropological literature on peasants. Most Western scholarship has emphasized the traditional quality of peasant thought and action. Robert Redfield put forward the classic statement of this view, contending that "in every part of the world, generally speaking, peasants have been a conservative factor in social change, a brake on revolution."[85] Charles Erasmus proposed the term *encogido syndrome* to characterize peasant attitudes as timid, withdrawn, and resistant to change.[86] Since Erasmus does not locate the source for these attitudes in the outside environment, one gets the impression that peasants are somehow plagued with a peculiar mentality that inhibits normal personality growth. Similarly, George Foster describes the peasant as holding an "image of the limited good" that sees resources as scarce and irreplaceable, such that one person's gain is the other's loss. This is said to result in fatalism, lack of "need for achievement," and a reluctance to cooperate in collective action.[87] The model is not unlike Richard Solomon's characterization of Chinese personality as dependent in dealings with authority and greatly fearful of interpersonal conflict with peers.[88] The difficulty with this picture of peasant apathy and inaction, of course, is that history is replete with cases not only of peasant passivity, but of peasant insurrection as well. Consequently, others have chosen to emphasize the "revolutionary" temperament of the peasant, who is pictured as uniquely prone to spontaneous violence.[89]

Missing from most theories of peasant temperament is an appreciation of the impact of environment and class position on attitude structure. Surely the particular resource configuration and one's access to it will have major implications for an individual's social perspective. As Gerrit Huizer has effectively demonstrated, peasants are variously apathetic or organizable depending on the circumstances.[90] There is, in other words, no characteristic or generalized peasant mentality that is basically different from that of other people.

To understand how peasants view the world and how they assess their own chances for influencing that world, attention must be directed to the concrete physical and social environments in which they are operating. The natural setting of Huai-pei, we have seen, was unstable in the extreme. Flood and drought posed continual threats to survival. This uncertainty, exacerbated by the recurrent scourge of warfare, made it difficult for inhabitants to undertake any long-term measures for improving their ecological situation.

At the same time, societal restrictions were comparatively light in this area. Although poverty was widespread and landholdings unequal, class differences were not so pronounced as in other parts of China. Tenancy was less prevalent and owner-cultivation the rule. Economic standings could be quickly reversed in time of natural disaster, generating a social fluidity not to be found in more stable regions. Furthermore, the low government profile in the area permitted the emergence of violent solutions to the problem of peasant welfare.

These observations may help to reconcile what at first appear to be contradictory descriptions of Huai-pei peasant mentality found in local gazetteers. Somewhat akin to the argument in contemporary scholarship over conservative versus rebellious peasants, gazetteers provide a picture that encompasses both views. On the one hand, Huai-pei peasants are described as fatalistic and lazy. On the other hand, they are pictured as belligerent and unruly. The apparent contrast in these views can perhaps be resolved by thinking of peasants as reacting simultaneously to two environments: natural and social. Toward nature, over which peasants in this area could reasonably expect to exert only minimal control, they exhibited a submissive approach. Toward their fellow inhabitants, who were probably seen as both more predictable and less formidable than the Huai and Yellow rivers, these same peasants were a good deal more aggressive.

References to the local populace as indolent and resigned to the dictates of nature abound in Huai-pei gazetteers. As the Lu-i gazetteer puts it, "Peasants here are not very diligent and leave things to fate. In the past there was a well-developed system of irrigation, but now the waterways have become obstructed. During the summer rains, this area turns into a flooded swampland. The peasants do nothing to avert the situation, crying out with folded arms."[91] The gazetteer of T'ung-shan County presents a similar description: "These people are at the mercy of natural calamities. They rely solely on the natural fertility of the soil, making no effort to improve it. The peasants are lazy and loath to engage in agricultural work. Once they've sown their fields, they don't bother to weed them. Since they neglect irrigation works, the people have no means of controlling the water level during flood or drought."[92]

The author of the Feng-t'ai gazetteer provides a vivid, if somewhat exaggerated, personal account of this lack of initiative among the Huai-pei peasantry:

Once I passed by the county city at the time of a mild drought and noticed the crops were all withering. By the side of the fields was a reservoir filled to the brim with water. I asked the peasants, "Why don't you draw the water and irrigate the fields?" Their reply was, "There's too little water for too much land. It wouldn't be enough to go around." I continued to press, "Wouldn't it be better to salvage even a few *mou* than to let everything wither?" The answer was, "We don't have the necessary tools." I asked, "Why not make some?" The peasants responded, "That's hard work and we're afraid the gains wouldn't be worth it."[93]

This reluctance to tamper with the natural environment is in striking contrast to the picture that has been drawn of peasants in more prosperous regions of the country. In South China, Evelyn Rawski has pointed to the certainty of commercial opportunity as a major stimulus to peasant initiative. There the prospect of a good market price encouraged cultivators to intensify by increasing inputs of labor, water, and fertilizer.[94] The difference in motivation is explained by an American observer in Huai-pei during the early twentieth century:

Amongst a people with years of good harvests at their backs, although a terrible flood is a dreadful calamity, when the shock passes there is a rebound and a vitality which makes for strenuous work in repairing the damage and building guards for the future, which is the normal recuperative power of a healthy people; but in North Anhwei and North Kiangsu this vital recuperative power is entirely lacking, killed by continuous years of failure and starvation. Year after year the crops are a failure by what appears an act of God, then the farm animals are eaten, then there is no seed for new crops, then the small farm is sold and the money soon expended, and the choice comes between begging and stealing, and often not even this choice, as there is but little to steal, and the strong take that.[95]

The overwhelming odds against winning in any battle with nature had made the peasants of Huai-pei understandably conservative in their approach to agriculture and economic innovation in general. At the same time, we find a much less passive picture when it comes to the question of *social* interaction. It is a rare gazetteer indeed that fails to mention the fierce and truculent nature of the Huai-pei peasantry. Sources concur in characterizing these people as quick to fight for the slightest material advantage. "Congregating and competing for small gains" is repeatedly cited as the primary vice of peasants in this area. More specifically, rural inhabitants are accused of an intractable propensity toward gambling, feuds, and banditry. The peasants are described as using their meager savings to stockpile weapons—spears, swords, and even guns—to buttress their positions in the recurring conflicts.[96] As the famous Ch'ing scholar-official, Wei Yüan, characterized the Huai-pei scene: "Land is neglected and the people are lazy but fierce. They are given to robbery, forming groups of a thousand people, each with its own leader. Murders and injuries occur daily. Thus the area is known as difficult to govern."[97]

Populations living under conditions of resource scarcity have frequently turned to intergroup aggression as one strategy for adapting to ecological crisis.[98] The small owner-cultivators of Huai-pei, perennially ravaged by natural catastrophe, conducted a continuing interclan and intervillage struggle for scarce resources. One can identify a certain class character to the modal strategies of predation and protection that evolved in this area. Yet until the basic ecological dilemma was resolved, class contradictions were in many ways obscured by this fundamental problem.

The impact of the environment on collective violence in Huai-pei was twofold. First, precarious ecological conditions had given rise to a certain configuration of economic, social, and political interactions that would shape patterns of group aggression in the area. Second, in times of natural disaster, reliance on these ongoing forms of collective action would intensify, as increased numbers of people found it necessary to seize or defend diminished resources by violent means.

3. Strategies of Peasant Survival in Huai-pei

Huai-pei peasants, we have seen, lived in a highly unstable natural environment. The resultant insecurity cast a dark shadow upon economic, social, and political life in the area. With productive opportunities severely constrained, peasants turned to alternative means of promoting and safeguarding their survival. Many households pursued the familiar strategies of controlling family size, borrowing from others, or moving elsewhere in an effort to obtain or conserve scarce resources. Such solutions, common to peasants the world over, assumed a particular form in Huai-pei that was conducive to the emergence of a diverse array of more aggressive strategies. These violent adaptations to a hostile environment can, for the most part, be subsumed within two broad categories. The first category includes offensive attempts to seize the resources of others: the predatory strategy. The second is composed of efforts to guard against such attacks: the protective strategy.

Although the motivation for these strategies was personal survival, their effect was to provide peasants with valuable experience in cooperation, mobility, and high-risk behavior. It is often assumed that sideline pursuits work primarily to sap rebellious potential.* Missing from this view is the point that adaptive strategies are more than simply income boosters. Far from

*For example, James Scott has commented, "To the degree that the marginal opportunities open to the peasant do in fact alleviate short-run subsistence needs, to that degree they tend to reduce the likelihood of more direct and violent solutions" (1976, p. 204).

an inevitable fetter upon revolt, involvement in short-term migration, banditry, militia, and the like can actually organize peasants for more dramatic steps. It is important to remember that these adaptations to the local environment evolved and persisted over generations. Although conditioned by the physical and social backdrop, these were by no means automatic, "knee-jerk" responses to set stimuli. Peasants learned to cope with their predicament in a cumulative history of trial-and-error experience, passing on these traditions to their progeny through oral history, folklore, and direct instruction.

Like all human beings, peasants are not entirely autonomous individuals. Their range of activity is dependent upon and limited by social circumstances and traditions. Conflict over scarce resources is not comprehensible on an individual basis alone. Both the pattern of resource distribution and the struggle for a readjustment of this pattern necessarily involve wider social units. Much of the following discussion of peasant survival strategies will therefore be concerned with identifying the levels of social organization at which particular strategies were employed. Collective action implies organization, but this may be variously based upon kinship, settlement, class, friendship, occupation, or a number of other ties. Only after having clarified the underlying structures of action can we proceed to the central issue: the relationship of these strategies to peasant rebellion.

Recent theories of group conflict stress the importance of "mobilization"—the process whereby the discontented muster resources for the pursuit of common goals.[1] Collective survival strategies constitute important means of peasant mobilization, thereby facilitating the possibility of rural rebellion. Case studies of the Nien and Red Spears in Chapters 4 and 5 will show how, at two specific times in history, ongoing predation and protection were transformed into outright rebellion. Under the pressures of severe natural disaster and political crisis, regular survival strategies could generate antistate activity. Such dramatic, rebellious expressions should not, however, blind us to the pragmatic and continuous character of these local patterns of survival. An ecological perspective on peasant revolt does not deny its political nature. In the first place, national policies played a role in creating many of the problems with which Huai-pei peasants had to cope. Lack of proper dike maintenance by the central government was largely responsible for the devastating flooding of the region. Administrative irrationalities made possible the practice of smuggling. Lax security contributed to the growth of banditry and the need for private forms of defense. Periodic tax increases and marauding government soldiers furthered the protective response. In the second place, rebellion by definition involves opposition to government authority and is therefore a political act. Nevertheless, such opposition is often peripheral to an explanation of how and why traditions of rural violence evolve and persist. For the peasants themselves, armed revolt is often an extension of familiar strategies for making a living, turning into an antistate position only reluctantly and under outside pressure.

STANDARD HOUSEHOLD STRATEGIES

Peasant households sought to cope with the problem of scarcity by controlling family size and composition, borrowing from others, and the like. Periodically family members or entire households would also move outside the Huai-pei area in search of additional resources. These "sedentary" and "mobile" solutions were standard patterns that may at first appear quite unrelated to more aggressive survival strategies. In fact, they did have an important bearing on the likelihood and style of collective violence. Typically adopted at the level of the household— the primary production-consumption unit of any peasant economy—these mundane responses are common to many peasant societies. The form and consequences of these solutions to resource scarcity differ, however, and it is these differences that help to define the nature of peasant action in specific local areas.

Sedentary Solutions

One of the most prevalent and tragic solutions to peasant poverty is the killing of infants. In China, where males were the favored offspring for both cultural and economic reasons, infanticide was primarily directed against girl babies. Whereas boys might be expected eventually to contribute to family income, girls were seen simply as liabilities who had to be reared and then married off at considerable expense. Widespread female infanticide resulted in a glaring imbalance in the sex ratio, males outnumbering females by a sizable margin.[2]

For the mid-nineteenth century, figures from Hsüchou Prefecture in Kiangsu suggest an average of 129 men for every 100 women.[3] The disparity continued into the twentieth century. Table 7 gives figures from a field investigation conducted in sixteen north Anhwei villages in 1932. These statistics show males outnumbering females in the early years, with the ratio reversing itself among the elderly. Although in peasant societies female life expectancy is often lower than that of males because of higher mortality during the childbearing years, here we see no indication of that trend. Rather, the proportion of women increases steadily over the life cycle. It thus seems likely that the imbalance in sex ratio was due to female infanticide. Figures from eighteen northern Anhwei counties in 1934 range from a low of 108 to a high of 150 males per 100 females. The mean for the area as a whole was 123 men for every 100 women.[4]

This sex ratio imbalance was not extraordinarily high by traditional Chinese standards, yet the figures suggest that as many as 20 percent of Huai-pei males may have gone unmarried. Although individual peasant families were pursuing a rational policy in rearing sons who were expected to augment household income, the social impact of this policy was a serious surplus of single young males. The dryland wheat farming practiced in Huai-pei, we have seen, was an extensive form of agriculture

Table 7. Percentage of Males and Females in
Northern Anhwei Villages, 1932

Age group	Pct. male	Pct. female
Under 7 years	55%	45%
7–14 years	54	46
15–54 years	53	47
55+ years	49	51
AVERAGE	53%	47%

Source: Yang Chi-hua, 1933.

unresponsive to increased increments of human labor. Few family plots were large enough to absorb the labor of many sons. Although some of these unmarried men were able to sell their services to more affluent families as hired workers or servants, unemployment was a chronic problem. The existence of this huge contingent of single men had major consequences for the pattern of intergroup conflict. "Bare sticks," as unmarried males were popularly termed, provided a principal source of recruits for both predatory and protective movements in Huai-pei. Smugglers, bandits, crop watchers, and militiamen alike were drawn in large part from their ranks. Thus the practice of female infanticide, though motivated by a family's need to restrict resource consumption, also helped contribute to particular forms of resource competition.

Despite efforts to control family size, many households continued to suffer economic difficulties. A flood, famine, wedding, or funeral could push peasants below the margin of survival, forcing them to borrow grain or money to weather the crisis. If an investigation conducted in four northern Kiangsu villages in 1943 is representative, nearly one-half of all households were in debt. About 80 percent of these debts had been incurred to provide food for immediate subsistence needs. Most of the other borrowing was a response to weddings, funerals, or illness. Less than 5 percent of the debts were for productive purposes such as irrigation improvement or the purchase of seeds, tools, or draft animals. Borrowing from relatives was common, since such loans might carry a more favorable rate of interest.[5]

Besides borrowing from creditors to tide themselves over in immediate crises, peasants organized loan associations as a means of insurance against hard times in the future. Although often based on kinship, such groups involved a level of cooperation higher than the nuclear family, bringing together friends and relatives in a collective strategy for coping with economic insecurity. "Old people societies" were formed to help with the burden of funeral expenses. Dues were pooled and then used to defray the cost of mourning clothes, coffins, and funeral arrangements as the need arose. "Fur garment societies" were organized to provide participating peasants with warm winter coats which were beyond their individual means. Members paid annual dues which were used to purchase one or more coats each year. The group disbanded when all participants had been duly provided for. In addition to these specialized societies, groups created to provide more general types of loans were also common. These associations, or yao-hui, typically met once a year, at which time members drank wine and threw dice to determine the precedence for borrowing.[6] Only a thin line separated the yao-hui from the hua-hui, or illegal gambling societies, which were also prevalent in the area. Gambling had long been a favorite pastime for Huai-pei peasants during the slack season. As the gazetteer of Po County commented, "Gambling constitutes the most serious and harmful vice of the local people."[7] Those who engaged in this practice usually did so with very little capital, so that losers often had no means of making good their debts. As we will see in the case of the Nien, losses at the gambling table were a potent motivation for the move to open banditry.

Incurring debts was obviously only a temporary palliative, one which could readily lead to greater poverty as interest on the loan accumulated. Many peasants thus sought relief beyond the creditor or loan association, in the outside world.

Mobile Solutions

Throughout human history, one common method of alleviating the problem of too large a population for too little food has been migration. Not a few Huai-pei residents adopted this "exit" solution to rural poverty. Mobility was a way of life for Huai-pei villagers, a clear consequence of the difficult environment in which they lived. Chronic unemployment drove many to seek seasonal support elsewhere during periods of agricultural slack. Sudden natural disasters forced whole communities to evacuate their homes on a moment's notice. Gazetteers state that in time of calamity poor peasants "rushed to abandon the land," leading women and children down across the Yangtze in search of food.[8] Shouldering a few belongings, they would trudge off to a temporary refuge where they might wait out the trouble back home. This meant that the Huai-pei population was in a continuous state of transiency and flux. Although not every member of every family was on the move every year, many people did in fact migrate both seasonally and in response to unforeseen ecological crises.

Whether individual or group, seasonal or in response to sudden disaster, mobility was a normal feature of Huai-pei peasant life. The fact that mobility was both continuous and temporary (in the sense that peasants returned home whenever possible) gave it a special importance with respect to the development of collective action. Migration, because of its disruptive and unsettling consequences, frequently militates against group action. In Huai-pei, however, migration did not involve a sharp break with familiar patterns of organization. An integral part of household economic activity, migratory experiences could enhance rather than inhibit the emergence of collective action and group conflict.

In the mid-nineteenth century, southern Kiangsu—particularly the city of Shanghai—was the destination for many Huai-pei migrants who sought seasonal work as coolie laborers, porters, rickshaw pullers, and the like. Few jobs were available, however, and most of the new arrivals were forced into the ranks of the beggar army of Shanghai. Numbers swelled with the onset of natural disaster. A description of the phenomenon appeared in the October 4, 1865, *North-China Herald:*

> They have come from the northern part of this province, where the country has been devastated by locusts, and are traveling with a passport, given to them by the chief magistrate of the place from which they have come—specifying the reasons for their traveling, and testifying to their good character, declaring that they are good, but *distressed* people.
>
> In times of scarcity of provisions—occasioned by inundation, drought, locusts, and the like, when the government is unable to supply the means of sustenance—such licensed bands of beggars are by no means uncommon to China. As the food cannot be brought to them—there being neither the money to purchase it, nor the ways and means of transporting it if bought—necessity requires that the distressed people should go to the food.
>
> In this land begging is moreover no very dishonorable profession, and when, as in this case, a passport is given to the beggars, they go in high spirits and are very bold; yet they rob nobody, take no denials, grow stout, and when the calamity is passed they usually return quietly to their native places—having traveled perhaps over half the length of the empire.[9]

As this description makes clear, begging in ecologically more stable areas constituted a recognized route for pursuing one's living in a society with few productive options outside agriculture. Begging was often a seasonal phenomenon—an alternative adopted during periods of agricultural slack as a regular method for supplementing family income.*

Seasonally mobile peasants created a fluid population not eas-

---

*In Feng-yang, Anhwei, the practice of begging evolved in an interesting fashion. This county, birthplace of the first Ming emperor, was devastated by turmoil that preceded the founding of the dynasty. To repopulate his home county, the new sovereign forced more than fourteen thousand affluent people from south of the Yangtze to settle permanently in Feng-yang. Any who returned to their homes were to be severely punished. Since the displaced persons had a strong desire to visit their family graves, they masqueraded as seasonal beggars to make the risky journey home. In time, it became a regular custom to depart in winter and return for spring planting. The practice had originated because people in Feng-yang had enough money to travel, but over the centuries it became in fact what it once had pretended to be, a winter occupation of the poor for supplementing annual income (Inoue Kobai, 1923, pp. 273–74).

ily subject to government control. Throughout the Ch'ing dynasty, memorials and edicts proliferated with regard to the problem. In 1815, a report on conditions in Anhwei by Manchu official Na Yen-ch'eng stressed the importance of conducting an annual census of all mobile peasants—the so-called shed people or *p'eng-min*—during the periods when they returned to their native villages. In 1822 and again in 1824, imperial edicts were issued to the effect that "shed people" must be investigated one by one, with a responsible supervisor chosen for every ten households and accurate family registers posted on all doors. [10]

Local gentry bemoaned the difficulties of instituting the *pao-chia* security system in Huai-pei. As one gazetteer stated the problem, "The people are not attached to their land and there are many wanderers without regular occupations. They may leave for months at a time without returning home. Thus 30 to 40 percent of the dwellings are occupied by outsiders. These intruders may stay for months and are neither easily expelled nor easily incorporated into a security system." [11]

Periodic movements of large numbers of people opened the way for a good deal of dislocation in Huai-pei, inhibiting government efforts at tight supervision. The result was not chaos, however, for regularized mobility induced a kind of structure of its own. Although usually conducted as a household strategy, migration often generated higher levels of social cooperation and conflict. A revealing illustration of this process is provided by the *hu-t'uan,* or lake associations, which developed as a result of serious inundations in the area. [12] Massive flooding of the Yellow River in 1851 caused two lakes on the Kiangsu-Shantung border to overflow, submerging all the surrounding land on the western shores of these two lakes. The inhabitants of the area (P'ei and T'ung-shan counties in northwest Kiangsu) fled en masse to escape the calamity.

Four years later the Yellow River again burst its dikes, this time inflicting its greatest damage a few miles north of the previous flood. Inhabitants of the southern Shantung area were hardest hit, and disaster victims rushed down across the border by the hundreds of thousands to seek refuge in neighboring Kiangsu. There they found the abandoned lands which had been inundated in 1851, but which by now had partially dried into fertile silted terrain. The newcomers from Shantung erected shacks and industriously set about cultivating the unoccupied lands. Their hard work paid off and soon the immigrants were enjoying bountiful harvests. This prosperity was reflected in the organization of twelve defense leagues, called lake associations, to protect their newfound wealth. With official approval, the settlers constructed forts and stockpiled weapons to safeguard their livelihood against outside intrusion. The immigrants successfully fought off waves of rebel incursions and remained happily settled in their new homes for nearly a decade.

At this point, however, former inhabitants of the region who had fled the 1851 floods began to reappear on the scene. Seeing that their now fertile lands had been claimed by others, the returned natives filed indignant complaints with the local authorities. When no official help was forthcoming, fighting erupted between the original occupants and the immigrant lake associations. The conflict escalated in late 1865 with an incursion of Nien rebels from Anhwei, who found supporters among unruly elements in the *hu-t'uan*. The area was on the verge of revolt, and order was restored only when government troops marched in to arrest and execute more than one thousand lake association members. Two *hu-t'uan* found guilty of having harbored rebels were disbanded and their lands confiscated by the government and redistributed to the original owners.

As the example suggests, life in Huai-pei was extremely fluid. An unstable natural environment resulted in massive population movement both out of and into the area. In the late nineteenth and early twentieth centuries, the urbanization of South China also drew large numbers of Huai-pei residents out of their villages to seek temporary employment. In 1935 the Ministry of Industries reported that more than 50 percent of rural families in northern Anhwei had lost some of their members by migration to cities—the national average being only 13.5

percent. Young unmarried males formed the bulk of the emigrants.[13]

Armies were another outlet for the surplus population. Huai-pei had historically served as a major recruiting ground for government soldiers in times of national crisis. Although military service paid poorly in terms of salary or provisions, the life of the soldier promised travel and adventure as well as the opportunity to prey upon distant populations. A military career was usually brief, however. After completing a campaign, the troops would be summarily released and ordered to return to their native villages. Accustomed to a life of violence, and seldom able to find regular employment at home, demobilized soldiers were likely candidates for banditry.[14]

AGGRESSIVE SURVIVAL STRATEGIES

Peasants in Huai-pei, we have seen, employed a variety of conventional methods for dealing with the problem of scarcity. These standard and, for the most part, officially sanctioned activities in turn generated a number of more aggressive approaches. It is important to emphasize that no hard and fast line can be drawn between the conventional methods and the more dramatic strategies of predation and protection. As a foreign observer in bandit-infested Honan noted in 1927:

> Personally, after having talked this over with numbers of foreigners as well as Chinese, I am inclined to believe that there really is no distinction as between "bandits" and "people" further than that by bandits are meant those who are at the time under arms and "on the war path" and by people the women and children and the aged who carry on small businesses in the poorly stocked markets or till the land. But that the people are really the fathers and mothers and sisters and brothers of the bandits, and profit by their activity insofar as those who are active in the profession divide their gains with the folks back home.
> On the other hand, there is ample evidence that some of the inhabitants, at least on occasions, rebel against being interfered with by anyone. For one comes upon towns which are "sealed"; and have been so for weeks or months. By this is meant that all the gates are closed and

banked up behind with earth, so that the wall is, to all intents and purposes, a continuous structure, and no one who does not belong to the community is allowed in under any circumstances. Communities which adopt this measure may be reinforced by soldiers or Red Spears or both. I have heard of places that had held out in this manner for months, refusing admittance even to the military on official business.[15]

Ordinarily the relative absence of state interference in Huai-pei meant that peasants were fairly free to devise their own methods for ensuring subsistence. When agriculture failed, competition for scarce resources intensified. The hungry staged attacks on those with goods; the latter responded defensively. And thus was set in motion a kind of parochial dialectic between predator and protector. Periodically, however, if violence escalated to an unacceptable level, if the central treasury were seriously depleted, or in times of foreign invasion, outside actors might enter the picture: government soldiers, state officials, or Japanese or warlord troops. Their tactics of harsh repression or heavy taxation could drive predator and protector together into a united front against this common enemy from the outside. Although such a synthesis was always fraught with tension, it furthered the potential for massive rebellion in Huai-pei.

PREDATORY STRATEGIES

It is frequently noted that peasants are normally inhibited from rebellious activity by the tyranny of work and the pressures of custom. The young surplus population of Huai-pei—unemployed and often well traveled—were less subject to these restrictions. Having engaged perhaps in periodic excursions out of their native villages as beggars, soldiers, or hired laborers, they had acquired valuable exposure to new ways. Denied regular work at home, these bare sticks were on the face of it classic "marginal men"—impoverished and with no stake or position in conventional society. In reality, however, the very fact that Huai-pei regularly reproduced this "marginal" class gave its members a certain recognized social place. These young men, we remember, had been reared as part of a household strategy for survival. Although unmarried, they remained a part of their natal families, to whom they might return periodically with remittances of resources secured in their outside activities. For this reason, the predatory strategy—staffed predominantly by such bare sticks—was organized largely along familial lines. Smuggling activities were frequently conducted by lineage, bandit gangs generally encompassed kinship networks, and feuds were often between competing clans. Thus predation need not be seen as the domain of solitary individuals, forced into asocial behavior by their lack of communal bonds. Precisely because these figures were not only "marginal," but also an integral part of the structure of peasant society, their predatory ventures were a form of collective action with strong rebel potential.

Smuggling

Smuggling was an illegal form of seasonal mobility which took peasants to other areas in an effort to supplement their inadequate agricultural income. It differed from begging, migrating, or soldiering in that it was a seizure of resources officially deemed off-limits to the people involved. Smuggling is by definition illegal, and it is this criminal aspect of the behavior that differentiates it from officially sanctioned mobility. In attempting to seize control over resources to which they had no legal access, smugglers were engaging in a type of predatory activity that blended easily into theft, banditry, and open revolt. As early as Huang Ch'ao's uprising in 874–85, salt smuggling was a prelude to rebellion on the North China Plain.

The peculiarities of the government salt monopoly during the Ch'ing made the illegal transport and sale of salt an extremely lucrative occupation for peasants in the Huai-pei area. Official regulations divided the country into eleven salt zones. Only certain types of salt could legally be sold and consumed in particular zones at fixed prices. The way the boundaries were drawn, central and eastern Honan and the one county of Su in northern Anhwei were "Ch'ang-lu salt" districts, whereas the rest of northern Anhwei was restricted to the inferior "Huai salt." To make matters worse, the foul-tasting Huai salt was the most expensive variety of all.[16] In the early nineteenth century, each *chin* of Huai salt cost 40 to 50 *wen*, whereas the more palatable Ch'ang-lu variety sold for only half the price.[17] Enterprising peasants in the Huai districts thus used the winter slack period to travel to the Ch'ang-lu zones, load up on salt, and return home to sell the illicit variety at a sizable profit.

Because of the danger inherent in this illegal enterprise, salt smugglers enlisted the services of armed guards to accompany them on their perilous journeys. In 1815, imperial censor T'ao Chu[18] memorialized that salt smuggling along the Honan-Anhwei border was being conducted behind a shield provided by people popularly known as "Red Beards." These strongmen were said to be remnants of the White Lotus Rebellion who now engaged in armed robbery for a living. Their nickname derived from the fact that, in traditional Chinese opera, red beards were part of the stock make-up for the role of the fierce, lawless character. These people often supplied protection for more than a hundred salt carts a day, receiving a fee of 200 *wen* per cart. If the revenue from smuggling proved insufficient to support the extravagant feasting and gambling parties to which they were accustomed, the Red Beards undertook plundering expeditions to secure additional goods. On these forays they gathered into groups, each of which was known as a *nien*, organizational units that T'ao described as ranging in size from a dozen to several hundred people. The Red Beards-cum-*nien* were said to have stolen goods, seized women, and committed a host of sadistic atrocities on innocent victims. They were described as well armed and as posing a major challenge to local peacekeeping efforts.[19]

As we will see in Chapter 4, the Nien Rebellion was in many ways intimately linked to Huai-pei salt smuggling. Subsequent rebellions in the area were also connected to conflict over the prized resource of salt. In 1898, for example, an uprising involving some thirty thousand peasants in Kuo-yang County began with an attack on the market town's largest salt shop. Centered in the same county that had produced the Nien half a century before, these latter-day rebels also set up a five-colored-banner system and chose an alliance commander in obvious imitation of the Nien pattern.[20] Problems with salt continued into the Republican period. In 1928, Hsü-i County in Anhwei was plagued with more than a thousand "salt bandits" who took advantage of the poorly maintained Huai River system to plunder stranded salt boats as they ran aground on the accumulated silt.[21]

The Huai-pei salt traffic provided a tempting opportunity for poor peasants to augment a meager income. During the Republican era, opium smuggling was also a lucrative profession in this area.[22] As a regular seasonal activity, smuggling was well organized, often according to lineage.[23] The high-risk nature of the enterprise made it imperative for participating peasants to cooperate closely; such cooperation was most easily effected along kinship lines. The fact that the activity was in direct defiance of government authority meant that it was but a short step from smuggler to full-fledged rebel. Thus smuggling was a form of organized predatory behavior especially conducive to antistate movements.

Banditry

Even nearer than smuggling to rebellion was organized banditry. Huai-pei was for centuries known as a hotbed of Chinese banditry. Here, where natural disaster and warfare swept the countryside repeatedly, large numbers of peasants took to the "greenwoods" (*lü-lin*) with equal regularity. Throughout the late Ch'ing and Republican periods, scarcely a day would pass without newspaper and government reports of organized brigandage in the area. Within Huai-pei itself, certain locations were particularly prone to bandit occupation. Frequent flooding turned the marshy shores of Lake Hung-tse into an especially fertile breeding ground for brigands. Provincial and county borders were another favorite refuge.

Ineffective government control made the choice of banditry viable. Huai-pei, like Taiwan or northern Shensi, was one of those backwaters of the Chinese empire traditionally regarded by the government as incorrigibly recalcitrant. Officials dreaded assignment to this unruly area and, if they had the misfortune to receive such a post, usually tried to endure the tenure with as little local involvement as possible. Along county and provincial borders the problem of banditry was especially acute. Since officials in each district preferred to pass the buck to their neighbors rather than cooperate for effective control, bandits moved back and forth across jurisdictional boundaries with impunity. In 1823, Anhwei governor T'ao Chu characterized the zones of bandit activity as the "three no-governs" (san pu-kuan), where county, prefecture, and province all denied responsibility for law enforcement.[24] T'ao repeatedly memorialized, to no apparent avail, on the need for official cooperation along the provincial borders of Anhwei-Kiangsu-Honan-Shantung, where banditry was rampant. This region continued to serve as home for many of China's bandits on into the Republican period.[25]

Government ineptitude was itself partially a product of the natural setting. Take as an example an incident that occurred along the Kiangsu-Honan border in 1872. The magistrates of neighboring counties in the two provinces met to adjudicate a case in which a dry-goods store had been plundered by bandits. The problem was that the village in which the incident took place had no tax registers or property deeds, these having all perished in massive inundations some years back. After the flood waters subsided, people in adjacent counties had bought and sold property in ignorance of the earlier provincial boundary line, and it was now unclear to which jurisdiction the village belonged. Only after a lengthy investigation were gravestones unearthed that identified the village as part of Yung-ch'eng County in Honan.[26]

Natural and political factors worked in concert to make Huai-pei an unstable ecosystem especially hospitable to banditry. In addition to contextual causes, an ongoing popular tradition among the peasants themselves played a vital role in perpetuating an awareness of and propensity for banditry. As one indication of this tradition, we have the testimony of the famous Ch'ing general Yüan Chia-san, who was horrified to discover on an inspection tour of Huai-pei the existence of extremely ornate temples dedicated to none other than Tao Chih, the notorious bandit chief of Chinese legend.[27] The profession of banditry thus apparently did enjoy a certain popular prestige.

Folk songs and folk tales recently collected by historians working in this area offer further evidence of a living tradition of social banditry.[28] The stories are rich in matters of strategy and tactics, suggesting that oral literature was an important means of transmitting practical knowledge from one generation to the next. That Huai-pei bandits considered themselves a part of such a tradition is suggested by their widespread adoption of similar titles and practices. It was common for bandit chiefs to assume names borrowed from the heroes of popular literature, to organize their forces under a system of five banners, and to distribute turbans and tasseled spears to their followers. In addition, bandits in this area developed a distinctive set of expressions to describe their activities, a vernacular which showed surprising stability over time.[29] Thus there existed background conditions and a conscious tradition conducive to the growth of banditry in Huai-pei. Yet the question remains as to what this banditry was like and how individual brigands coalesced into organized groups to pursue their common interests.

Bandits often began their journey into crime at the level of petty thievery—robbing graves or individual households by night, seizing crops from unwatched fields, and so forth. Once the group obtained sufficient arms and personnel to pose a credible threat, however, they would escalate to more audacious activities. Frequently bandits set up operations in local markets, requisitioning lavish food and drink from the surrounding populace and extorting protection money from shopkeepers and merchants. Another favorite activity was to lie in wait along trade routes and swoop down upon unsuspecting travelers, robbing them or demanding some set fee for safe passage. Sometimes bandit groups even managed to take control of government customs passes, assuming the authority to levy taxes at will.

One of the most common ways in which Huai-pei bandits acquired money and goods was by kidnaping hostages for ransom. This practice was directed primarily against the well-to-do, since these families could best afford handsome compensation. Huai-pei bandits often demanded their ransom in opium, which served as a prime medium of exchange in the late Ch'ing and Republican periods. Those who insisted upon this form of payment were known as *hsiang-chu,* or "trunk masters," and government reports are replete with references to their bold runs across the Huai-pei plain.[30] Even more colorful terms were used to differentiate kidnaping according to the victim involved. In the case of female victims, the act was termed "seizing a goddess of mercy"; in the case of wealthy males, it was "grabbing a fat pig." The ransom price would vary according to the chief's appraisal of the financial means of the household involved. The time limit imposed on payment was also variable. In the case of virgin girls, a special "quick ticket" (*k'uai-p'iao*) might be required if the young woman were to be reclaimed before nightfall. In addition to opium, payment could be demanded in cash, grain, arms, or horses.[31]

During the Republican period, foreigners also became prized targets for kidnap. Perhaps the boldest such instance was an international incident in May 1923, when thousands of armed bandits converged upon the Tientsin-Pukow Railroad as it approached Lin-ch'eng station in southern Shantung. Three hundred passengers, including thirty foreigners, were taken hostage in a bid to c.d the military siege to which the bandits' mountain lair was being subjected by government forces at the time.[32] A decade earlier, bandit chief Pai Lang ("White Wolf") had adopted similar tactics, seizing thirteen foreign missionaries on a foray into northern Hupeh. The practice was repeated by his band on a smaller scale in Anhwei, Honan, and Kansu.[33]

Whether such activities represented an incipient anti-imperialism is uncertain; that they were an effort to garner lucrative ransom seems indisputable.

In addition to relying on robbery, extortion, and kidnap, some large and well-organized groups of bandits were sufficiently bold and powerful actually to occupy cities. The famous Honan bandit Lao Yang-jen was an example. Popularly known as the "old foreigner" because of his height and curly hair, this bandit led a force of over ten thousand to occupy a whole string of cities in Honan and Anhwei during the 1920s.[34]

Bandit gangs numbering in the hundreds and thousands were not uncommon in Huai-pei. For the Republican period, the picture has been reasonably well documented. In 1925, Shantung was reported to have had forty-seven major bandit chiefs with a total of more than seventeen thousand regular followers. In Honan Province, some fifty-two bandit gangs were said to include fifty-one thousand regulars. Hsüchou district in Kiangsu harbored close to five thousand bandits; in one Anhwei county alone there were ten gangs with several hundred followers in the early 1930s.[35]

Who were these bandits and how did they organize themselves? In answering these questions, we must keep in mind that there were at least three types of bandit outfits, differing in size, composition, geographical scope, and durability: the ad hoc gang, the semipermanent gang, and the bandit army.

The simplest bandit group—the ad hoc gang—was a regular institution in the Huai-pei countryside. This was the small, seasonal gathering of local yu-min who drifted into occasional brigandage for economic reasons. The yu-min were chronically unemployed persons, usually young males, who milled about their local market towns gambling, committing petty theft, and the like. These were the surplus sons of poor peasant families, unable to secure a steady occupation within the confines of their unproductive home economy. For them, the world of banditry constituted an appealing alternative to a life of aimless hunger.

In fact, their participation in brigandage was often a regular family strategy whereby younger sons would serve as seasonal bandits to augment household income. Bandit gangs composed entirely of *yu-min* were temporary, small-scale operations of a dozen or so people that seldom ventured far from home. At harvest time, the members would disband to lend a hand with the farm work.

In bad years, when flood or drought depressed the harvest, ad hoc gangs could evolve into a second type of bandit outfit: the semipermanent gang. Unable to pursue even a seasonal occupation on the land, the bandits began to operate year-round. They selected some safe base from which to conduct their plundering forays, activities that began to spread farther from home to areas less struck by natural disaster.

As banditry took on a more permanent form, it attracted a new type of member. On the leadership level, the *yu-min* were superseded by another group that may, for lack of a better term, be called the "village aspirants." Rural Huai-pei generated a certain number of ambitious young men, and less frequently women,* of relatively affluent families who found their plans for advancement thwarted by the powers that be. These were usually not the offspring of landed gentry, for whom educational and bureaucratic advancement was within reach, but the children of moderately well-off owner-cultivators to whom such channels of mobility seemed far less promising. Unschooled but enterprising, these individuals faced a bleak future in the vil-

---

*Women bandit leaders were less common, but certainly did exist, in both the Ch'ing and Republican periods. For examples from Huai-pei during the late nineteenth century, see NC, vol. 2, pp. 202–88; vol. 4, pp. 210–49. In the Republican period, Huai-pei's best-known female bandit was "Mama Chao," who led a force of six or seven hundred bandits, all of them women, in southern Shantung (Ho Hsi-ya, 1925, p. 19; Nagano Akira, 1931, p. 68). Interviews with former residents of the area suggest that there were in fact many more women outlaws than the written record would have us believe. In Anhwei's Shou County, for example, a woman bandit known as "Two-gun Chang" was famous for wielding a pistol in each hand. She is said to have come from a respectable middle peasant family and to have stolen from the rich in neighboring areas to assist the poor of Shou County.

lages of Huai-pei. Since legitimate entrepreneurial opportunities were extremely scarce, some of the aspirants chose instead to seek their fortune in the world of crime. Often the aspirants were actively coaxed into brigandage by some unfortunate brush with the law. Like Hobsbawm's "noble robber," they might begin their bandit careers as victims of injustice.[36] Occasionally their subsequent activities also reflected an ethic of social banditry: righting wrongs, robbing the rich to assist the poor, and performing other acts of peasant justice associated with a Robin Hood—or *Liang-shan-po*—image. Chang Lo-hsing, commander of the Nien alliance, was apparently an outlaw of this sort. Pai Lang, perhaps the best-known bandit of the Republican period, demonstrated similar tendencies. Both Chang and Pai came from families with sizable landholdings, Chang's father owning some 140 to 150 *mou* and Pai's about 200 *mou*. Both were illiterate peasants who engaged in a variety of nonagricultural pursuits before turning to open banditry. In each case, their fateful brush with the law stemmed from involvement in gambling and interclan feuds. Both carried out individual acts of chivalry and tried to impress upon their followers the importance of discipline and social justice.[37]

The semipermanent gang was based upon a patron-client relationship between village aspirant leaders and *yu-min* followers. The bandit chief used his own influence and resources to offer security and material welfare to the otherwise destitute drifter. The *yu-min*, for his part, reciprocated by carrying out plunder and performing symbolic acts of deference to the leader.* Chieftains brought to the group crucial assets with which to get the enterprise underway. In the case of the Lin-

---

*Scott and Kerkvliet (1977, p. 443) deny the applicability of a patron-client link to the bandit context, noting that the bandit chief is newly arrived with little claim to higher status, and not culturally sanctioned. The typical Huai-pei case would seem at variance with this. In Huai-pei the chief usually did come from a relatively secure family and thus brought to banditry a set of resources quite different from those of his followers. Furthermore, there does seem to have been a strong subculture of legitimacy to sustain the bandit leader. Interviews with former residents confirm the fact that in Huai-pei the role of "noble bandit" was considered a quasi-respectable one for frustrated youths.

ch'eng railroad brigands, for example, the two brothers who founded the gang did so by using the proceeds from selling their family lands to purchase horses and arms.[38] Once the group was in operation, the plunder of the followers supplied the wherewithal to continue. The chief did not lose importance, however, for it was his responsibility to negotiate the necessary protective alliances to keep the gang afloat. The followers provided the economic basis of survival, and the chieftain contributed political resources to the arrangement. It was his duty to serve as a kind of power broker for the group, effecting advantageous coalitions with prestigious individuals, competing gangs, or other potential allies.

Sometimes the hard-core followers of a bandit gang were related to the chief by blood. The impoverished nephew was an especially common source of committed clients. Members of the gang who were not actually related often underwent sworn brotherhood ceremonies and addressed one another with fictive kinship titles. Bandit chief Wu Ju-wen, an important brigand operating along the Anhwei-Kiangsu border in the early Republican period, claimed more than one hundred "adopted sons" among his entourage.[39] Newcomers to bandit gangs were often assigned new names, one character of which was uniform for all members of their same age or seniority, the same pattern as was used for siblings and cousins in a regular extended family. Thus the gang did provide a kind of surrogate family for the yu-min who attached themselves to it. The structure of the group was highly authoritarian, however, since the chief had final responsibility for all major decisions and held the power of life or death over his subordinates.[40]

In his role as power broker, the bandit chief made short-term alliances with other gangs. According to these arrangements, each chief retained autonomy with respect to his own subordinates but was expected to coordinate tactical plans with other cooperating chieftains. These alliances were the backbone of the third major type of bandit group, the massive bandit armies that staged periodic raids on market towns and administrative centers. Bandit armies were especially likely to emerge in times of chronic famine, attracting to their ranks large numbers of starving peasants from the surrounding countryside. If particular coalitions proved especially successful, the chieftains might agree to cooperate on a longer-term basis. In this case, they would make a formal alliance, usually selecting as their commander the chief with the largest following. Often the resulting coalition took on a quasi-military organizational structure, assuming divisions such as brigades, battalions, and the like. Some armies adopted formal disciplinary codes and a kind of martial law.[41] Even in these cases, however, the alliances remained in reality cellular and segmented, with primary loyalties continuing to operate at the level of the gang, rather than the army. Military codes were honored mostly in the breach, and discipline was seldom strictly enforced. Since tactical cooperation really pertained only among chiefs, alliances did not involve a basic restructuring of gang commitments. The coalition was always uneasy, with great potential for disharmony and fissure.

Understanding the composition of bandit gangs and armies is crucial in assessing the adaptability of this survival strategy to peasant rebellion. Without such inspection, banditry might appear a natural candidate for incorporation into wider antistate movements. It was, after all, an enterprise that organized huge numbers of peasants into an aggressive and mobile mode of action. It was led by individuals with concerns that transcended personal or parochial boundaries. What could have been simpler than to convert this ongoing tradition into outright rebellion?

From the perspective of the state, of course, the very existence of banditry augured rebellion, inasmuch as it was an open defiance of official authority. Particularly in China, where the Mandate of Heaven sanctioned the possibility of a commoner rising to assume the throne, the political potential of brigandry must have seemed especially strong. Looked at from the bandit side, however, another picture emerges. Large-scale banditry, we have seen, was an uneasy composite of three distinct layers of rural Huai-pei society. Each of these elements entered the activity for its own reasons, and each implied a different degree of commitment to brigandage as a way of life. The poor peasant who joined up with a marauding bandit army was the least tied to this survival strategy. His allegiance was short-lived and purely pragmatic. Plunder was for him a means of supplementing, but not supplanting, an inadequate income. By contrast, the *yu-min* participants demonstrated a stronger allegiance to banditry as an occupation. These individuals might owe their entire livelihood to the bandit gang and were thus unlikely to abandon it unless offered a secure alternative means of survival. Finally, the bandit chieftain had joined the movement for yet a third set of reasons. His motivation stemmed less from temporary or chronic poverty than from a desire to enhance his own position. The aspirant's commitment to banditry was dependent upon its being able to facilitate honor and impact in a wider world than his own village could offer.

These three layers of participation thus implied quite different sorts of motivation and commitment. For our purposes, the crucial point is that none of the three was inherently rebellious. Temporary gain, permanent livelihood, and individual prestige were all a far cry from an attack upon either the personnel or the structure of state authority. Add to this the intrinsic weaknesses of bandit organization—the patron-client basis of the gang, the loose, cellular quality of intergang cooperation, the fleeting attachment of ordinary peasants—and one appreciates the difficulties involved in any effort to convert banditry to the cause of rebellion.

What complicates the picture somewhat is the pivotal role of the bandit chief. This individual, we must recall, was largely interested in expanding his own power. The scope of the chieftain's control depended upon the kinds of outside coalitions he was able to forge. Such coalitions were seen not only as a necessary source of protection for plundering activities, but as steppingstones to a wider world of power and fame. Although ambitious chiefs effected alliances according to strictly pragmatic criteria, the character of the allies had potentially important implications for the subsequent direction of the bandit movement. If the leader's most promising friends were rebels, then it was quite possible that he would change the rhetoric, and sometimes the substance, of his activity to an antistate position. Nien leader Chang Lo-hsing, as Chapter 4 will show, offers a prime example of this process. In his search for broader sources of support, Chang effected a crucial alliance with the Taiping rebels which was intended to transform his bandit army into an anti-Ch'ing movement. Similarly, in the Republican period it was assistance from Sun Yat-sen's camp that pushed bandit chief Pai Lang toward open revolt. When much-needed arms and military advisors were forthcoming from the revolutionaries, Pai's pronouncements took on an increasingly political tone.[42]

These examples suggest that it was indeed possible for bandit leaders to assume a rebellious position. If wider political circumstances were such that rebels constituted the most available allies, then banditry could change from pure plunder to antigovernment revolt. Historically speaking, however, these situations were relatively rare. Since the state usually constituted the most promising power domain, it was far more common for ambitious bandits to turn in this direction. Government cooptation of bandit chiefs was frequent in traditional China. "Pacification," complete with official position, was such a common government tactic that more than a few bandit leaders probably saw their outlaw career as a quick means of attaining bureaucratic rank.[43] The popular novel Shui-hu chuan provided a well-known model of this very pattern. In fact, the phenomenon of pacification was so frequent that a folk saying arose: "If you want to become an official, carry a big stick"; i.e., be a bandit.[44] Talking softly, however, was evidently not required. Exactly when to surrender was nevertheless a delicate calculation, since the larger one's following, the higher official title one might expect to be offered. Thus there was always a countercurrent at work drawing bandit chieftains away from government control. Because his behavior was not firmly rooted in either economic need or political commitment, the chieftain often assumed a chameleonic quality, vacillating between the worlds of official-dom and crime in a continuing search for personal gain. Bandits did display a certain consideration toward the people who lived near their base of operations. As the Chinese proverb puts it, "A rabbit never eats the grass around its own hole." Outlaws were obviously dependent upon the good will and pro-tection of local inhabitants and were usually related to them by blood. It was thus common to share booty with poor friends, relatives, and protectors back home.* For most peasant partici-pants, however, banditry was a survival strategy born of des-peration. Whether or not it also exhibited a sense of social justice depended in large part upon the level of affluence and security a particular group managed to attain. Outlaws who did enjoy some degree of safety tended to be both more selective in their targets and more generous in sharing the booty. When starva-tion no longer loomed, it is plausible that brigands would con-sciously try to fashion their behavior on a social bandit model. A popular song recorded in one gazetteer reflects this process:

> Bandits make a stir,
> Impoverishing the wealthy, enriching the poor;
> They kidnap for ransom and eat all they can hold;
> Then the leftover silver they give to the old.[45]

Nagano Akira, a Japanese journalist stationed in China during the 1930s, has left us with some of the most informed firsthand accounts of Chinese banditry for that period. Nagano argues strongly in favor of a social bandit characterization of the groups he investigated. As evidence, he quotes from the proclamation of a large bandit gang in Yen-ch'eng, Kiangsu: "We signal the masses of the green forest to assemble for one end—liquida-tion of the corrupt elements in our society. The common folk are our concern and communal property our goal. First we must

---

*Edward Friedman (1974a, p. 164) has noted that the government was finally able to suppress the bandit army of Pai Lang ("White Wolf") only by terrorizing the brigands' families. Their relatives were killed, farms confiscated, and homes burned to prevent the bandits from blending back into the peasantry.

beat to death all greedy officials and evil rich, destroying the root of China's trouble and transforming this into a pure new world."[46] As further indication of a rudimentary class consciousness, Nagano cites a song popular among the notorious railway brigands of Lin-ch'eng, Shantung:

> Upper classes, you owe us money;
> Middle classes, stay out of our affairs.
> Lower classes, hurry to our mountain lair,
> Here to pass the years with us.[47]

Apparently some bandit groups thus did evidence a redistributive ethos. Nevertheless, the dominant motivation for involvement in banditry remained the promise of immediate gain. Even the Lin-ch'eng bandits, for all their radical rhetoric, ended up negotiating a deal with the government whereby their chieftain would be made a brigade commander and allowed to reorganize his followers into the army in exchange for the release of their foreign captives.[48]

In conclusion, banditry was a complex variety of predatory behavior that incorporated a number of contradictory strains. For most of its participants, the enterprise represented an effort to secure resources in response to sudden or endemic scarcity. In this sense, banditry was only a more organized form of other aggressive strategies for survival that had evolved on the Huai-pei plain. Precisely because of this higher level of organization, however, banditry was sometimes liable to take a more politicized direction. Depending upon the types of coalitions that their chieftains forged, bandit gangs could move toward either open rebellion or calculated capitulation. The outside context was crucial in presenting opportunities and obstacles for wider involvement.

Feuds

An equally complex type of predatory violence in Huai-pei was the feud, an enduring form of contention between families and villages. Local gentry being few and far between in this area, conflict resolution was correspondingly deficient. Competition among inhabitants fostered bitter, deadly disputes conducted along clan and community lines. Like salt smuggling and banditry, feuds were usually organized by kinship, as part of a household or clan strategy to improve its livelihood at the expense of competitors. More than these other forms of predatory activity, however, feuding also involved aspects of the protective response. Because parties to the feud were roughly co-equals, with each engaging in aggressive assaults on the other, both sides found it necessary to build up their defenses. As protective measures proceeded, feuds often incorporated whole villages. Settlement in Huai-pei was often by clan, and defense was most effectively conducted at the community level. The fact that certain of the disputes revolved about issues that affected entire villages (for example, water rights or territorial boundaries) also helped to organize the violence on a communal basis.

More clearly than in other forms of predation, we can see in the feud an attempt not only to seize scarce resources, but also to eliminate fellow competitors. In this respect, the feud closely resembled primitive warfare. However, its occurrence in peasant, rather than primitive, society lent the phenomenon rebellious potential. Despite its essentially private character, feuding had wider implications. For one thing, this form of predatory behavior encouraged the militarization of peasant families, thereby enhancing the possibility of armed action on a larger scale as well. Furthermore, when rebellions did get underway in the area, they were shaped in important ways by these homely roots. Revenge could escalate to draw in increasing numbers of combatants, but the resulting conflict never entirely outgrew the pattern of underlying feuds.

The making of armaments for private use flourished. In 1815 in Ying Prefecture, along the Honan-Anhwei border, a village ironsmith was running a lucrative business producing guns for the local populace. The county magistrate reported that repeated efforts to confiscate the weapons had failed miserably, both because of the high economic value of the guns and because peasants feared official investigation if they turned in the weapons as requested.[49] As one gazetteer noted, "The riffraff take along knives and swords whenever they venture outdoors. These persons gather into groups of desperadoes who are quick to pick a fight. As a result, ordinary peasant families must also stockpile weapons."[50]

Ethnic feuds were one motivation for the private arsenals. In 1852, the governor of Anhwei memorialized that Muslims and Han Chinese in this area were making their own spears and swords for use in combat against each other.[51] Often, however, the disputes involved no such ethnic overtones.

During the late Ch'ing, reports on feuds were a frequent theme in memorials to the throne submitted by the provincial governors of Anhwei, Honan, and Kiangsu. As described in these documents, the conflicts typically originated as disputes over scarce resources between individuals. The controversies then quickly escalated into armed confrontations fought, for the most part, along kinship lines.

A few examples from the Huai-pei region of Anhwei illustrate the flavor of these feuds. In June 1845, for instance, the governor of Anhwei presented a memorial describing a case in a village in Huai-yüan County. The trouble began when livestock belonging to an escaped criminal trampled and devoured beans growing on his neighbor's land. Seeing the damage to his crops, the neighbor initiated a heated argument. When the ex-criminal consulted his paternal uncle for advice, the uncle decided that the dispute provided an excellent pretext for a feud. A number of relatives were notified, and the following day thirteen of them—some armed with guns, some without weapons—marched on the home of the victim. The neighbor, assisted by several of his relatives, rushed out to meet the intruders. A fight ensued in which many on both sides were wounded or killed. Bystanders who tried to mediate were also injured in the fray.[52]

In October 1848 an armed feud between two families in Shou County was reported as having developed out of a quarrel over the price of a cow. The owner demanded 13,000 *wen*, whereas a prospective buyer would offer only 12,700. In March 1849, a feud in Huai-yüan stemmed from an argument over repayment of a debt. Wang Yüan-k'o owed Shao K'uei-shen 160 *wen* in cash from a loan for the purchase of firecrackers. One day Shao ran into his debtor on the street and asked for the money. Wang responded with loud curses. The next day Shao called together four of his relatives. Armed with spears, they set out to start a fight. Wang and his neighbor were both killed in the melee.[53]

These examples, brief as they are, give some indication of the origins of Huai-pei feuds. The conflicts developed out of controversies between individuals over scarce resources: crops, animals, money. From these modest beginnings, interclan wars were generated to buttress the individual disputants' claims.

Eventually communal feuds took on a life of their own. An illustration is provided by a dispute that had endured for generations between the Wang and Kuo family villages in Shang-ch'iu, Honan. In 1844, Kuo villagers amassed armed groups of raiders to plunder and kidnap residents of two neighboring villages inhabited by members of the Wang clan, extracting ransoms from more than a hundred families. In 1847, Kuo villagers again went on the offensive, this time stealing wheat from the same Wang community. The theft was reported to the county authorities, whereupon two of the raiders were apprehended. As a result, the Kuo clan harbored an even deeper grudge against the Wangs. In 1850 one of the imprisoned Kuo raiders escaped from jail and stole some millet from the Wang village. Again the government was notified, at which point the Kuo clan amassed more than a hundred members, armed with spears and swords, to stage a retaliatory offensive against the Wangs. One member of the Wang clan was seriously wounded and one Kuo killed in the melee. Not content to let the matter rest, several of the Kuo masqueraded as officials to launch a surprise attack upon Wang households, forcing open doors, breaking windows, and looting at will.[54]

Disputes over water use were a common source of lingering intercommunity feuds. In the summer of 1932, for example, such a conflict flared up along the border between the counties of Hsiao in Kiangsu and Su in Anhwei. When inhabitants of Hsiao County drained two riverbeds, thousands of armed Su villagers responded by filling in the trenches dug by Hsiao in order to keep their own land from flooding. A similar struggle occurred in the same area in the fall of 1933, in part because enduring animosities had yet to be settled.[55]

Although feuds were usually conducted on a clan basis, often pitting whole lineage settlements against each other, disputes within the kinship network also occurred on occasion. In 1850, for example, we have an account of such a case in Su County concerning an unemployed peasant, Wang Chia-pao, who tried to borrow money from his kinsman Wang Chia-hsiu. Chia-hsiu, who was in mourning at the time, reprimanded Chia-pao for the impropriety, ridiculed his lack of a steady job, and summarily refused the loan. Infuriated by these insults, Chia-pao gathered eleven followers to attack his relative's home. They robbed the house of money and carted Chia-hsiu off to an empty lot north of the village where they proceeded to gouge out both his eyes. When the eldest son arrived to rescue his unfortunate father, his eyesight was extinguished as well. A year later Chia-hsiu's second son ran into Chia-pao at market and cursed him vociferously, whereupon Chia-pao seized the youth with the intention of gouging out his eyes also. In response to the impassioned pleading of a crowd who gathered in the marketplace, Chia-pao released the son but avenged the insult by another attack on the family home in which he stole horses and donkeys that were later sold for cash. Four months later yet another assault was staged. This time Chia-pao made off with dishes, pots, and clothing.[56]

An interesting sidelight on these cases is that all were reports of lawsuits filed by the self-declared victims. The initiators were individuals whose persons or property had been harmed or stolen and who used the lawsuit as a means of regaining, or preferably improving upon, their loss. It is important to point out, however, that such people were not only the wealthy or landed gentry. In 1849, for example, a case was filed by a young tenant farmer in response to a bandit attack. Local officials, bribed by the bandit's relatives, took advantage of the litigant's illiteracy to avoid filing a complete report on the incident. Eventually, however, the full facts of the case were brought to light and the victim was compensated for his losses.[57]

Local gazetteers confirm the fact that lawsuits were filed by all sectors of rural Huai-pei society—although with differing frequency and success, one would certainly suspect.[58] That lawsuits were often a strategy for aggressively gaining at the expense of others, rather than a simple effort to redress loss, is borne out by the gazetteer accounts: "The people are frugal, wear rough clothing, and eat coarse food. However, they often gamble and file court cases. Households may easily be bankrupted in this way. Those who are able to take their complaints to the higher courts are regarded as local heroes. Relatives and friends think it normal to give money to support these ventures, which are pursued in hopes of profit."[59] If the cases reported by the provincial governors are any indication, many Huai-pei lawsuits were filed in connection with armed feuds. After loss on the battlefield, a trip to the county magistrate might be a next step in the conflict. Since legal recourse was, however, a less predictable and a potentially disastrous move, most disputes were settled out of court.

Feuds thus usually remained a private form of competition. Nevertheless, they did organize people, typically along kinship lines, to pursue their interests by violent means. To be sure, the feuds of Huai-pei were not so elaborate as the massive armed battles (hsieh-tou) of southeastern China. There a more commercialized economy and powerful lineage structure had made possible the development of a sophisticated and expensive type of vendetta that involved hiring mercenaries, performing religious ceremonies, and so forth.[60] Despite its comparatively modest proportions, however, feuding in Huai-pei did provide peasants with experience in collective violence. Emergent rebellions, we will see, took advantage of such rivalries to gain supporters from among the competitors. By the same token, the form the rebellions assumed—their geographical spread, definition of enemies, level of political consciousness—was shaped in many respects by those roots in local feuds.

Like banditry, feuding bore a two-sided relationship to rebellion. On the one hand, it schooled peasants in the practice of group violence, a skill that might under certain historical conditions be channeled into more rebellious directions. On the other hand, feuds were inherently divisive, establishing deep animosities that could surface during the course of a rebellion.* In the case of both the Nien and the Red Spears, continuing feuds sapped the vitality of the rebel movements and undermined effective cooperation for wider political goals.

PROTECTIVE STRATEGIES

Predatory activities, we have seen, were methods for aggressively increasing the assets of some individuals and groups at the expense of others. The origins of these activities may be linked to local problems of resource scarcity, but the subsequent directions of particular predatory movements were highly dependent upon the wider political context. The protective strategy can also be traced back to endemic competition among Huai-pei inhabitants. Those who found themselves under attack rose to the challenge with a variety of countermeasures. Surplus resources were used to sponsor village guards, crop-watching associations, community defense leagues, and fortification projects.

Compared to the predatory strategy, protection was typically organized by community, rather than by kinship. In single-

*Lamley notes that feuds helped give rise to all four of China's major mid-nineteenth-century rebellions: Taiping, Nien, and Northwest and Southwest Muslim. However, he also finds that in the areas of southeast China where *hsieh-tou* were most highly developed, large-scale rebellion was uncommon. Apparently, in those areas the conflicts were too intense to permit cooperative struggle against the state. ("Hsieh-tou: The Pathology of Violence in Southeastern China, *Ch'ing-shih wen-t'i*, 3, no. 7 [1977]: 31–32.)

lineage settlements the distinction was of course irrelevant, but in multisurname villages the community can usually be identified as the dominant unit of organization. Since predation often threatened all members of a victimized community, the residents devised cooperative measures of defense.

As with the predatory strategy, the form, strength, and political coloration of such activities were intimately connected to the larger society. Just as outside forces played a critical role in attracting or alienating bandits, so they also had a decisive impact upon the allegiances of protective groups. Official support was crucial in encouraging the evolution of local defense. However, when governments tried to extract more resources in the form of higher taxes, these same protective units could rapidly turn their energies toward open revolt.

Crop-watching

The threat of crop theft was the cause of a good deal of defensive activity in rural Huai-pei. Since stealing from a wheat field was an almost irresistible temptation to the hungry, cultivators found it necessary to provide protection for their ripening crops. The likelihood of theft was exacerbated by the fact that peasant dwellings were clustered together into compact villages a good distance from many of the fields. Although a central location evened out the travel time to the scattered holdings where peasants worked, this settlement pattern had the side-effect of leaving fields unprotected by the security of a nearby dwelling. As a result, when harvest time drew near, peasants would send family members out into the fields at night to take turns guarding the household plots. Some affluent families hired regular crop watchers to do the unpleasant task for them. The practice was known as *k'an-ch'ing*, or "watching the green." Often several families with contiguous holdings cooperated in hiring a guard to protect all their crops until ready for harvest.

When harvest time finally arrived, unemployed laborers would converge upon the local market town in search of temporary work. Large landholders contracted with these laborers by the day, leading them to the fields to help cut the wheat. Additional crop watchers were often hired to make certain that no stealing occurred in the midst of the harvest activity. This variety of crop-watching was known as *k'an-pien*, or "watching the borders."[61]

As the harvesting proceeded, in many places it was customary to permit poor peasants from the surrounding countryside to go through the fields gleaning leftovers. The practice, intended as a concession to the impoverished, was the root of many a dispute between gleaners and landowners. In some areas, the difficulties associated with this custom led to the emergence of more formal institutions. In Lu-i County, for example, the evolution of crop-watching associations was directly traceable to gleaning:

At harvest time, women from impoverished families descended upon the fields to seize any leftovers. The more cunning sometimes used gleaning as an opportunity for theft. Time and again quarrels and lawsuits occurred over this problem. As a result, the community determined that gleaning was to be prohibited. Anyone who pilfered grain or let loose animals [to graze on the property of others] would be punished severely. These decisions resulted in the *lan-ch'ing-hui*, or crop-protection association.[62]

By the early twentieth century, crop-watching had in many places changed from a family to a village responsibility. Sometimes the job was performed on a rotating cooperative basis, but more commonly guards were hired by the crop-watching association to carry out the task. Expenses were borne by the villagers, payable in direct proportion to the amount of their holdings.[63] The individuals hired to serve as watchmen were usually the landless poor who had no regular source of support. By hiring some "idle, worthless fellow in the village (not infrequently a thief he is)"[64] the crop-watching association provided an alternative livelihood, thereby channeling potentially lawless behavior into a socially beneficial mode.

Several village studies conducted in North China during the later Ch'ing and Republican periods point to the formation of crop-watching associations as indicating a heightened degree of solidarity and cooperation in the villages of this area.[65] However, Japanese scholar Hatada Takashi presents a quite different explanation for the phenomenon. In Hatada's opinion, crop-watching associations were evidence not of village growth and development, but rather of village decline. His interpretation is based primarily upon investigations sponsored by the South Manchurian Railway that Hatada helped to conduct in six North China villages from 1940 to 1944. According to informants, the organization of crop-watching activities escalated in direct response to the threat of theft. Thus the switch from family- to village-based systems was primarily a defensive reaction against increased robbery, rather than a positive reflection of village dynamism. In Hatada's analysis, the emergence of crop-watching associations was linked to a deterioration in peasant livelihood during the late Ch'ing and Republican eras: growing concentration of landholdings, dissolution of the single-lineage settlement, decline in village finance, and so forth. As rural poverty increased, so did the incidence of theft, and hence the need for protection. Although the peasants originally tried to conduct crop-watching on a household basis, family plots were usually scattered in small parcels here and there, so it was extremely difficult for one household to guard them all. Crop-watching associations were formed as a more effective means of carrying out the onerous chore. Furthermore, since the most persistent thieves were not outsiders, but impoverished members of the village itself, the practice of providing gainful employment for these individuals was a boon to the other inhabitants as well. In short, in Hatada's view the evolution of crop-watching was a gradual and multifunctional strategy for dealing with the effects of rural poverty.[66]

Significantly, the process was soon coopted by local governments. By the turn of the century, it was common for counties in North China to instruct their villages to form crop-watching associations. The idea was that, by cutting down on the percentage of the harvest lost to theft, more would be made available for taxation. Furthermore, since villagers were quite willing to pay to protect their fields, the county government saw the crop-watching association as an effective vehicle for general tax collection. In many areas, "crop-watching fees" became the center of village finance, only a fraction of which actually went toward the expense of crop-watching operations.[67]

The government thus found it expedient to systematize and convert to its own purposes a practice by which peasants tried to protect their insecure livelihoods. In this respect, the development of crop-watching associations resembled that of local militia—another process that evidenced the overlay of official policy upon preexisting ecological strategies.

Militia

Whereas crop-watching was designed to protect the outlying fields, other measures were required to defend property within the village. Since the local government was of little assistance in this matter, responsibility for village defense devolved upon the rural inhabitants themselves. Wealthy households hired personal vigilantes—usually the local riffraff—to provide protection. In addition, whole villages cooperated in organizing for common defense. One traditional village defense institution was the night watch. Watchmen patrolled the streets at night and, at two-hour intervals, sounded a gong, the noise of which was intended to scare off prowlers.

Private vigilantes or night watchmen by themselves were, however, inadequate for the defense needs of most Huai-pei villages. The prevalence of large-scale banditry meant that villagers found it necessary to organize from among themselves groups of armed guards, or militia, to provide the requisite protection. Leadership and funding for these defense forces came from the wealthier inhabitants—gentry, landlords, or rich peasants.

An example of a particularly successful defense league was one directed by Niu Fei-jan of Ts'ao-shih-chi, Anhwei. Niu, a degree holder, in 1853 organized the local militia in opposition to growing Nien activity in his area. For a decade, he, his son, and a cousin actively fought against the Nien. Their work was so esteemed by the government that they were officially dubbed the "Niu Family Army." In 1863, Niu Fei-jan played a leading role in pacifying a Nien chieftain in the area who then proceeded to betray Nien commander Chang Lo-hsing to the authorities. For this deed Niu was rewarded with a high bureaucratic position.*

The militia was one of those key institutions in China which to some extent represented a convergence of the interests of state and society.[68] For rural inhabitants, a viable defense structure meant protection of their livelihood against the threat of banditry. To the government, the militia was a means of maintaining its mandate in the face of rebellion.

Official encouragement of local defense was forthcoming when the regime found itself unable to cope with serious peasant unrest. Thus in 1853, with the northward advance of the Taiping rebels, the Ch'ing government ordered the formation of militia throughout the Huai-pei area. It is important to keep in mind, however, that official support during times of crisis was being superimposed upon a preexisting pattern of rural protection. Although state and society shared certain concerns in the matter, tensions reflecting the two strains were inherent in the institution of the militia. To the villagers, self-defense was a weapon against predatory threats to property. In cases where the threat was posed by plundering bandits, those under attack shared with the state a common interest in combating the problem. Often, however, it was the government itself that played the role of predator by demanding resources from the countryside. At such times the militia constituted an effective vehicle for furthering peasant livelihood at government expense.

An illustration of the rebel potential of the defense corps was found in Hsü-ch'ang, Honan. In 1854, a militia had been estab-

---

*Kuo-yang-hsien chih, 1924, 12/51. Niu's militia was probably related to the Old Cows, a secret society–defense league (described in more detail in Chapter 4), which carried out bitter opposition to the Nien. One Nien folk tale (Nien-chün ku-shih chi, 1962, p. 225) suggests such a connection. The Niu militia was located in approximately the area described by Liu T'ang (NC, vol. 1, p. 349) as Old Cow territory.

lished there in reaction to the intrusion of the Taipings. The following year the militia decided to turn its attention to government intrusion as well. For years, government troops had passed through Hsü-ch'ang on their way to military engagements elsewhere. In the past, the troops had hired carts from the local peasants at the rate of one liang of silver per one hundred *li*. Now, under the auspices of the new defense corps, the community demanded one liang per day per cart, regardless of the distance traveled. The government stepped in to thwart the proposal, but not without provoking a major riot in which several officials were killed.[69]

In the mid-nineteenth century, the proliferation of militia was associated with a dramatic rise in the frequency and scale of tax resistance in Huai-pei.[70] The relationship was twofold. In the first place, the surcharges levied to support the organization of militia were a cause of considerable resentment. In the second place, these same militia in turn offered an organizational base for opposition to government policy.

Massive tax riots were occasioned in part by a steady fall in the price of grain during the first half of the nineteenth century.[71] It has been estimated that prices dropped by about one-half between the years 1815 and 1850, creating an almost 100 percent appreciation in the value of silver.[72] Since taxes were paid in cash, peasants were now forced to sell nearly double the amount of crops in order to be able to pay the same taxes as previously. When one adds on the new surcharges that were being demanded in this period, the magnitude of the burden is readily apparent.

It was in areas where tenancy was low and freeholding peasants numerous that tax riots tended to be most frequent.[73] Higher taxes were of concern to all landholders—large landlords and small owner-cultivators alike. The newly created self-defense forces, led by local landlords and gentry and staffed by ordinary peasants, thus constituted an effective vehicle for tax resistance. In contrast to the secret society, the militia was free to recruit its numbers openly. Under the pretext of local defense, peasants were encouraged to stockpile weapons and participate in military training. The result was a powerful force that could be mobilized to promote local interests when these conflicted with government demands. In 1859, the Manchu prince Seng-ko-lin-ch'in reported that all of Shantung was ablaze with tax revolts instigated by the local militia. Hundreds of cases have been recorded of militia leading assaults on county offices, burning tax registers, and killing magistrates and other officials.[74]

In addition to carrying out what were essentially defensive acts against tax collection, the militia sometimes engaged in outright predatory activities themselves. Ironically, the state's promotion of the militia had brought into being a weapon that could be used for plunder as well as protection. The very existence of this institution in the Huai-pei countryside opened new organizational opportunities for both types of survival strategy. As if to spite a social scientist's search for order, bandits now began to assume the guise of regular militia, secreting their predatory designs behind the cover of protective legitimacy. Government-sponsored militarization during the late Ch'ing gave birth to powerful institutions that could turn from their officially prescribed functions to tax resistance, banditry, and open revolt.

The importance of defense forces to collective violence did not end with the demise of imperial China. During the Republican era as well, self-defense leagues were a crucial basis for local resistance. In the chaos of the 1920s, locally sponsored village militia mushroomed to combat bandits and warlords in the Huai-pei countryside, often moving to tax revolt in their effort to maintain control over precarious resources. In the late 1930s, when the Japanese occupied much of Huai-pei, the central government once again instructed local communities to organize self-defense groups in response. Newspapers of the time are replete with accounts of these forces turning to predatory activities. In 1939, all of Anhwei Province was ordered to establish militia units to resist Japanese intrusion.[75] The vice-commander of the northern Anhwei self-defense league, a young man by the

name of Chou T'iao-fan, used his position as a front for organized banditry. Chou forced peasants in his jurisdiction to
grow opium, which he then sold at considerable profit to himself. For several years, the vice-commander instructed his subordinates to kill, plunder, and kidnap for ransom.[76]

The militia stood as a kind of bridge between the government
and the peasantry. As power brokers in the countryside, village
defense leagues were intended to mediate the interests of state
and society. When those interests proved irreconcilable, however, militia could serve to channel mass action in opposition to
government demands.

Fortification

Intimately connected to the emergence of militia was the establishment of fortified communities. To facilitate local defense, villagers erected walls and constructed stockades around their
threatened settlements. Throughout Chinese history, the wall
has been an architectural response to conflict. Simple town walls
of pounded earth date back to Lung-shan settlements of 2000
B.C. Subsequently the structures became more massive and enclosed greater expanses of territory. Walls were built to fend off
bandits, to define the borders of warring states, and to insulate
the so-called civilized world from the barbarous outside.

The particular type of fortification associated with the rise of
the militia during the late nineteenth century had precedents in
practices developed during the White Lotus Rebellion. Local
notables instructed the peasants to construct earth fortresses in
which to store grain and take refuge. The idea was that when
rebels approached there would be nothing in the fields for them
to steal, no place to rest, and no people to threaten. Moats were
dug around the fortresses and gun turrets built at the corners to
make them virtually impervious to rebel incursion.[77]

In Huai-pei, construction of these fortified communities may
have begun with the White Lotus insurgency, but it mushroomed in response to the Nien and Taipings in the mid-
nineteenth century. The fortresses were known in the Huai-pei

area as *yü-chai*. The term has an interesting etymology. Although the word *chai*, or stockade, was common throughout North China, the character *yü* had a more parochial meaning. Originally the word referred to land that was effectively protected by dikes against the Huai River. During the late Ch'ing, the meaning was extended to describe the heavy fortifications constructed against banditry and rebellion under gentry supervision.[78] As maladministration of the river system increased, so grew the need for defense against predatory attack. A term that at one time had been reserved for protection from the physical environment was now applied to protection from human competitors.

A cyclical theory of village fortification has been proposed by G. William Skinner, who suggests that each dynastic decline triggered a process of community closure at the local level. According to the theory, during the height of a dynasty's vigor, rural villages were relatively open. In response to the many opportunities for upward mobility, individuals moved out of and back into their rural communities with considerable frequency. Conversely, the onset of dynastic decay caused villages to close their doors in defense against an increasingly threatening and insecure environment. "Coercive closure," as Skinner terms the process, involved a sequence of steps: formation of crop-watching societies, expulsion of outsiders, militarization of local systems, and fortification of key areas.*

In Huai-pei in the late nineteenth and early twentieth centuries, the process of community closure was well underway—a direct response to the ecological and political instability of the period. Although construction of fortifications was periodically endorsed by the state, it was fundamentally an expression of parochial interests. Local residents rushed to erect walls and

---

*Skinner, 1971. Skinner's point about decreased movement in and out of the community during the period of closure is less applicable to Huai-pei, where seasonal migration as beggars, salt smugglers, and bandits seems to have increased in response to ecological insecurity. Although mobility for educational or commercial purposes may have declined, periodic forays to obtain scarce resources intensified.

stockades when their property was threatened by attack. Construction of *yü-chai* thus neatly mirrored the level of predatory activity in the area. The general pattern is illustrated by data culled from the gazetteers of six Huai-pei counties which have recorded the dates when fortresses were built in their areas (see Table 8). As the table shows, the greatest period of construction occurred during the late Hsien-feng and T'ung-chih reigns (1856–66), when the Nien and Taipings were most active in the area. The early Republican period then witnessed another rise in construction, as Pai Lang, Lao Yang-jen, and other bandits marched across Huai-pei. Unfortunately, most of the gazetteers that included these data were published too early to present an accurate indication of the trends after the turn of the century. However, we know from other accounts that forts continued to be built in opposition to warlords and marauding troops on into the Republican period. It is probably safe to assume that the construction of new forts and repair of dilapidated ones escalated during this period far faster than the table would suggest.

The building of these massive forts had important implications for the configuration of spatial boundaries in Huai-pei. As peasants arranged to store a part of their crop in its granary, the stockade began to assume a host of economic functions. In time, the *yü-chai* effectively displaced local markets in some areas. Once-prosperous markets turned into ghost towns as commerce shifted to the safety of the walled fortress.[79]

This accretion of economic importance was soon translated into political status as well. In the 1860s, the *yü-chai* replaced the rural town as a quasi-administrative unit in most parts of Huai-pei. By the Kuomintang period, the *yü-chai* was formally recognized as a level of rural administration, with 3,721 of these units in the Huai-pei portion of Anhwei Province alone.[80] Encompassing an average of 400 to 500 households, the *yü-chai* occupied a slot one step above the village in the hierarchy of rural administration. In Kuo-yang County, for example, the 221 *yü-chai* in operation in 1925 had jurisdictions ranging from 3 to 79 villages, the average being about 25 villages.[81]

Table 8. Construction of Fortified Communities in Huai-pei

	County						
Year	T'ung-shan	P'ei	Sui-ning	Feng	Che-ch'eng	Hsiang-ch'eng	Total
1807	1						1
1846	1						1
1850	5					5	10
1853					1	1	2
1854						5	5
1855					1		1
1856	4				2	2	8
1857	6				1	5	12
1858	9		31	5	3	17	65
1859	17		11		12	5	45
1860	27	1	25	16	9	10	88
1861	9	2	7	20	9	24	71
1862	28	1	12	1	16	36	94
1863	7		3		1	8	19
1864	2	1	1	1		3	8
1865	2	1	3			1	7
1866	4	1	2		3	3	13
1867	1	1	1			1	4
1870						1	1
1871	5						5
1875			1			1	2
1880	2						2
1890	1						1
1891	1						1
1894	1						1
1909	2						2
1910						3	3
1911	8					12	20
1920		46					46
No date	23		6	1		36	66
TOTAL	166	54	103	44	58	179	604

Sources: T'ung-shan-hsien chih, 1926, 10/1–30; P'ei-hsien chih, 1920, 16/9–10; Sui-ning-hsien chih, 1887, 6/35–51; Feng-hsien chih, 1894, 2/7–11; Che-ch'eng-hsien chih, 1896, 2/15–19; Hsiang-ch'eng-hsien chih, 1911.

The method of operation of these forts and the extent to which they constituted permanent living quarters as opposed to emergency shelters varied from place to place. The differences seem due in large measure to the magnitude and distribution of resources in particular locales. In areas of poor, freeholding villages—which were most typical of Huai-pei—*yü-chai* were usually temporary refuges managed cooperatively by all members of the community. However, in places where there was severe landholding concentration, such that one or two families controlled great tracts of property, the construction of forts was likely to be considerably more lavish. Since these affluent households had much to protect and sufficient means to do so, they would build massive fortifications within which they and their subordinates lived permanently.

To illustrate the freeholding pattern, we have the case of Lao-wo, a large village in eastern Honan which included some 400 households. In 1938 the village learned of a bandit gang numbering over 1,000 which had plundered ruthlessly in the area. The villagers congregated in their earthen fort at night in self-defense. Some two miles in circumference, the fort was divided into 35 sections, each of which was guarded by 10 members of the community on a rotating basis. In addition to the 350 peasants on stationary duty, there were 8 mobile units which took turns patrolling around the fort. Within the stockade, peasants slept in dwellings they themselves had constructed. A few of the more affluent used bricks, but most dwellings were made of wheat stalks, and some peasants simply laid out straw mats on which to spend their nights, clutching their rifles as they slept. At one point, Lao-wo joined with neighboring villages to try to combat the bandits directly. Although they managed to mobilize nearly 1,800 peasants in this engagement, the villagers were unable to suppress the menace. As a result, the peasants of Lao-wo were forced to continue their nightly routine of taking refuge in the fort.[82]

In cases where the *yü-chai* were essentially owned and operated by wealthy landlords, the system was somewhat different.

This second pattern has been vividly described for certain sections of northern Kiangsu where land concentration was especially pronounced. The walls of these forts were often constructed of brick or stone, rather than earth. Cannon towers were erected at the four corners of the stockade. In the center of the encirclement was a tiled mansion with its own cannon tower, the home of the large landowner. All around the fortress chief lived the several hundred tenant households who cultivated his lands. Outside the fort were a number of tiny satellite villages, some of whose inhabitants also tilled the fortress chief's lands.[83]

According to observers who conducted field work in the area in 1930, these were extremely self-contained communities, permeated with a thoroughly medieval atmosphere. The fortress chiefs, who were also the commanders of the local self-defense corps, assumed titles such as "King of the Underworld Kuo," "Hegemon Li," and the like. Their militia comprised primarily tenant farmers, sometimes supplemented by disbanded soldiers or other peasants in need of employment.[84]

The *yü-chai* under these circumstances operated as autonomous kingdoms, the fortress chief in command of both economic and judicial matters. Militarily such forts constituted a serious challenge to the local government. In Kiangsu's P'ei County, for example, in 1930 the county administration itself controlled only eighteen rifles—eight under the militia and ten under the public security office. By contrast, one single fortress chief in the county possessed thirty-four rifles and, when he cooperated with two adjacent forts led by kinsmen, could control fifty-three rifles, nearly three times the government stock. Often several fortresses did join forces to resist the authority of the county administration. They would then refuse to pay taxes and would assume full independence from government control.[85]

Regardless of whether they were initiated and managed by small owner-cultivators or by rich landlords, the forts were essentially a means of promoting security and survival in a threatening environment. Once these structures were built, however, they themselves constituted an important part of the setting to which peasants had to adjust. The *yü-chai*, we have seen, came to assume both marketing and administrative functions in rural Huai-pei. Furthermore, the very physical presence of these walled communities had an important effect upon collective survival strategies in the area. Although they were products of human activity, the forts became, in a real sense, a feature of the Huai-pei ecosystem.* As such, *yü-chai* were an important weapon for predators as well as protectors. Operating on such flat terrain, Huai-pei bandits found the walled fortress a useful substitute for the swamp marsh or mountain lair that their brethren in other geographical regions chose as home base. Just as the construction of fortified communities was an essential method of protection against bandit attack, so the occupation of these same fortifications became a key tactic for successful banditry in Huai-pei.

CONCLUSION

There was a kind of dialectic at work in the relation between the predatory and protective strategies of survival. On the one hand, the two strategies were polar opposites. Predation was an aggressive attack upon the resources of others; protection was its direct countermeasure. On the other hand, these approaches implied a mutual dependency in which they simultaneously presupposed and limited each other. Although the strategies were fundamentally antagonistic, they provided opportunities for cooperation as well as competition. At times, one mode would pass into the other—militias turned to plunder or bandits

---

*Clifford Geertz explains this same process with reference to the example of the Eskimo's igloo, which, he explains, "can be seen as a most important cultural weapon in his [the Eskimo's] resourceful struggle against the arctic climate, or it can be seen as a, to him, highly relevant feature of the physical landscape within which he is set and in terms of which he must adapt" (1971, p. 9). As a Chinese scholar described the Huai-pei landscape in 1930, it was "nothing but windswept, dry, dusty fields on which were planted a veritable forest of earthen forts" (Wu Shou-p'eng, 1930, p. 70).

settled within walled fortresses. At still other times, the two would even join hands, with bandits and defense leagues making common cause in opposition to yet a third enemy: the state. Widespread and long-lasting rebellion in Huai-pei was born of this peculiar synthesis. The alliance was always fragile, however, inasmuch as it represented two contrary sets of interests and approaches. Particular rebellions had roots in either the predatory or the protective strategy. Large-scale movements necessarily drew to their ranks adherents of the opposite mode, but they could not entirely overcome their origins in the process. The synthesis was never complete, and was often rife with conflict.

The notion of a dualistic tension is implicit in much of the scholarship on traditional Chinese society. The terms of the dialectic are usually defined from the perspective of the ruling elite, however. Thus the dichotomy is typically posed as one of "order versus chaos," "orthodoxy versus heterodoxy," or "state versus society." In this view, the tension in the system arises out of conflict between the government's demand for conformity and the propensity of peasants and local gentry toward an unruly independence. In adopting this perspective, scholars mirror the outlook of the documents they study. It is the *yin* and *yang* as seen from the top that is being applied to society at large.

Although data on the peasant perspective are obviously less accessible and often altogether nonexistent, we do have information about peasant behavior. Building our theory of rebellion from the bottom up, we begin with the notion of peasants adapting to a particular environment, developing individual and group strategies on the basis of the paucity or surplus of their resources. By looking at rural collective action, we can identify a dialectic operating by its own rules at the lowest levels of society.

Chapters 4 and 5 will present case studies of rebellions born of the predatory and protective strategies of Huai-pei peasants. A central theme will be the interplay, at once generative and self-destructive, of each strategy with its opposite over the course of the movements.

4. Predators Turn Rebels: The Case of the Nien

Predatory activities of smuggling, feuds, and banditry were, we have seen, adaptive survival strategies for poor peasants in Huai-pei. An ongoing phenomenon, predation escalated during periods of natural calamity. Ad hoc bandit outfits grew first into semipermanent gangs and then into massive bandit armies that razed the countryside in search of a living.

Mid-nineteenth-century Huai-pei witnessed a dramatic rise in predatory aggression, a clear reflection of worsening ecological circumstances. Local militia and earthwall fortifications then sprang up in response to the growing threat. Competition might have remained at this parochial level had it not been for the involvement of outside actors: the central government and the Taiping rebels. These external forces merged predators and protectors in a common antagonism toward the state. What began as simple predation was pushed into a rebellious posture. But bandit origins could not be entirely overcome and, for most participants, the movement continued to be a means for securing household income rather than a self-conscious effort at toppling the dynasty.

The Nien Rebellion was a major peasant movement that effectively precluded government control in Huai-pei for more than a decade (1851–63). Although somewhat overshadowed by their contemporaries, the Taipings, the Nien are well known for their mobile warfare which decimated the Manchus' crack cavalry division and killed its commander, Prince Seng-ko-lin-ch'in. For years the entire North China Plain was subjected to periodic Nien incursions as hundreds of thousands of the mounted rebels darted from one plundering expedition to the next.

What are the origins of this enormous insurrection? Why did such massive numbers of Huai-pei peasants join the Nien forces? In seeking to answer these questions, most studies of the Nien have focused less upon the participants themselves than upon the wider political context. The rebellion has been explained as part of a general trend toward regionalism in nineteenth-century China, as a response to the government corruption that accompanied imperial decline, and as a reaction against the deleterious effects of imperialism and increased land concentration attendant upon the Opium Wars.[1]

Every major social action is in some sense a reflection of the wider historical setting in which it develops, but a preoccupation with the larger scene at the expense of attention to the actors themselves runs the risk of "overdetermining" one's explanation. Without denying the importance of evaluating the Nien's place in history, it would seem that there is room for a more microscopic approach to the rebellion as well. Although national events had major significance for the timing and evolution of the rebellion, the contention here is that the origins and activities of the Nien are inextricably linked to ongoing processes of adaptive competition within the Huai-pei region.[2]

In interpreting the Nien as an outgrowth of a local struggle for scarce resources, this chapter proposes an explanation somewhat at variance with the commonly held view of the rebellion as essentially a secret-society operation. Most studies have suggested that the movement was an expression of the White Lotus Society, a group of heterodox sects that had inspired countless rebellions throughout North China.[3] Evidence for such an argument is, however, circumstantial at best. Although scattered hints of White Lotus influence can indeed be found, these do not add up to a compelling case in favor of secret-society direction. White Lotus sects constituted simply one of many allies to whom the Nien were drawn in their continual search for support. The origins of the uprising lie not in anti-Manchu millenarianism, but rather in a highly pragmatic effort by vast numbers of Huai-pei inhabitants to seize and sustain a livelihood. Likewise, the turn from banditry to outright revolt is explained less by the attraction of a revolutionary secret society than by the exactions of the government itself. The movement arose out of a dialectic specific to the Huai-pei countryside; subsequent developments then reflected the intrusion of outside forces more than any "natural" rebelliousness on the part of local society.

NIEN ORIGINS

The word *nien* referred in Huai-pei to a band of people formed for the purpose of plunder. The precise origins of the term are obscure, but the usage probably stemmed from the written Chinese character's other meaning, "to twist." Since bandits generally conducted their raids at night, they used torches (*yu-nien*) made by twisting pieces of cloth which were then soaked in oil and ignited. This explanation for the origins of the term *nien* is provided in numerous sources.[4] Alternative interpretations say the term originally referred to the loading and transporting of carts by salt smugglers or to religious ceremonies of one sort or another.[5] Regardless of the exact etymology, it is clear that by the early nineteenth century the term had come to refer to groups of bandits, ranging in size from a few people to several hundred, located along the Honan-Anhwei border. Unlike simple ad hoc bandits (*t'u-fei*), the *nien* apparently operated as semipermanent gangs. Such brigands were accused in official documents of having "formed *nien*" (*chieh-nien*) in order to carry out their predatory activities.

Whether *nien* was a name the brigands themselves used is open to question. Some accounts suggest that the term was bestowed by outsiders, whereas others describe it as a self-appellation.[6] In any case, it is certain that the term did not refer to a unified movement. For example, the gazetteer of Chin-hsiang, Shantung, notes that in 1852 "local *nien*" (*t'u-nien*) were active in the area. However, the groups led by Chang Lo-hsing, usually considered the main Nien movement, are referred to in the gazetteer not as *nien*, but rather as "Anhwei bandits" (*wan-fei*).[7]

The exact origins of the bandits themselves are only a little less hazy than those of the term by which they came to be known. The earliest dating would place the Nien in the K'ang-hsi period (1662–1722), but this ex post facto periodization is not corroborated by other sources.[8] A more credible version puts the start of the Nien at the close of the White Lotus Rebellion in 1805.[9] Imperial censor T'ao Chu in an 1814 memorial referred to the Nien as organizational units of the "Red Beard" bandits said to have been active along the Honan-Anhwei border for a decade. T'ao described the Red Beards as escaped White Lotus rebels, a statement that has formed the basis of subsequent speculation linking the Nien to the secret society. At the same time, T'ao mentioned no religious activities and made clear that the brigands were interested in plunder rather than proselytizing. Organized in Nien groups with as many as a thousand members, the Red Beards were said to have stolen money and women and to have committed various indecencies in the local marketplaces. Their money came mainly from acting as armed protectors for the salt smuggling ventures common in the region. When that income was insufficient, the Red Beards resorted to outright plunder.[10]

Whereas T'ao Chu linked the early Nien to White Lotus remnants, a contemporary official described them as disbanded soldiers from the imperial forces that suppressed that same rebellion. According to this version, multitudes of Huai-pei peasants had been recruited as government braves for the campaign against the rebellion then raging along the Szechuan-Hupei-Shensi border. After the uprising was quelled, the recruits were discharged and ordered to return to their homes in Huai-pei. Accustomed to military adventure and unable to find regular work in their native villages, the demobilized soldiers turned to a life of brigandage.[11] This explanation for a link between the Nien and the White Lotus Rebellion seems more creditable, inasmuch as we do know that large numbers of Huai-pei peasants fought on the government side in the campaign, and since there is no indication that the early Nien were outsiders to Huai-pei, or that they practiced the White Lotus faith.

In any case, whether former rebels, soldiers, or both, the influx of people was an important addition to ongoing forms of predatory activity in the area. Since the mid-eighteenth century, officials had been concerned about the growth of societies of outlaws in the Huai-pei border region. In 1755 and again in 1757, it was reported that bands of armed ruffians, calling themselves the "Smooth Sword Society" (shun-tao-hui), gathered at markets and temple festivals to drink, gamble, and fight duels. Although no evidence was found to implicate the group as a heterodox sect, members were known to have engaged in robbery and extortion.[12] Reports of similar outlaw groups, referred to variously as "sword-dragging bandits" (i-tao-fei) or "sword-concealing bandits" (yeh-tao-fei), continued to be registered over the succeeding years. As T'ao Chu described the origins of these armed societies:

The prefectures of Hsü, P'ei, Huai, and Hai in Kiangsu adjoin the provinces of Anhwei, Honan, and Shantung along a jagged borderline. Bandits appear and hide in this area. Furthermore, the local inhabitants are strong and fierce by nature, skilled at wielding weapons. Cases of physical assault and murder amount to twice the number found in other places. . . . Investigation has shown that originally the bandits were nothing but unemployed persons who behaved with impunity. Having no restraints imposed upon them, gradually, three to five in number, they joined together to extort money. At the slightest pretext, they would draw their swords. The foolish and cowardly, afraid of their power, dared not challenge them. Consequently they grew arrogant and more disrespectful of the law. After a time, they turned into vicious groups of brigands who brandished weapons.[13]

It was in the context of a long tradition of armed predatory societies such as these that the Nien took root and developed into a formidable fighting force.

EARLY NIEN MOTIVES AND ACTIVITIES

Although the Nien got underway at the conclusion of the White Lotus Rebellion and probably did absorb individuals who had been connected in one way or another with that uprising, their own activities did not reflect secret-society inspiration. After the suppression of yet another White Lotus uprising in 1813, which had managed the incredible feat of penetrating the Forbidden City itself, the ruling authorities were especially alert to any suspicion of "heterodox" behavior. Thus it is significant that the early Nien were officially characterized as "less threatening than heterodox bandits, who form massive associations and advocate rebellion." Ch'ing legal codes accused the Nien only of robbery and not of the more serious crime of propagating heterodox religion.[14]

Although the authorities feared a possible merger between the Nien and local religious sects, they were careful to distinguish the groups in official documents. In 1822, a discovered White Lotus rebel, Chu Feng-k'o, from eastern Honan, fled across the border into Ying Prefecture, Anhwei. Officials noted with concern that the Ying district was a favorite refuge for fugitive rebels:

Ferocity is the rule in Ying Prefecture. There are Nien bandits and smugglers who, although they do not practice religion or recruit disciples, are useful contacts because of their reputation and local influence. It is rumored that in Ai-t'ing-chi, located about 160 li southwest of Fu-yang city, there are many Nien bandits. This is where rebels like Chu seek refuge. About 15 li north of Ai-t'ing-chi is a village called Ma-chia-tien . . . the bandit leader Ma P'i-hsien is chief of countless Nien in that area. In the western part of the county . . . Nien bandits and salt smugglers flock into groups. If they are not arrested soon, it is possible that the religious followers in hiding will join the Nien bandits to stir up great trouble.[15]

Although the specter of a Nien–White Lotus alliance weighed on the imagination of the authorities, they clearly distinguished the Nien from religious rebels aiming to bring down the state. In 1830, a circuit intendant in Honan reported that since assuming office he had supervised the arrest of a White Lotus rebel and 53 followers, as well as some 50 Nien. In the province as a whole, 215 Nien, 103 ordinary bandits, and 110 White Lotus disciples had been apprehended.[16]

The inspiration for early Nien activities derived less from secret-society influence than from ongoing patterns of predation in the area. Searching for the cause of growing Nien strength, the governor-general of Anhwei and Kiangsu remarked that "peasants in Huai-pei have traditionally been unruly, a natural consequence of bad soil and endemic poverty. Large numbers of wandering unemployed persons move about, form groups, and turn to plunder. In summer, when sorghum grows tall, bandits hide in the fields and stage surprise raids on unsuspecting passers-by."[17] In 1815, a county magistrate with many years of experience in Huai-pei classified the "trouble makers" of this area into three categories: bare sticks, smugglers, and bandits. Bare sticks were unemployed villagers who tried to overcome their poverty by engaging in petty crime. The more daring of them set up gambling operations in the local markets, brandished weapons in broad daylight, and "killed at the slightest pretext." Sometimes they came into conflict with the second group of Huai-pei predators, the smugglers. Usually, however, the two groups cooperated, the smugglers depending upon bare sticks for protection. The third group of trouble makers, the bandits, formed armed units known as *nien* who stole crops and animals and kidnaped for ransom. The magistrate estimated that there were thousands of these various outlaws in the Huai valley. Despite their different activities, they had arisen from common origins. When one calculated that each outlaw was also the member of a family, it was apparent that tens of thousands of people were benefiting directly or indirectly from these predatory activities. If the brigands were to renounce their lawless ways, the countryside would be left with massive numbers of households lacking alternative means to supplement an inadequate agricultural livelihood. It would be unnatural to expect them quietly to starve to death, concluded the magistrate.[18]

Drawn from the ranks of the chronically unemployed, the Nien engaged in all the activities normally associated with the predatory strategy. Table 9 presents a summary of early Nien activities, as reported in contemporary official documents.

Table 9. Nien Activities Prior to 1845

Date	Province(s)	Activities	Source
K'ang-hsi (1662–1722)	Shantung	Robbery	NC 1:1
1797	Honan, Anhwei	Gambling, robbery	NC 1:309
1808[a]	Honan, Anhwei, Shantung	Robbery	SCSH-CC 99/30
1809[a]	Honan	Robbing travelers	CSL-CC 217/35-36
1809[a]	Honan, Anhwei, Shantung	Gambling, robbery	CSL-CC 218/22
1811[a]	Honan	Robbing rich, giving to poor	CSL-CC 246/2
1814[a]	Anhwei, Honan	Robbery	NC I:378
1815[a]	Anhwei, Honan	Salt smuggling protection, robbery, rape	NCPC:6
1815	Honan	Armed feuds	CSL-CC 308/16
1815	Anhwei, Honan, Kiangsu	Stealing crops and animals, kidnaping	NCPC:29
1818	Shantung, Anhwei, Honan, Kiangsu	Robbing travelers, killing officials	CSL-CC 344/14-15
1818[a]	Shantung	Robbery, salt smuggling	SCSH-CC 102/4-5
1820	Honan	Robbery	SCSH-CC 102/7
1821[a]	Shantung	Robbery	SCSH-TK 80
1821[a]	Honan, Anhwei, Hupeh	Robbery	CSLC 37/37
1822	Anhwei, Honan	Salt smuggling	SCSH-TK 80
1823	Honan	Robbery, extortion, murder	NCPC:13
1823[a]	Honan, Anhwei	Robbery	SYT-TK 3/7/22
1824[a]	Honan, Anhwei, Hupeh	Robbery	WCT-TK 4/10/28
1830[a]	Honan	Salt smuggling, feuds, robbery	SCSH-TK 82
1832	Hupeh, Honan	Robbery	NCPC:33
1832	Hupeh, Honan	Wounding soldiers	CSL-TK 222/20-21
1836	Honan	Trying to kill soldiers	CSL-TK 283/7

(continued)

Table 9. Nien Activities Prior to 1845 *(continued)*

Date	Province(s)	Activities	Source
1842	Hupeh, Honan	Killing officials	CSL-TK 380/2
1842	Kiangsu, Anhwei, Honan	Killing soldiers	CSL-TK 382/23
1842	Kiangsu	Stealing money, clothes	CSL-TK 383/4
1842	Kiangsu, Anhwei	Robbery	SCSH-TK 86
1842	Honan, Hupeh	Robbery	CSL-TK 385/2
1843	Anhwei	Salt smuggling	CSL-TK 389/29
1843	Honan	Killing an official	CSL-TK 391/2
1844	Kiangsu, Honan	Salt smuggling	SCSH-TK 86

^aRefers to reports of "Red Beards" in addition to, or in place of, Nien.

Many of these early Nien were *yu-min*, drifters who mingled in market towns to while away the time. According to some accounts, Nien leaders were at one time known as "table chiefs" (*cho-chu*) in reference to their control over local gambling operations. Often those who gambled did so with very little capital. One loss could sink them deeply into debt, thereby opening the door to more serious crimes.[19]

Salt Smuggling

Salt smuggling was one of those more serious offenses. As described in Chapter 3, northern Anhwei was a center for smuggling, since it was a meeting point for the Huai and Ch'ang-lu salt districts. The single county of Su belonged to the Ch'ang-lu district, whose salt was both less expensive and more palatable than the Huai salt to which the rest of the province was restricted. A further inducement to smuggling was the fact that in the mid-nineteenth century Su County was permitted by law to sell 20,893 *yin* of salt, whereas neighboring Po was authorized to sell a mere 5,033 *yin*, and the six counties of Ying Prefecture (Po, Meng-ch'eng, Fu-yang, Ying-shang, Huo-ch'iu, and T'ai-ho) all together were allowed only 24,216 *yin*.*

An-hui t'ung-chih, 1877, chap. 79. The *yin* were certificates that permitted the purchase and sale of salt. During much of the Ch'ing period, 1 *yin* was fixed at

As a result of these inequities, peasants from northern Anhwei found it profitable to travel to Su County or to nearby Honan or Shantung to purchase salt for resale back home. During the 1850s, one string of cash could purchase a full thirty *chin* of Ch'ang-lu salt, which after being smuggled back to northern Anhwei sold at the rate of twenty *chin* per string.[20] For many peasants, smuggling was a seasonal occupation, carried out during the slack periods as a means of supplementing income.

Over time, salt smuggling operations in northern Anhwei came to be centered in the market town of Chih-ho-chi, conveniently situated near the dividing line of the Huai and Ch'ang-lu zones. Thanks to the town's proximity to several different county and provincial jurisdictions, government control was lax. Smugglers returning from expeditions to the Ch'ang-lu district sold their stock to middlemen in Chih-ho-chi for transport down the rivers to neighboring towns and villages.[21]

One of the most important effects of salt smuggling was to break down regional barriers and permit Huai-pei peasants to establish a wide range of personal contacts. These geographically dispersed relationships proved very important to the subsequent spread of the Nien uprising. Furthermore, the enterprise of smuggling provided peasants with valuable experience in mobility and the art of evading capture. The significance of these skills—acquired through generations of practice—became clear in the guerrilla tactics of the Nien Army, which kept government forces at bay for decades.[22]

The early Nien were connected to salt smuggling in two ways. Some were smugglers themselves, and others served as guards for those who conducted the actual traffic. An inherently dangerous activity, smuggling generated its own demand for adequate protection. Groups of armed guards were therefore formed to provide this service. Nien commander Chang Lo-hsing was the leader of one such band of strongmen known as the "eighteen spears," a force that in fact included some fifty to

---

364 catties in the Huai zone; under T'ao Chu's reform of 1832, it was standardized at 400 catties (Metzger, 1962, pp. 4, 26).

one hundred people.[23] Chang came from a village located about twelve *li* to the northwest of Chih-ho-chi. His was a major clan in this area, encompassing eighteen neighboring villages. Chang's own family was fairly affluent, his father owning about 150 *mou* of land. Chang Lo-hsing was the youngest of three sons. The eldest son having died at an early age, Lo-hsing and his brother Min-hsing each inherited half of their father's holdings. Chang Min-hsing soon married a woman from a wealthy clan in a nearby village and was then able to purchase over 300 *mou* of additional land. He thereupon moved to another village more convenient to the newly acquired fields, leaving his younger brother Chang Lo-hsing as the sole family representative in their native village. The size of the Chang clan gave Chang Lo-hsing considerable local influence.[24] With many of his poorer clan members engaged in salt smuggling, "village aspirant" Chang Lo-hsing began to assume the role of patron for these kinsmen. Since the Chang family village was located right along the road to Yung-ch'eng County, it was a natural stopping point for peasants operating the route between Yung-ch'eng and Chih-ho-chi.* Along this route, smugglers transported their loads in wheelbarrows that could carry twenty to thirty packages of salt. One package per cart was the price for Chang Lo-hsing's protection. The service was so effective that the local officials found it in their interest not to interfere with smugglers who had affixed Chang's seal to their wheelbarrows.[25]

Although smuggling was simply a means of augmenting income for most of the poor peasants who engaged in it, the fact that it was conducted in defiance of government authority rendered it an important steppingstone to outright rebellion. As the Nien developed, it was hardly surprising that many of their chieftains should have been drawn from the ranks of salt smuggling leaders. The term for Nien chieftain, "excursion

*Legend has it that Chang Lo-hsing was also involved in gambling (Ma Ch'ang-hua, 1959, p. 24). An account published in Taiwan by a representative to the National Assembly from Kuo-yang County explains Chang's move to rebellion as a response to government efforts to shut down his lucrative gambling operations (Wang Fan-t'ing, 1975, p. 15).

leader" (*t'ang-chu*), had apparently been used originally to designate the person in charge of a smuggling foray.*

Plunder, Kidnaping

Like most predatory outfits in Huai-pei, the Nien gained the largest share of their income from plunder. Robbing traveling merchants was an especially common occupation. One of the earliest and most enduring Nien groups was situated on a small mountain in southern Honan, a spot that had been a favorite bandit lair for generations thanks to its strategic location near the borders of six different counties. Just below the mountain was a trail leading to a nearby market. Merchants traveling this path could easily be spotted from the bandit hideaway and relieved of all their wares.† Similarly, in 1846 southern Shantung was said to be rife with Nien from northern Kiangsu who robbed merchants passing through the area. The stolen goods were quickly sold to nearby outlets in Kiangsu, Honan, or Chihli. Capture of the bandits was extremely difficult, inasmuch as any potentially incriminating booty had already been disposed of by the time local authorities caught up with the culprits. Officials admitted that the bandits maintained cordial relations with the great majority of local inhabitants, who were simply too poor to constitute appealing victims.[26]

Not all stolen loot was sold for cash. Many Nien groups seized grain and animals which were then transported home to share with their families. There are scattered indications of social banditry in some of these ventures. In 1853, for example, the governor of Anhwei reported that Nien in Ling-pi County had been robbing official grain envoys and distributing the goods to poor peasants in the area.[27]

*This interpretation of *t'ang-chu* is found in Ma Ch'ang-hua, 1959, pp. 16–17. Based on field investigations in northern Anhwei, Ma et al. suggest that the rendition of *t'ang-chu* in many official documents as the homophone meaning "sect leader" reflected a misunderstanding of the local dialect.

†FL 1/24–26. This same mountain stronghold, located in Pi-yang County, was the site of bandit Pai Lang's ("White Wolf") defeat of General Chang Hsi-yüan in 1913. It was also the place where bandit Lao Yang-jen held out until warlord Wu P'ei-fu agreed to enroll him in his army in 1923. (Billingsley, 1974, p. 80.)

Kidnaping for ransom provided another major source of Nien income. After seizing victims from well-to-do homes, the bandits issued notices with a ransom demand based on their assessment of the family's financial means. The practice was known in Huai-pei as "nailing" (*ting-ting*). In 1848, when members of a small group of fifteen Nien were apprehended in Suining County, Kiangsu, they confessed to having kidnaped eight persons during their one-month career. Female victims were often sold outright, or ransomed in exchange for horses.[28]

Feuds

In carrying out their acts of smuggling and plunder, the Nien came into conflict with many groups and communities. Parties to the conflicts were not random, but tended to reflect long-standing patterns of feuding. The steady illicit salt traffic from Yung-ch'eng to Chih-ho-chi, for example, had created certain lasting animosities among inhabitants of the two areas. Since sheep-grazing was common in Yung-ch'eng, the smugglers from Anhwei often combined their salt ventures with sheep-rustling. In the winter of 1851–52, one of Chang Lo-hsing's kinsmen, accompanied by eighteen followers, tried to steal more than one hundred sheep on their way home from smuggling, an offense for which they were all imprisoned. Chang Lo-hsing, at the time involved in a smuggling operation north of the Yellow River, returned home to assemble a large force that surrounded the city of Yung-ch'eng and succeeded in freeing the prisoners. As a result of the incident, Chang's reputation as a local leader was markedly enhanced.[29]

After this showdown, the rustlers went back to Yung-ch'eng to steal more sheep. This time the opposition was prepared. A large group of Yung-ch'eng inhabitants, led by a local degree holder, pursued the culprits. Their heads wrapped in white turbans, the Yung-ch'eng posse chased the rustlers to a bridge, where fierce fighting broke out between the two sides. The melee resulted in the death of three martial arts teachers from Yung-ch'eng and the drowning of a member of the Nien contingent from Chih-ho-chi. To avenge the demise of their comrade, the Nien returned to Yung-ch'eng and slaughtered thirty relatives of the degree holder who had led the chase against them.[30] Feuds between residents of the two counties of Yung-ch'eng and Po (where Chih-ho-chi was located) had been a problem for years.[31] In response to the continuing attacks, relatives of Yung-ch'eng inhabitants who had been injured during the Nien incursions organized a self-defense group known as the "Old Cow Society" (lao-niu-hui). Members of the group, said to have numbered in the tens of thousands, wore white robes and hats and carried banners of the same color.* It was apparently this defense group, led by local degree holders and martial arts teachers, which had countered the Nien sheep-rustling intrusion in 1851–52.†

The white garb of the Old Cows suggests that the protective association may have had White Lotus connections.‡ Certainly,

---

*NC, vol. 4, p. 33. In this source, the title of the group is given as "Cow Head Society" (niu-t'ou-hui). However, inasmuch as the name "Old Cow Society" is found in most sources, it appears the more creditable. One contemporary official called this group the "Mourning Hat Society" (hsiao-mao-hui) in obvious reference to its members' white garb. However, the same author also used the more common term Old Cows when describing an encounter in which five thousand of the group killed some one thousand bandits (NC, vol. 3, p. 9).

The name "Old Cow Society" was not unique to Huai-pei. In the 1840s a group with the same name was operating near the Great Wall. This society also was a private self-defense force organized to protect villagers in the area against bandit attacks. The name was taken from the fact that the group had gotten underway with a feast that involved the slaughter of an old bull. The society was so successful in eliminating banditry that it was officially recognized by the government and its name changed to "Agency for Public Peace." (Hsiao Kung-ch'üan, 1960, pp. 310–11.) The Huai-pei Old Cows had adopted their name in honor of their founder, a wealthy landlord by the name of Niu Keng, whose surname meant "cow" (NC, vol. 1, p. 349). For an interesting interpretation of folk tales about the Old Cows in Huai-pei and their connection to the Nien, see Jenner, 1970.

†As Chang Lo-hsing declared in his confession, "In 1851–52, we fought with the Old Cows in Honan's Yung-ch'eng" (Ma Jung-heng and Liu Shou-i, 1962, p. 4). See Appendix A for a translation of the entire confession.

‡As Daniel Overmyer (1976, p. 95) notes, an imperial edict was promulgated in 1259 prohibiting heretics from forming "societies [of those who wear] white clothing (pai-i-hui)." Overmyer suggests that the term white clothing societies may well have referred to the White Lotus. The Yung-ch'eng gazetteer records that there was a "white clothing shrine" (pai-i-ts'u) in the county seat (Yung-ch'eng-hsien chih, 1901, 5/16).

several folk stories about the Old Cows stress the religious coloration of the group. To enter the society, prospective members had to drink charms and pronounce incantations so as to become possessed by spirits. Such rituals were said to make members impervious to bullets. Regular breathing exercises and martial arts routines were also required. At set times, participants would assemble with their yellow-tasseled spears for formal inspection.[32] What is fascinating about these accounts is the very close resemblance they suggest between the Old Cows and the Red Spears of half a century later. The latter group, another village association formed in opposition to rampant banditry, was also noted for secret charms, breathing exercises, spirit possession, martial arts performances, and so on. Like the founders of the Old Cows, most Red Spear leaders were relatively affluent local notables who organized self-defense units to protect personal and village property from predatory assault. Conflict between the Nien and Old Cows persisted until the suppression of the Nien.*

The trouble between Yung-ch'eng and Po was not the only case of Nien involvement in feuds. In addition to community-level disputes, various Nien engaged in more personal conflicts. An example was "Ch'eng the pockmarked," one of the most powerful of the early Nien leaders, whose base of operations was in Shou County, Anhwei. During the years 1845–51, Ch'eng staged plundering raids throughout northern Anhwei, seizing animals and holding people for ransom. Often he took refuge

---

*Feuds between the two areas did not end with the conclusion of the Nien Rebellion, however. As recently as the 1960s, communes in this same location were reported to be embroiled in conflict: "The Kaochuang Commune of Honan and the Tiehfo Commune were separated only by a stream. . . . Liu Shao-ch'i's revisionist proposal that the counties, communes and brigades conserve their own water influenced the two communes and each concentrated on its own projects. Tiehfo Commune built its own waterlock and dam. During the flood season, water was held back by the lock and could not flow into Kaochuang's fields. So the Kaochuang peasants went and broke open the lock and dam. This angered the Tiehfo people. For a number of years the two communes feuded." (Chung Wen, 1972, pp. 29–30.) We may assume that the lines of conflict were set not only by Liu Shao-ch'i's "revisionism," but by enduring animosities between members of the two communities as well.

from the authorities at the home of the Kao brothers, two Nien leaders based in nearby Ho-fei County with whom Ch'eng was on friendly terms. Independently and jointly, the three leaders carried out attacks on individuals against whom they harbored grudges, killing one man who had refused to sell the Kao brothers an ox on credit and another who had demanded repayment of a long-standing debt.[33]

Nien chieftains themselves were not immune from such assaults. In 1851, Ch'eng was subjected to a raid by the neighbor of a fellow whom he had swindled out of some money. Ch'eng called on the Kaos to help muster a force of more than a hundred Nien to wreak revenge. The neighbor's house was damaged and many of his hired laborers wounded in the attack.[34] Examples of these personal feuds run through the story of the early Nien movement. In 1850, for instance, a devastating raid was launched by a Nien leader whose elder brother had been refused a sale of bean curd on credit.[35]

Besides engaging in community and individual conflicts themselves, the Nien took advantage of other ongoing feuds to enhance their position. One of the most enduring such feuds was the ethnic struggle between Muslims and Han Chinese in northern Anhwei. In 1830, a bloody fight between the two groups had resulted in the complete destruction of a large mosque in Ying Prefecture. In 1852, hundreds of Chinese and Muslims in Ying, Feng-yang, and Shou engaged in a conflict that left countless dead on both sides. Nien bandits were said to have taken advantage of this turmoil to plunder wantonly. In the summer of 1853, as the governor of Anhwei was reviewing the progress of militia development in Shou, he received word of renewed ethnic fighting. Muslims in Fu-yang, including a local garrison leader, battalion commander, and two braves, had attacked the militia offices in a market town, killing a brave and two watchmen and making off with all the weapons. A Han Chinese against whom one of the Muslims held a deep grudge was beheaded, his heart dissected and strung from a pole. In addition, several Chinese homes were looted and the inhabitants injured. Although the county magistrate temporarily quelled the disturbance, in another month there were renewed rumors of an imminent Muslim attack. Han Chinese grew increasingly uneasy, and the father of the man who had been so brutally killed in the previous encounter now assembled over a thousand people to exact revenge. In the midst of this chaos, Nien began to gain strength throughout the area, recruiting new members to their ranks.[36]

The intermingling of ongoing feuds and emergent Nien banditry made it a confusing situation for government peacekeeping attempts. In 1854, the Ch'ing general Yüan Chia-san cautioned his troops not to interfere with peasants who were involved only in feuds—which included much of the Huai-pei populace—but to concentrate all their efforts on bandits instead.[37] In practice, the distinction was virtually impossible to discern. Nien were also local inhabitants, and their activities were intimately related to the configuration of local violence—feuds included—occurring in Huai-pei.

The connection to ongoing patterns of collective violence is well summarized in a poem about the Nien written by a member of the gentry in Ku-shih, Honan, a center of early Nien activity. In classical rhyme, the poem relates the Nien to a thousand-year-old tradition of belligerence in the Huai valley. This was a society in which "children carry swords, adults shoulder guns, and desperadoes gather by the hundreds to kill in broad daylight." As the poem explains, the more chivalrously inclined of these outlaws, ready to avenge any injustice, were known as Nien. There were strong and weak Nien, large groups and small. All of them plundered and all were quick to pick a feud. When two Nien chieftains had a disagreement, one issued a letter of challenge, setting the date for a confrontation. Three days before the scheduled encounter, one group of Nien would display their military might outside the gate of their opponents. The following day the other Nien group would do likewise. At the appointed time, the two contingents marched to an open field, whereupon friends and relatives tried to intervene as peacemakers. If all negotiations failed, a vicious battle ensued with swords, guns, and cannon. At the conclusion of the fight, corpses were duly buried, the officials were not notified, and grudges lay smoldering for subsequent revenge. The poet concluded that more stringent laws or stricter officials would do nothing to eliminate the fundamental problem. Subdued at one time, the trouble makers would reemerge at another. As he explained, "I was born in this place and well do I know its ways. The land is poor, its inhabitants witless and crude. They gamble for a living and sell smuggled salt. . . . When people have no dependable property, how can they have a dependable spirit?"[38]

Conflicts between Nien chieftains, known as "family feuds" (ch'iu-chia-tzu), were especially fierce affairs. According to one official who witnessed these events, when a Nien leader was defeated his entire village was often razed by the victors. If a Nien chieftain chose to flee rather than face a challenge, the local notables would usually try to reach a settlement with the challenger so as to avoid the destruction of their village. Lavish feasts were prepared and large sums of money tendered in an effort to appease. If the payment was adequate, the village in question would be spared, although the house of the escaped Nien chieftain might still be looted and burned.[39]

One example of this type of dissension within Nien ranks was reported in Hsin-ts'ai County in 1845. A Nien chief in the county had led sixteen followers to stage a robbery in which they had made off with a sizable haul of animals, clothing, and bedding. All of this loot was handed over to the leader, who had promised to sell it and distribute the proceeds among his followers. When the chieftain reneged on the agreement, his betrayed subordinates decided out of spite to join the ranks of a rival Nien leader. Emboldened by this addition to his force, the rival leader launched a surprise attack on the first chief's home, demolishing his dwelling and seriously injuring numerous relatives.[40]

RELATIONS WITH THE GOVERNMENT

The early Nien movement was a conglomeration of geographically dispersed, often feuding, autonomous groups. In

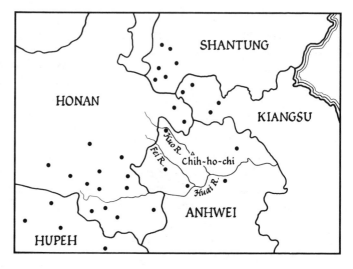

Map 2. Counties of Nien Activity, 1805–45. (Chih-ho-chi is a market town, not a county.)

1851, when both a major Nien chieftain in Anhwei—Ch'eng the pockmarked—and the main leader in Honan—Chiao Chien-teh—were separately captured and subjected to intensive questioning, it was determined that the two Nien contingents were in no way connected. These were independent outfits of seasonal and permanent outlaws who gambled, feuded, smuggled salt, plundered, and kidnaped for ransom.

Although their existence was clearly an outgrowth of the unstable and unproductive environment in which they lived, the choice of banditry was feasible only because of weak government control in Huai-pei. The bulk of Nien lairs were situated near administrative borders to facilitate rapid escape from one jurisdiction to the next as the occasion required (see Map 2). Local officials often found appeasement easier than strict law enforcement. When lawsuits involving Nien robberies were brought before them, many magistrates simply reimbursed the victims from the state treasury and summarily dismissed the cases.[41]

A key factor behind Nien expansion was the tacit or active support of many government officials. In some cases, Nien members actually managed to infiltrate the ranks of the yamen runners and were thus able to keep their comrades informed of any planned government moves against them. Higher officials, generously bribed by their local Nien groups, sometimes provided regular refuges for Nien on the run. A powerful Nien chieftain in Honan, Li Shih-lin, plundered government salt boats under the protection of the local authorities. Li was the adopted son of the militia director who, in turn, bribed the county magistrate to desist from pursuing the brigands. Another nearby Nien chieftain had an agreement with his local magistrate as well. Whenever the bandits returned to the county, the magistrate used their presence as an excuse to levy taxes, ostensibly to support a militia in self-defense. In reality, the money went straight into the magistrate's own pocket. When the bandits departed peaceably, the magistrate reported a military victory to the provincial governor.[42]

Another instance of government connivance in Nien activities was registered by a twenty-six-year-old man in Hsi County, Honan. According to the complaint, a Nien bandit had been robbing members of the man's village for some time under the protection of several local government officials with whom the bandit shared his loot. In early 1849, the bandit summoned over two hundred Nien followers for a raid. Armed with guns and cannon, they stole money and animals, burned down the litigant's house, and kidnaped his uncle. Bribes to the county magistrate were reported as having delayed full disclosure of the case.*

In certain places, the Nien succeeded in entirely supplanting the regularly constituted government authority. The result could actually be a considerable improvement for some of the local residents. In Honan's Ku-shih County, for example, poor people seeking a settlement of their problems flocked to the local Nien chieftain for help. A member of the gentry, puzzled by this phenomenon, asked the people why, when there was a county

*WCT-TK 29/6/2. A graphic example of the government abuse rampant in Huai-pei is found in the testimony of an eighty-three-year-old hired laborer in Sui-ning County, Kiangsu, whose son had been the victim of such mistreatment. As the man related the incident to the provincial authorities: "In the first month of this year [1848] a clerk in Hsi Keng-nan's grocery store was robbed by a bandit on a red horse who made off with money and clothing. Hsi reported the matter to the county magistrate who ordered his underlings to capture the culprit. The yamen underlings forced Hsi to pay a bribe for their services. Then, when they were unable to come up with the real criminal, these underlings seized my son. Seeing that he had a horse of the same color as the bandit, they dragged him to Hsi's store, intimidating the grocer into falsely 'recognizing' my son as the criminal. Wrongly accused, my son cursed Hsi, who in revenge ordered the underlings to torture my son into a confession. Copper wires were forced into my son's nose until he fainted. Upon reviving, he still refused to confess. Subsequently my son was taken to the county offices for further interrogation. Hsi then bribed the gatekeeper to have the magistrate torture my son again. He died of wounds inflicted from this torture. When I filed a lawsuit, the corpse was inspected and found to be covered with several hundred wounds. However, Hsi again bribed the officials to cover up the matter and pretend that my son had died of illness. A few months later a bandit was captured in Fu-yang who confessed to the grocery store robbery. My son has been unjustly accused, but still the local authorities do nothing. Thus have I come in desperation to the capital." (WCT-TK 28/9/19.)

yamen every 100 *li*, they insisted upon going to the Nien instead. Replied the peasants:

The officials in their yamen are like gods in a temple. You never really
get to see them. Their gatekeepers are more ferocious than demons.
You need money to lodge a complaint and even then the official may
not approve it. If he does approve, there is no guarantee that his underlings will carry out the orders. And every step along the way requires
money. One lawsuit can bankrupt an entire family. But when we go to
the Nien, without wasting a cent the case is decided and justice done
within the day.[43]

Despite this tendency to assume government responsibilities
in some places, there is little evidence that the early Nien were
actually rebels, consciously aiming to topple or supplant the
Ch'ing rulers. The great majority of Nien activities centered
around economically motivated crimes, and any ideology was
limited to a rough notion of peasant justice. During this period,
when the Nien did kill soldiers or government officials, the act
was seldom premeditated and was usually committed in self-
defense. In fact, a legal distinction was made between those
who "formed Nien" for plunder and others who were outright
rebels (*tsei*). In addition, however, the Nien were differentiated
from simple local bandits (*t'u-fei*), inasmuch as they were organized and enjoyed a formidable reputation in the Huai-pei
countryside.[44]

THE MOVE TO REBELLION

Over time, the organizational evolution of the Nien became
more pronounced, as previously autonomous groups coalesced
into larger and better-coordinated units. In 1853, Ch'ing general
Yüan Chia-san defeated a group of three thousand Nien who
had been plundering along the border between Fu-yang and Po
counties. The force had more than a hundred horses and carried
numerous battle banners on which were embroidered slogans
taken from folk literature. Interrogation of the captured Nien

revealed that fifty-eight formerly independent groups had cooperated in this venture. Four cannon, over two hundred guns, and countless spears and swords were confiscated.[45]

In other parts of Huai-pei, competing Nien chieftains were consolidating their forces as well. A leader in Huai-yüan gathered four or five thousand followers, rode in a great sedan chair, and assumed the title "King of the Western Huai." His entourage was said to have included several dozen body guards dressed in matching red uniforms, and over one hundred cavalry.[46]

Ecological Crisis

Much of the explanation for this transformation from small, independent gangs to huge bandit armies can be attributed to a series of extremely severe ecological crises which induced more and more peasants to the Nien side. Natural disaster was, of course, no stranger to the Huai-pei plain. Judging from the records of gazetteers in the area, during the first half of the nineteenth century individual counties experienced a flood, drought, or locust invasion on the average of every three to four years. Beginning in 1851, however, the scope, severity, and persistence of these catastrophes increased dramatically. Whereas previously it was rare that all of Huai-pei would be afflicted in any one year, or that individual counties would be affected for more than one or two years in succession, now both of these situations prevailed.[47]

One reason for the marked increase in natural disasters was the collapse of the Yellow River dike system. Years of inadequate maintenance finally met their test in a summer of exceptionally heavy rains in 1851. The result was a major breach of the dikes along the Anhwei-Kiangsu border. When the calamity did not elicit a full-scale repair, the river began its monumental northward shift. With continuing downpours, ruptures occurred in dikes all across the plain. Year after year, enormous areas of Huai-pei lay submerged under flood waters. Crops could not be planted, and increasing numbers of households found them-

Table 10. Natural Disasters in Nineteenth-Century P'ei County

Year	Disaster(s)	Effect(s)
1807	Rainstorms, hailstorms	Famine
1812	Drought	
1813	Drought	Famine
1821	Plague, rainstorms	
1826	Flood (waters over 5 feet deep)	Famine
1827	Locusts	
1832	Floods (over 100 days of rain)	
1833	Plague	Famine
1840	Flood	
1847	Earthquake	
1851	Break in Yellow River: great floods	
1852	Flood, earthquake	Famine
1853	Break in Yellow River: great floods, plague	
1854		Famine
1855	Break in Yellow River: great floods	
1856	Drought, locusts	Famine
1857		Famine, cannibalism, banditry
1858		Nien rebels
1859	Flood, earthquake	
1860	Flood	Nien rebels
1861		Nien rebels
1862	Locusts	
1863		Nien rebels
1864	Drought	
1865	Rainstorms	Nien rebels

Source: *P'ei-hsien chih*, 1920, 2/30.

selves with no store of grain and no prospects for harvesting any in the near future. More and more, these impoverished peasants turned to an ongoing solution: the Nien.

The gazetteer of P'ei County, Kiangsu—located in the heart of the Huai-pei flood zone—provides a good indication of the timing and consequences of natural calamities in the area. Table 10, which traces disasters back to the beginning of the nineteenth century, shows in 1851 a sudden escalation in frequency and effect.

Although the Nien had been active in Huai-pei for half a century, engaging in all the predatory pursuits common to the region, it was only in the 1850s that they assumed the character of a mass movement. Officials in charge of their suppression no longer described the Nien as bandit gangs, but rather as rebel armies attracting hundreds and thousands of followers. When ecological crisis impoverished increasing numbers of peasants, predation assumed an ever wider appeal. Now the Nien could operate not simply as gangs of individuals, but as families, clans, and whole communities.

Taiping Influence

As the movement expanded, leaders of the newly formed alliances took on increasingly pretentious titles and began to adopt a more overtly antagonistic position toward the government. One indication of this gradual move toward rebellion is provided in an 1853 memorial by Yüan Chia-san in which he reported that, although there were few Nien with hair as long as four or five inches, many were now donning red turbans in an attempt to mask the shortness of their locks. Growing one's hair in defiance of the regulations requiring a clean-shaven face and forehead was seen as a sure sign of revolt against the Manchu authorities. According to Yüan, the Nien in northern Anhwei would now loosen their queues, pull their hair out in all directions, and tie it with a piece of red cloth to look the part of genuine rebels.[48] That same year, a false prime minister's seal of office was discovered in the possession of several captured Nien in Meng-ch'eng, Anhwei. In Meng-ch'eng and Po, four Nien leaders were reported to have adopted imperial titles in 1853.[49]

Credit for this growing rebelliousness may be attributed in part to the entry of Taiping rebels into Huai-pei. The Taiping Rebellion was a massive millenarian movement, inspired by a militant brand of quasi-Christian doctrine, which had arisen in South China in 1851. Having established their Heavenly Capital at Nanking, the Taipings in 1853 launched a northern expedition that took them straight through northern Anhwei. As Chang Lo-hsing recounted in his confession, "In 1853 the Taipings attacked the Po area. After the city fell, bandits arose all around.

Only then did I . . . establish banners and take to plunder to make a living. I set up the yellow banner and called myself 'Everlasting King of the Han.'"[50] To assume the title "King of the Han" indicated not merely imperial pretensions, but a direct attack upon the legitimacy of the Ch'ing, who were, of course, Manchus and not Han Chinese. This had a more serious and explicitly rebellious tone than had most of the titles adopted by earlier Nien chieftains: "Big Cannon Chang," "Water Pipe Wei," "Cat-Eared Golden King of Hell Wang," and the like.[51]

Although the precise nature of Taiping-Nien connections at this time is not known, it is apparent that the southern rebels did exercise some influence upon the northern bandits. In 1854, two cooperating Nien chieftains in northern Anhwei proclaimed themselves Taiping kings and adopted banners that read "Army of the Taipings." They united a number of leaders from throughout Po, Meng-ch'eng, and Yung-ch'eng counties and set up headquarters at I-men-chi, a market town some forty *li* away from Chang Lo-hsing's stronghold at Chih-ho-chi. The I-men-chi Nien, who were said to have maintained friendly relations with Chang Lo-hsing's outfit, boasted an impressive military organization: battalion commanders, route captains, and so forth. When several members of this group were taken prisoner by the government, letters from the Taipings in Nanking were discovered among their possessions.[52]

Predatory-Protective Synthesis

The Nien was the only large-scale nineteenth-century Chinese rebellion that was not fueled by religious beliefs—in striking contrast to the White Lotus, Taiping, and Muslim uprisings. We can probably assume therefore that the example of an ideologically complex rebel force was significant in raising the level of Nien political consciousness. The real importance of the Taipings to the emergence of the Nien Rebellion, however, lay less in any direct instruction or inspiration than in the consequences of the Taiping advance for the predatory-protective balance in Huai-pei. The key to Nien strength, we will see, rested not simply in perpetuating predatory forms of aggression, but in a skillful incorporation of protective mechanisms as well.

For years, banditry in Huai-pei had elicited defensive reactions from the individuals, families, and communities subjected to assault. The Nien were no exception. In response to the emerging threat, local gentry—building on experience gained during the White Lotus Rebellion—organized militia and constructed fortifications. These local initiatives were strongly endorsed by the central government, which lacked the money or personnel to conduct an effective defense policy itself. In 1853, as the Taipings marched northward and the Nien took to bolder plundering, imperial edicts were issued instructing all provinces affected by rebel disturbances to drill local militia, build stout walls around groups of villages, and even conduct a scorched-earth policy to deny the rebels any supplies. The governor of Shantung immediately directed his entire province to institute defense measures. The following year, the practice was copied in Anhwei and Honan provinces as well. Villages were instructed to cooperate in establishing militia units, each of which was to be enclosed in a walled fortress. Thus were born the characteristic yü-chai for which Huai-pei became well known. Often the forts were built on the wasteland of market towns or large villages. According to official specifications, the walls were to be ten feet high, three to four feet in depth, and surround an area at least a mile in circumference. One or more moats and several hundred gun emplacements were also recommended. In a few years, thousands of yü-chai dotted the Huai-pei landscape. Most counties had at least one or two hundred of the walled fortresses in operation.[53]

The policy was not implemented without some difficulty, however. Militia organization was costly and burdensome. Good cropland being at a premium, peasants were reluctant to construct large walls or carry out a scorched-earth campaign that would endanger their scant holdings. Furthermore, neighboring villages often refused to cooperate in common defense. Rather than pooling resources, many insisted on going it alone. This dispersion of effort resulted in slipshod work—walls too low or moats too shallow to offer proper resistance. Structures intended to provide protection against Nien incursion became instead invitations to Nien occupation.[54]

Emerging forms of defense created new opportunities for Huai-pei predators, as was illustrated in a number of ingenious Nien ruses. In 1853, some two thousand Nien masqueraded as local militia to carry out a plundering foray in the Chih-ho-chi area. Similar disguises allowed Nien in Honan to steal a large cache of military supplies.[55] Far more serious than these clever stratagems, however, was the Nien capacity to absorb local defense institutions on a sustained basis. Ironically, the very fortresses and militia designed to deter the Nien were converted into the lifeline of the burgeoning movement.

This blurring of predatory and protective strategies cannot be credited entirely to Nien ingenuity; the government also played an important part in the process. The state's very encouragement of militia and *yü-chai* was, of course, a sign of its own weakness in the countryside. To deal with its incapacity, the court was anxious to shift the burden of local defense onto the inhabitants themselves, while at the same time raising taxes so as to strengthen the national army. The blow was thus a double one.

To make matters worse, government exactions did not end with the imposition of costly defense measures or higher taxes. The national army itself became a major source of rural suffering. The recruits for the army were bare sticks in need of a livelihood. Unlike many bandits, however, they were cut off from family ties and required to operate in foreign territory. As a result, their behavior was often callous or uncommitted. One military officer reflected candidly on the problem:

Who would have expected that the atrocities of the imperial army would be so much worse than the rebels themselves! Our food supplies are ample and our equipment sufficient, yet the troops shrink from contact with the enemy. The reason the rebels are so powerful is entirely due to the cowardly retreat of the official troops. When the masses see the army coming to provide protection, they cling to it like the Great Wall and entertain no thought of fleeing. But when the soldiers themselves run off before the rebels have even appeared, the masses cannot escape in time and are slaughtered by the millions.[56]

The cavalry of Prince Seng-ko-lin-ch'in were notoriously corrupt, demanding bribes before they would respond to requests for help. When the people complained of his troops raping and stealing, Seng-ko-lin-ch'in is said to have frowned and replied, "The soldiers have been away from home for a long time. It's best to make the people move to avoid them."[57]

Increasingly, these forms of oppression were met by popular resistance, the capacity for which had been inadvertently enhanced by official encouragement of *yü-chai*. Perhaps the most important way in which the Nien took advantage of the policy of local defense was by building heavy fortifications around their own communities. In this way, they created secure base areas, not easily uprooted by government attack. In 1855, Chang Lo-hsing initiated the strategy by constructing a massive earthwall around Chih-ho-chi. By the end of the year, Nien forts controlled all the area within about a hundred-mile radius of Chih-ho-chi. Other Nien leaders followed suit, some building massive forts more than three miles in circumference.[58] General Yüan Chia-san described a Nien fort he attacked in 1857 as having five cannon emplacements and two moats, the inner one twenty feet wide and the outer one five or six feet wide.* Although such forts were usually built by one Nien chieftain, they generally remained under Nien auspices despite changes in leadership. A *yü-chai* on the Meng-ch'eng–Su border was in 1860 already under its third Nien leader.[59]

A second way in which the Nien tried to gain from the fortification policy was by concluding peace treaties with fortresses

---

*Yüan Chia-san, 1911: 7/28. Folk tales suggest that some Nien forts were extremely elaborate in design. One fort in Kuo-yang County, commanded by Nien chief Kung Teh, is said to have been constructed as a maze in an eight-trigram pattern, with walls and moats arranged in a complex *yin-yang* motif (*Nien-chün ku-shih-chi*, 1962, pp. 106–08).

whose leaders were not Nien. In exchange for payment, the Nien would agree not to attack their communities. One interesting example of an unsuccessful effort at such an agreement occurred in 1855, when gentry in Yung-ch'eng attempted to reach an understanding with Chang Lo-hsing. Frightened by his ruthless plundering, they contacted Chang's brother-in-law to negotiate a peace settlement with the chieftain. All of them agreed to meet together in Chih-ho-chi to draw up the terms of the treaty. However, because the brother-in-law failed to appear at the scheduled meeting on time, the Yung-ch'eng delegation went in person to meet with Chang Lo-hsing. The result of their discussion was an agreement to pay the Nien 2,000 piculs of grain in return for a pledge not to attack Yung-ch'eng. Only after the gentry had returned home did the brother-in-law arrive. Perturbed that the settlement had not been his own achievement, he started a false rumor accusing Yung-ch'eng of preparing an attack against the Nien. Chang Lo-hsing, furious to learn of this apparent betrayal, made plans to besiege the city. Ten members of the Yung-ch'eng gentry who attempted to seek a truce were tied together by their queues and were on the verge of being killed when one protested, "We have come to negotiate. Please let us see the alliance commander." They were finally granted an audience with Chang, who released their bonds in exchange for an agreement to produce 1,000 strings of cash and 800 taels worth of opium by the following noon. The men returned home, but the city had now been deserted and they were unable to come up with more than a fraction of the demands. An emissary sent to request a delay was killed and the city attacked.[60]

A third way in which the Nien used *yü-chai* to expand their power was by enlisting the active cooperation of these communities. Preferable to a treaty of noninterference was, of course, a pledge of positive assistance. Ambitious militia captains were sometimes persuaded to move from a defensive posture to outright revolt. The captains had considerable leverage in such decisions, since fort rules usually required all inhabitants to register with the leader, who was authorized to call on their services as necessary.[61] As semi-independent powers in the countryside, the militia captains were free to cooperate with either the government or the Nien. Many chose the latter as the more promising ally.

An example of such support from a militia leader was the case of Liu Teh-p'ei, a lower degree holder in Tzu-ch'uan, Shantung. Liu first gained notoriety in 1859 when he posted notices around the city calling for a tax revolt. He was imprisoned, but managed to escape. Undaunted, in the winter of 1861 Liu and three other degree holders did manage to stage a successful tax riot. They led a force that surrounded the city, killed one county clerk, and threatened to loot the home of another. The magistrate himself died from shock as a result of the incident, and the government agreed to reduce the tax rate.[62] In 1862, the new magistrate ordered the organization of village militia to combat the threat of Nien incursion from the south. Liu took advantage of the directive to declare himself a militia captain. When the Nien did approach, Liu made a secret alliance with them. Together they robbed a pawnshop in Tzu-ch'uan, and as a result of the success of this venture, Liu's militia grew overnight. Wealthy households were assessed for financial support and Liu was able to offer volunteers an inducement fee, food, clothing, and a small daily salary. In this way, he managed to establish a whole network of militia bureaus under his personal direction. These rebel militia took control of taxes in all the villages they occupied. In concert with the Nien and local salt smugglers, they staged numerous attacks on government offices throughout the area. After killing the Tzu-ch'uan magistrate, Liu and his militia were finally quelled by the army in 1863.[63]

Another important instance of Shantung militia support for the Nien is provided by the "Long Spear Society," a private defense league started by a member of the Ts'ao-chou gentry in 1859. The Long Spears were initiated as a counterweight to the regular militia in the area, which had attained enormous, and often abusive, power since its origin in 1854. Although the formation of the Long Spears was officially sanctioned by the local magistrate, the group soon attracted numerous bandits to its ranks. By 1860, it had grown to a formidable force of twenty-five to thirty thousand, organized under a five-banner system. Belated government efforts to disband the group were to no avail. When the Nien entered the region, most of the Long Spears rushed to join them. A period of cooperation—a valuable boost to Nien operations in southern Shantung—persisted until the suppression of the Long Spears in 1865.[64]

The rationale behind a decision to ally with the Nien is not hard to fathom. In 1855, in all of northern Anhwei the government had only two thousand troops stationed in Ying Prefecture and three thousand in Feng-yang. In the entire province of Honan, there were a mere seventeen thousand regular soldiers. The force obviously was woefully inadequate to cope with the enormous numbers of plundering Nien in the area. Astute fortress leaders, anxious to effect advantageous alliances, were not easily attracted to the government side. Thus by 1858, the great majority of forts in the Meng-ch'eng, Po, Feng-yang, Ying, and Shou area were under the rebel banner. In 1862, the governor of Anhwei reported that there were at least two thousand Nien forts in Huai-pei, each with one to three thousand inhabitants. The Nien apparently were in at least nominal control of a population of some two to six million people.[65]

THE ORGANIZATION OF THE NIEN REBELLION

Nien expansion and endurance were made possible by the movement's close connection to social organization in Huai-pei. Although banditry was normally the pursuit of unemployed bare sticks, it is important to remember that such people were seldom completely divorced from normal social bonds. Ties between these mobile individuals and the more sedentary members of their households and villages were crucial in permitting the expansion of predatory aggression to wider organizational units.*

In the case of the Nien, the importance of such communal connections is readily apparent. In 1853, for example, the Hsieh clan—which included over a thousand households—succeeded in coordinating clan members from more than ten northern Anhwei villages in a massive Nien expedition. That same year the Ma clan of Chih-ho-chi turned an entire village into plundering Nien. In Honan's Hsia-i County, Nien chieftain Hou Huang-le led two hundred relatives with the same surname, and in neighboring Shang-ch'iu, chieftain Chang San's Nien following consisted of three hundred who shared his surname.[66]

These were far from isolated instances. Families, clans, and lineage settlements were at the very heart of Nien organizational strength. The relationship is well demonstrated for all of the main banner leaders who joined the Chih-ho-chi alliance of 1856. That occasion, on which a number of Nien chieftains agreed to recognize Chang Lo-hsing as their commander, is

---

*Many students of peasant rebellion have pointed to the importance of such human links between the home community and the outside. Jack Woddis has identified seasonally mobile peasants as the key constituent in many African rebellions, for example. Like their counterparts in Huai-pei, these people are predominantly adult males who leave their villages for brief periods. Migration is repeated time and again in the lifetime of the individual, his career alternating between short terms of outside activities and agricultural labor at home. Although the "worker-peasants" described by Woddis are able to find productive labor outside the village, and thus need not resort to seasonal predation, the basic motivation for mobility in the two areas is identical: an insecure and inadequate agricultural income. Interestingly, Woddis finds that in Africa it is the alluvial flood plains—geographically akin to Huai-pei—where seasonal migration is the most common. (1960, chaps. 1, 4.)

Eric Wolf has also stressed the importance of links between the village and the outside in his identification of the "middle peasant" as the critical leader in peasant revolt. Although the middle peasant himself remains on the land, he sends his children elsewhere to work. From them he learns the new ideas and methods capable of destroying the old order. (Wolf, 1969, p. 291.) However, as other scholars have pointed out, the linkage position is not limited to middle peasants. In many cases it is the mobile poor who play this pivotal role. See Edward Malefakis, "Peasants, Politics, and Civil War in Spain, 1931–1939," in *Modern European Social History*, ed. Robert Bezucha (New York, 1972), p. 198; and Woddis, 1960, p. 82.

usually interpreted as a watershed in the history of the Nien movement. The result of the meeting was the formal establishment of a system of colored banners. There were five main banners—yellow, blue, white, red, and black—under each of which was a myriad of subordinate banners, distinguished by different colored edges, shapes, and so on. Each of the subsidiary banners represented, in effect, a semiautonomous bandit gang whose hard-core membership was often related by blood. Inasmuch as subordinate chiefs typically controlled too few followers to undertake effective independent action, they found it useful to enlist under the aegis of a more powerful chieftain, often of the same clan.

The five main banner leaders who concluded the 1856 alliance were at the time the principal such chieftains in the northern Anhwei region. Their choice of Chang Lo-hsing as commander was a reflection both of his clan connections and of his reputation as a formidable bandit chief. In 1853, Chang had already led a large plundering expedition in which eighteen other Nien leaders cooperated. However, the disturbance had been quelled and Chang Lo-hsing temporarily persuaded to surrender to the government forces. Chang was subsequently ordered to subdue a bandit in Shou County and, as a result of his participation in this venture, was given an official rank. Briefly in 1854 he served as a commander in the Anhwei braves, thereby gaining valuable access to information on the strength and condition of government forces in the area.* However, because there was very little salary connected to the position, Chang returned home and resumed his plundering ways. In 1855, the magistrate of Su County sent a mission to convince Chang to surrender again. This time, however, he was unwilling to accede. Instead, in early 1856—on the advice of two degree holders in Mengch'eng—Chang rode by royal sedan chair to Chih-ho-chi, where

---

*KCT-HF 008670. The pattern of Nien leaders joining the official forces, becoming disgruntled with the lack of salary, and then returning to their plundering ways was common. See, for example, the confession of Nien leader Ch'en Yü-chen in Chin-tai-shih tzu-liao [Materials on modern history] (Peking, 1963), vol. 1, p. 29.

he assumed the title of alliance commander of all Nien in the area.[67] Sacrifices were offered, rules promulgated, and cooperating leaders agreed to take orders from Chang Lo-hsing.[68] Although the banner system over which he presided was in reality a loose confederation of more or less independent groups, each with its own parochial interests, Chang Lo-hsing attempted to overcome this disunity. As alliance commander, Chang made efforts to impose coordination, morale, and a certain political character to the movement. His designs are expressed in a public proclamation issued at the time of the historic meeting in Chih-ho-chi:

> Alliance Commander Chang hereby makes known his concern for all subjects: scholars, peasants, artisans, and merchants alike. . . . Ever since Magistrate Liu got together with Militia Captain Lu* they have substituted military might for sincerity and responsibility. Ruthless and greedy, they determine punishments according to bribes and treat the people with hatred. The energies of ten thousand families are exhausted to enrich their two households. The alliance commander, filled with concern, cannot stand idly by. For these reasons we rise up: to rescue the impoverished, eliminate treachery, punish wrongdoing, and appease the public indignation. This is the sentiment of the alliance commander and of his many comrades.
>
> However, wherever our troops go, you grab your treasures and run away in terror. Ruffians then take advantage of the situation to plunder freely. Left unattended, your houses are burned to the ground and nothing is left standing when you return. Although your actions are intended to protect, in reality they bring nothing but disaster. Every time our soldiers venture forth, the alliance commander admonishes each banner against plunder or rape. No clothing or grain may be taken from the poor. These regulations are posted everywhere and any offenders will be punished. To guard against oversight, several hundred special investigators have been dispatched to make a careful check. All our members now observe the rules and any infringements are unlikely. Everyone may peacefully carry out his work. . . . Any unruly soldiers should be reported to the inspectors, who will notify the alliance commander. Justice will be done and punishment severe. The

---

*Liu is apparently a reference to Liu Ying-chieh of Meng-ch'eng (*Meng-ch'eng-hsien chih*, 1915, 6/4) and Lu to the magistrate of Ying-chou (see Appendix A).

will of the alliance commander is to comfort the righteous. Have no fear![69]

Further evidence of Chang's intentions is found in a set of military regulations issued at the same time as this proclamation.* The military code is a list of nineteen prohibitions against such offenses as rape, indiscriminate plunder, disobedience to superiors, desertion, and the like. The punishment for the great majority of the crimes was execution. Charged with leadership responsibilities for an unwieldy amalgam of bandit groups, Chang Lo-hsing saw that the movement required a heavy dose of discipline. In reality, however, the autonomous and entrenched power bases of his allies made it impossible for Chang to exert full control.

The main leaders in the alliance were from large clans that dominated a number of contiguous villages. Chang Lo-hsing's own clan was the main lineage in eighteen neighboring villages. Su T'ien-fu was from an extremely large clan in Yung-ch'eng which boasted as many as one hundred villages under its domination. Kung Teh, leader of the white banner, came from a spot where thirteen neighboring villages belonged to the Kung clan. Red-banner leader Hou Shih-wei hailed from a lineage that included about a dozen villages, and the clan of the blue-banner leader, Han Lao-wan, counted half a dozen villages under its control. Four of these five main chieftains lived within a ten-mile radius of Chih-ho-chi, and Su T'ien-fu's home was located twenty miles away.[70] Their cooperation thus represented an important combination of communal strength in the area.

*Chiang Ti, 1959, pp. 244–45. Another example of Chang Lo-hsing's commitment to strict discipline is provided by an account in the gazetteer of Kuoyang County. In 1857, when Lo-hsing commanded his nephew Tsung-yü to lead a foraging expedition to the south, Tsung-yü is said to have asked, "What should I do if the soldiers refuse to obey orders?" Replied his uncle, "Kill them!" (*Kuo-yang-hsien chih*, 1924, 15/12.)

Although it seems certain that Chang was convinced of the need for discipline, any further interpretation of the 1855 documents as representing an identifiable ideological platform is questionable. For one such effort, see Tchekanov, 1960, pp. 197–299. The proclamations, in flowery imperial style, were obviously written by literati sympathetic to the Nien. It is uncertain to what degree they represented the actual thinking of Chang or other Nien chiefs.

Subsidiary banner leaders were also closely tied into local social structure. In 1856, when a group of Honan gentry traveled to
Peking to lodge a complaint against Nien activities, they ap-
pended to their petition a namelist of 211 Nien chiefs. Of the 110
for whom a native village was listed, 59 came from places with
the same name as their own surnames. Chang Lo-hsing, for
example, came from Old Chang Village; Hou Shih-wei from
Old Hou Fort; Ch'en Chia-hsi from Big Ch'en Village; and so
on down the line.[71]

Generally speaking, those of the same surname fought under
the same banner. People named Chang, for example, were
members of the yellow banner, whereas those named Hou usually enlisted under the red banner. In a case where a village had
more than one surname, clan loyalties sometimes took precedence. The village of Wu Earth-tower, located about seven miles
northwest of Chih-ho-chi, midway between Old Chang Village
and Old Hou Fort, was a telling illustration. Although Wu
Earth-tower was a small settlement of only a few dozen families,
it was occupied by two surnames—Wu and Hou—which
affiliated with two separate banners. Related by marriage to an
important yellow-banner leader, Chang Chen-chiang, the Wu
family enlisted under that standard. The Hou, of course, linked
up with the red banner of their kinsman Hou Shih-wei.[72]

Not surprisingly, individual Nien leaders relied heavily on
close relatives as trusted lieutenants. Chang Lo-hsing's top ad-
visor was his nephew Chang Tsung-yü; Kung Teh's closest
comrade-in-arms was also a nephew, Kung Ta-mu; Su T'ien-fu
was assisted by his younger brother Su T'ien-hsi.[73] These bonds
were crucial in solidifying relationships within banners. Loyalties to clan and village imbued the Nien with a localistic orientation that greatly facilitated their endurance.

REBELLION AS SURVIVAL

Organized along kinship lines, the Nien conducted regular
peasant lives within their earthwall fortresses. In places where
natural disaster and warfare had not totally destroyed the possi-

bility of farming, agriculture was still the main economic activity of most Nien communities. However, even in areas where the land was fit for cultivation, the yields were seldom sufficient to cover the inhabitants' basic needs. Thus, after harvest time the local chief would call up all idle males in the community to participate in seasonal forays. Loot garnered on these expeditions was divided up among participants after the triumphant return home to the safety of their walled fortresses. As the governor of Honan described the Nien, "When they go out they burn and plunder; when they return they till the land once again."[74]

The principal targets of Nien plunder were the relatively unscathed parts of Honan, Shantung, and northern Kiangsu. From northern Anhwei, Nien groups followed three main routes of plunder, which matched the familiar salt smuggling paths of earlier days. One went via Kuei-teh and Lu-i into Honan, another through Tang-shan and Yung-ch'eng across the Shantung border, and a third via Lin-huai and Su northward into Shantung and Kiangsu. Nien went out simultaneously in these different directions and, even within routes, divided into smaller units so as to evade government detection. The expeditions were massive, nevertheless. In 1860 one contingent returning through I County in southern Shantung was described as including a thousand cavalrymen and several thousand soldiers on foot. Singing as they journeyed homeward, these Nien were said to be protecting a stolen booty of "several hundred carts of grain and tens of thousands of animals."[75]

The purpose of these forays was to garner from more prosperous areas the food so desperately lacking at home. Nien predatory activities were thus directly related to individual and community survival. A detailed account of Nien livelihood which clearly demonstrates the adaptive significance of the rebellion is provided by Liu T'ang, a degree holder from Honan who at the age of sixteen was taken captive by a group of Anhwei Nien with whom he lived for almost three months.[76] Inasmuch as Liu's story provides a rich and unique insight into daily Nien life, it will be told in some detail here.

In November 1858, a group of Nien from Anhwei began staging attacks in Liu T'ang's native area of Fu-kou in eastern Honan. Liu's father, a traveling merchant, upon hearing the news, hurried home to collect his two sons for an attempted escape from the threatened area. Not far from their home village, the three encountered a band of Nien who robbed them of all their money. Continuing to flee, they were set upon by another Nien group who demanded their outer clothing. Thus relieved of any worldly possessions, the unfortunate trio soon met up with yet a third band of Nien. Having neither money nor clothes with which to bargain, they now had no choice but to surrender to the bandits.

The banner chief of this particular group of Nien was a man by the name of Yao Feng-ch'un from a village in Meng-ch'eng, Anhwei. Yao came from a peasant family, had been both a local bandit and a soldier, and now was compelled by poverty to join the Nien. Despite his profession, the banner chief is described as an upstanding and sensitive individual. Whenever he saw houses burned or women taken advantage of, Yao cried out in anguish to halt the atrocities. Even so, he was not above ordering Liu T'ang's father to select one of his sons to be taken prisoner by the Nien. Since the elder son was married, it was tearfully determined that Liu T'ang, the budding scholar of the family, would be the victim.

Young Liu, somewhat comforted by the banner chief's promise of safety for his family, followed the Nien on their journey homeward to Anhwei. The weather being extremely chilly, the Nien gave Liu a stolen jacket, overcoat, and pair of trousers. The blue coat trailed on the ground and the thin white trousers looked like women's attire, yet Liu had no choice but to wear the ill-fitting garments to keep out the bitter cold.

In the Honan village where Liu spent his first night on the road with the Nien, the well had run dry. As there were no vessels for making tea, his companions used a porcelain jug to boil stagnant water from a pit. When finally the water began to boil, sugar stolen from a nearby village was added. The result was a sweet solution with an overpowering stench which Liu found impossible to swallow. Noodles were also very scarce, so the Nien would grind dry wheat into large slabs which were then roasted over a hot fire. Before the wheat cakes were even cooked through, they were greedily consumed. Liu recognized that these individuals were truly on the verge of starvation, a state he had never witnessed in his sheltered days at home. Seeing that the boy was unable to stomach this meager fare, the banner chief kindly gave him three pieces of dried bean curd taken from a nearby market. As they were eating, a stray pig happened to trot by and was immediately seized by the hungry bandits, who pulled off its legs, skinned it, and plunked it in the porcelain jug to boil in the sugary water. Just as soon as the blood ceased running, the pig—still squealing—was hastily consumed. More than a little depressed by his raw experiences of the day, Liu briefly entertained the idea of trying to escape. However, after witnessing the beheading and cremation of an attempted run-away from a nearby camp, Liu quickly dropped the idea and re-signed himself to this life of detention.

After a day's delay due to opposition from a local militia force, the Nien reached the western shores of the Fei River near their home base in northern Anhwei. At this point they received word that each banner chief was to send two cavalrymen and three foot soldiers to besiege an enemy stronghold in the area. When the men had been deployed to their posts, the carts bearing the stolen loot from their foray in Honan were ordered to go ahead and cross the river toward home. However, as soon as they saw the carts going on ahead, the Nien soldiers who had been instructed to surround the enemy fort decided to desert their posts and, in defiance of orders, follow their booty. The blockade broken, members of the enemy camp streamed out of their fort in hot pursuit, and the fleeing Nien were forced to abandon countless carts in the middle of the river. Liu managed to scramble onto one of the few carts that made it safely across.

After this harrowing adventure, Liu learned that the forts on the western shores of the Fei River were all controlled by that long-standing enemy of the Nien: the Old Cow Society. The

Nien in this area lived in fear of the Old Cows and at night a watchman patrolled the Nien camp beating his gong and crying out, "Stay alert, do not drowse; keep on guard against the Old Cows!"

Finally, on the fourth day after Liu's capture, the group arrived back at their home base, a small village surrounded by an earthen wall with one gate to the south, complete with wooden drawbridge. The village was known as Chia Family Encirclement since most of its residents were named Chia. The banner chief occupied a two-room thatched hut with his wife and aged mother, his father having been killed by bandits. Home from the expedition, the Nien were greeted by all their relatives. Having returned safely, they prepared a celebration feast of what they considered a very special treat: plain white noodles. Poor Liu had always turned up his nose at this type of food. Now, faced with no alternative but starvation, he forced down a bite and found it delicious!

Besides Liu, there were two other young boys in the camp who had been taken prisoner on earlier expeditions. One was a peasant lad from southern Shantung who toiled diligently—cutting grass, feeding the horses, gathering firewood, and so on. The other was an educated youth from a part of Honan very near Liu's own home. Liu himself spent much of the day moping, thereby evoking considerable sympathy from the banner chief's mother. The chief himself, knowing Liu's love of reading, scoured more than a dozen villages to find him a book. All he could come up with in this desolate area was a small pocket dictionary.

In time, Liu learned something of the organizational structure of his captors. The chief who had taken him prisoner, Yao Feng-ch'un, was actually only a minor banner chief (*hsiao-ch'i-chu*). Most such chiefs were in charge of about thirty-five cavalrymen and a dozen or so foot soldiers. The lesser chiefs were subordinate to a major banner chief (*ta-ch'i-chu*) who might count from ten to one hundred such minor chiefs under his command. All plundered loot, except for that given to the banner chiefs,[77] was divided up among the participants in the raid—usually on the formula of two parts to cavalrymen and one part to foot soldiers. Yao Feng-ch'un's major banner leader was his uncle, Yao Teh-kuang, who at the time of Liu's arrival was participating in an important Nien offensive with Chang Lo-hsing in Huai-yüan County. In Teh-kuang's absence, his nephew Yao Hua had been left temporarily in charge.

During Liu's stay at the Nien village, Teh-kuang's son, Yao Hsiu, who had been accompanying his father at Huai-yüan, did return home at one point. Yao Hsiu's family included a wife, a daughter, an infant son, and a concubine who had been seized on a previous plundering expedition. The daughter, aged seventeen, took an immediate liking to Liu T'ang. She had once been betrothed to a young man named Wang. The Wangs, however, had not joined the Nien, the two families became enemies, and the marriage was called off. Before long, Yao Hsiu's wife had banner chief Yao Feng-ch'un question Liu as to his marital status and whether he might be interested in remaining with the Nien and marrying into the family. When Liu answered in the negative, the matter was never raised again.

Daily meals in the Nien village consisted of lentil or sorghum noodles. Wheat was never a regular feature of the diet and seldom were there vegetables, with the exception of an occasional pepper. The land in this particular locale could no longer be farmed and showed few traces of human habitation. Most households were small, having lost many members to the rampages of bandits and soldiers. The depleted villages then merged, several dozen of them building a common wall in self-defense. Although wild animals were surprisingly abundant, all grain had to be secured from outside. The Nien stole grain on plundering forays, then sold the surplus in their home areas for a very low price. Cash earnings from such a trip were quickly depleted, especially since few banner chiefs could resist frequent trips to market to drink and vie for prestige. In less than a month's time, the money would all be gone and another expedition called together. Before setting forth on these trips, participating banner chiefs consulted to determine the size and strategy of the foray.

One day a group of Old Cows moved across the river into Nien territory to hunt the wild animals there. Ecologically more favored than the Nien's, the Old Cows' own land was all under cultivation and thus without any such prey. They converged upon a deserted village whose wall was still standing, set fire to the three remaining houses inside, blocked the gate with nets, and captured more than a hundred rabbits hopping out to escape the blaze. Although the Nien did not interfere with this particular intrusion, a few days later they decided to stage a retaliatory raid on the Old Cow fort. Each participant in this venture was to receive an equal share of the booty. The banner chief's wife strongly encouraged Liu to go along. However, a sudden flare-up of a foot infection precluded his participation.

At the time of Liu T'ang's capture, his father had been clearly informed of the exact location of the Anhwei fort to which the boy was being taken. However, since the father's sense of propriety prevented his entering bandit territory in person, he went instead to Po County, some 120 *li* away, to try to get some information about his son from a used-clothing merchant there. As it happened, just at the time of his visit, an old man had come to the merchant with clothes for resale. The man turned out to be an uncle of the banner chief, charged with disposing of stolen goods. Liu T'ang's father had the old man take a letter back to his son, requesting a reply and promising to return at New Year's to collect him. A couple of days after a reply had been sent verifying the boy's good health, the banner chief led Liu T'ang off to a village about 80 *li* from Po. There he was put in the hands of an innkeeper who was instructed to feed him at the chief's expense. The chief's parting words to Liu were, "Your father will be here shortly. When you see him, tell him that the Yaos treated you well and took not a cent." With these words, Yao Feng-ch'un tearfully departed.

After several days' delay, Liu went to Po in the company of the banner chief's uncle. They spent one night at Chih-ho-chi, the central Nien headquarters, where Liu was impressed with the storytelling, operas, and other signs of activity. When they finally reached Po County, Liu's father had already returned home for the holidays. However, the clothing merchant, after being persuaded of the boy's identity, gave the uncle some silver—Liu T'ang's first indication that he was, in fact, being ransomed. Thinking back on the banner chief's words, Liu wondered whether the chief too had been deceived by his uncle's designs.

In any event, Liu was forced to wait for his father for about a week in Po, during which time he learned the economic importance of the city to the Nien, both as a source of goods and as a market for stolen loot. Nien took their booty there for resale, and merchants from the city also went regularly to outlying Nien forts to purchase stolen goods. Finally, 80 days after his capture, Liu T'ang was reunited with his family. In reflecting upon his stay with the Nien, Liu concluded that they really had been forced into banditry by hunger and were not recalcitrant rebels at heart.

Liu's story is a revealing description of Nien success in wedding a strategy of predatory plunder to existing social organization. Aggressive modes of survival were being effectively combined with ongoing family and village life. Far from marginal individuals, the Nien acted as households, clans, and communities. One striking aspect of Liu's account is the apparent absence of any conscious rebelliousness on the part of those among whom he lived. Located only twenty miles from the center of the movement in Chih-ho-chi, these Nien seemed concerned with but one enemy: their local competitors, the Old Cows. Even at the height of Nien strength, survival in one's home environment was for most followers a more potent motivation than antagonism toward the state. Although major banner chief Yao Teh-kuang was in fact off at Huai-yüan participating in a joint Nien-Taiping venture against the Ch'ing, the majority of his subordinates remained parochial predators, striving to secure a livelihood under the most inhospitable of circumstances. As a Nien folk song poignantly presented their rationale:

> This year famine,
> Next year flood,
> Grass, roots, tree bark gone for food.
> Deep in debt,
> When the debt comes due:
> One picul is repaid as two.
> If not for the Nien,
> How could one stand?
> Let's join Old Lo to claim the land. [78]

THE LIMITS OF A PREDATORY REBELLION

The Nien derived strength from a merger of predatory and protective strategies. The movement had grown rebellious to the degree that endemic competition among Huai-pei inhabitants was superseded by cooperative efforts against the state. The synthesis was never complete, however. Some communities—such as the more affluent Old Cows—would continue stubbornly to adhere to their protective stance in resistance to the growing predatory movement. Even aspiring fortress chiefs and militia captains who did find it advantageous to join the Nien were quick to surrender whenever such a move appeared more likely to offer advancement.* And the predators themselves, despite alliances with protective institutions, never fully outgrew

*Perhaps the most notorious intermittent Nien supporter was the ambitious and opportunistic Miao P'ei-lin, a militia captain who had by 1859 gained control over several thousand forts and hundreds of thousands of people in the Huai valley. Although Miao at first cooperated with the government effort against the Nien, he did not find the official rewards sufficient. Thus in 1861 Miao decided to rebel. He ordered his forces to attack government strongholds and proceeded to make contact with both the Nien and the Taipings. Together with his new allies, Miao staged massive raids across the Huai-pei plain. In 1862, Miao returned once more to the government side. As evidence of his loyalties, he carried out several sudden attacks on Chang Lo-hsing's Nien forces and in the spring of 1862 captured the famous Taiping leader Ch'en Yü-ch'eng. For these deeds Miao was exonerated of his earlier crimes and ordered by the throne to resume his offensive against the Nien. Before long, however, Miao's relations with the government again deteriorated, and he returned to rebellious activities until his suppression in 1864. For details of Miao's colorful story, see NC, vol. 1, pp. 288–95.

their undisciplined methods of plunder and assault. These drawbacks prevented a smooth alliance between the Nien and Taipings and worked against the movement's development into a disciplined attack on state authority.

A discussion of Nien-Taiping relations helps to highlight some of the shortcomings of the Nien as a rebellious movement. The earliest contact between the two groups, we may remember, occurred in 1853, when the Taipings' northern expedition took them directly into the heart of Nien territory in northern Anhwei. Although the Taipings apparently left an impression on the Nien with whom they came in touch, no formal alliance was concluded. This was a time when the Taipings were at the height of their strength; cooperation with a motley group of local Anhwei bandits probably seemed a liability to be avoided. Three years later the situation had changed dramatically. The Taipings suffered from serious internal dissension and severe military losses. Inasmuch as the Nien had also undergone a series of defeats, it was to the advantage of both groups to effect an alliance.

The coalition was arranged in 1856 through the mediation of a former Nien turned Taiping: Li Chao-shou. Li himself had a colorful background and career. From a major clan in Ku-shih, Honan, Li's own family was poor. In place of book learning, Li spent his childhood acquiring the traditional acrobatic skills of Chinese robbers. He developed into an accomplished young thief and, because of his hairless head, was well known in the area as the "bald bandit." His thievery landed Li in three county prisons where he was cruelly mistreated. Upon his release in 1854, Li took advantage of the emerging Nien movement to amass his own following of several hundred people who plundered along the Honan-Anhwei border. Although nominally pacified by a militia captain, Li was never one to obey orders. As a result of his unruly behavior, the militia captain decided to execute Li. Word of this plan leaked out, however, and Li preempted the plot by killing the captain and taking control of the militia himself. He immediately surrendered to the Taipings and served for several years as a trusted lieutenant of Taiping leader Li Hsiu-ch'eng.[79]

Li Chao-shou's surrender to the Taipings was crucial in effecting an alliance between the Nien and Taiping movements. In 1856, Li—who maintained communications with Nien commander Chang Lo-hsing—sent Chang a message encouraging his allegiance to the Taipings. Chang Lo-hsing, having just suffered several military setbacks, was happy to accept the invitation. In late 1856, the northern Anhwei Nien forces thus formally merged with the Taipings. In early 1857, several large Taiping and Nien contingents jointly attacked the city of Huo-ch'iu in the first major instance of Nien-Taiping cooperation.[80]

Chang Lo-hsing's coalition with the Taipings, though motivated by practical military considerations, also reflected on his part a growing seriousness of purpose. No longer was the alliance commander content with conducting seasonal plundering raids from fortified communities. After concluding the pact with the Taipings, Chang led his troops south of the Huai River to cooperate full-time with the "long-haired rebels." This critical decision, expressive of Chang's own rebelliousness, created severe strains within the Nien movement. When heavy government opposition forced them into retreat, the Nien leadership was at irreconcilable odds over what course to pursue. Chang Lo-hsing, now spurred on by dreams of capturing the Mandate of Heaven, insisted upon remaining south of the Huai to continue joint struggles with his Taiping allies. A dissident faction of the Nien, led by blue-banner leader Liu E-lang, advocated giving up these taxing military encounters in favor of returning home to Huai-pei. The reasoning behind Liu's stand was plain. In the course of the past year's cooperation with the Taipings, Nien losses—especially within the blue banner—had been great. In late 1857, the besieged Nien had been forced to kill their own horses for food. Severe plague then dealt a heavy blow. By the thousands, corpses of Nien soldiers were thrown into the Huai River.[81] Furthermore, during this period, Miao P'ei-lin and other unfriendly militia captains had been taking advantage of the Nien's absence from Huai-pei to stage a series of crippling attacks on their home communities.

When no compromise between the blue-banner chief and his superior could be reached, Chang Lo-hsing murdered Liu E-lang and his nephew Liu T'ien-t'ai. The assassinations, however, only intensified Chang's problems. As a result of the incident, some forty to fifty thousand Nien returned to northern Anhwei to the familiar security of their earthwall forts and traditional survival strategies.[82] After 1858, Chang's fragile alliance was sundered into two distinct camps. The troops of Chang and Kung Teh, now a minority force, were centered south of the Huai in Huai-yüan, Anhwei. The majority of Nien were based back in their various forts throughout Huai-pei, continuing the age-old pattern of predatory plunder.[83] In late 1858, Chang set about unifying the movement in a desperate effort to sweep through Huai-pei, continuing on north toward ultimate victory. This futile effort to rally his less ambitious brethren is seen in the following proclamation issued from Huai-yüan:

Alliance Commander of the Great Han Chang hereby makes known: at the time of the Chih-ho-chi uprising all our brothers swore to live and die together. I was chosen as alliance commander, and everyone agreed to cooperate with one heart and to fight the enemy together. Let us seize the cities, open new territory, incorporate our country's heroes, plot for the great enterprise, and glorify our followers as an expression of our alliance.

When our troops went south . . . our army expanded greatly and the enemy fled in disgrace. Then we moved north, and attacked . . . a host of other cities. These deeds, though accomplished by men, were the will of heaven. Now let our brave chieftains lead our men northward to take Su, Ling, Meng, Po, and Ying, heading straight for the Yellow River to open the borders in hopes of becoming hegemon. Contemplate the rewards, the feudal privileges, the glory, the boundless joys of leisure—is this not beautiful? Those who think only of temporary security, who return home doggedly to hold their earthwall forts, who know only plunder, and who benefit just themselves—in the long run theirs is a suicidal policy. Time after time I have issued this call. . . . Many Nien chieftains have journeyed to Huai-yüan, ordered their troops, and carried out attacks. . . . The enemy forts temporarily surrendered, but the situation was soon reversed.

The enemy ships may come at any time to attack Huai-yüan; at any moment their horses may gallop in. Our troops are not prepared to stand in their way, still less to stage an offensive. Here will lie our defeat. Looking at the current situation, I ask those of you peacefully sitting in your earthwall forts, thinking only of yourselves, are your hearts truly at peace?

On the day that you receive this proclamation, decide to carry it out at once. Those who wish to achieve greatness, put in order your troops and horses and with singleness of purpose make ready for a northern expedition. Those who insist upon stubbornly defending your earthwall forts, suit yourselves. The alliance commander is fixed in purpose and resolution. To persuade you, I have prepared this special proclamation.[84]

Chang's proclamation proved less than persuasive, however. Most of the Nien chose to remain in their settled communities, venturing forth only as necessary to seize additional resources. Chang Lo-hsing himself began to weary of his unsuccessful efforts to rally the movement behind a united front with the Taipings. Plagued with serious problems of their own, the Taipings apparently had not proven overly hospitable to their northern allies. As Chang complained in his confession, "I lived with them for several years. But because their treatment was not good, I returned to my old village." Disillusionment was mutual. Taiping leader Li Hsiu-ch'eng explained in his confession to the authorities, "Although we had the allegiance of Chang Lo-hsing, his men accepted our titles and ranks, but not our orders."[85]

While the Taiping Rebellion was a critical factor in the growing ambitions of Chang and other Nien chieftains, the Taipings did not succeed in improving Nien discipline or organization, clarifying their ideals or program, or overcoming their propensity for seasonal plunder. Despite Commander Chang Lo-hsing's titular authority, he was never in a position to demand the absolute allegiance of subordinate Nien chieftains. The dispute between Chang and Liu E-lang was but one instance of this. Subordinate banner leaders had a calculus of decision-making and a scope of action quite independent of their superior's designs. White-banner leader Sun K'uei-hsin, for example, at one point surrendered to General Sheng Pao in hopes of attaining high government position. Finding his official rewards unsatisfactory, Sun subsequently returned to the Nien. Nevertheless, this return did not guarantee his steadfast allegiance to Chang Lo-hsing. In 1858, rather than remain with Chang south of the Huai, Sun took his large group of followers home to Po. Likewise, two months later Nien chiefs Liu Kou and Ch'en Ta-hsi also had a falling out with Chang Lo-hsing. Together with Sun they plundered across the Honan-Shantung border in apparent defiance of Chang's orders.[86] Chang's inability to forge his subordinates into a unified movement was a direct result of the power bases of these various banner chiefs. Owing their strength less to affiliation with the rebellion than to the support of their families, the minor banner leaders were naturally inclined to abandon the rebel cause whenever it conflicted with the demands of their home communities.

Sometimes the clan composition of the Nien Army was reflected in feuding reminiscent of the early Nien. In 1862, for example, a minor Nien chief in Hsiang-ch'eng, Honan, exchanged letters with his local magistrate expressing a desire to surrender. When the chief's superior learned of the correspondence, he murdered his subordinate. The family of the slain chief responded in turn by killing the commanding chieftain. Feuds between relatives of the two Nien leaders continued for some time.[87]

Although the Chih-ho-chi alliance had facilitated a change from simple banditry to an antistate position, the transition was far from complete. Many Nien in Honan Province had never participated in the 1856 alliance in the first place. Ch'en Ta-hsi, one of the most powerful Nien leaders in Honan, owed no formal obedience to Chang's commands. Ch'en had been a commander in the braves before joining the Nien. He set up several forts around his home village and often allied with local bandit gangs for joint plundering forays.* Such groups of Nien continued to carry out their independent ventures, free of subservience to higher command. Even those units that did pledge allegiance to Chang's authority tended, we have seen, to pursue their separate interests.

The Nien were possessed of a dual composition: plundering forays and fortified communities. Although the synthesis of these two strains accounted for the durability of the movement, in the end each implied a style and purpose at odds with the development of a unified, committed challenge to the state. Predatory origins had imbued the Nien with an intermittent and unbridled form of behavior that militated against coordination and discipline. The subsequent incorporation of the protective *yü-chai* exacerbated the tendency toward autonomy. Fortified lineage communities were like a myriad of independent kingdoms. Living as clans behind their protective walls, most Nien were reluctant to abandon their homes for a permanent rebel life.

The real test of the rebellion's strength came in 1863, with the destruction of the Nien's home base in Chih-ho-chi. Chang Lo-hsing, betrayed by a subordinate Nien chieftain, was captured and executed. Hundreds of forts in northern Anhwei responded to this loss by surrendering to the government.† The authorities, chastened by their experience with the rebellious *yü-chai*, set about trying to divest fortress chiefs of their power. In line with this policy of returning authority to the government, a new

*NC, vol. 2, pp. 243–49. Although it appears that most Nien chiefs in Honan (for example, Chao Hao-jan, Li Yüeh, and Li Shih-lin) were closer to pure banditry than their more rebellious counterparts in Anhwei, relationships with local bandits were not always cordial. One bandit in southeastern Honan took an intense dislike to a Nien chieftain in his area. The bandit led a raid against the Nien chief's village and was instrumental in his capture. (NC, vol. 1, pp. 332–34.)

†The death of Alliance Commander Chang Lo-hsing was not the only reason for the massive surrender. Cut off by government troops from their sources of plunder, many forts were in desperate circumstances. In 1863 the people of Meng-ch'eng were reduced to eating boiled leather, bark chips, and the pulverized bones of the dead. A pound of human flesh was reported to be selling for a hundred cash. (NC, vol. 1, p. 294.)

county—Kuo-yang—was established. The county seat was placed at Chih-ho-chi, and parts of the four contiguous counties of Meng-ch'eng, Po, Fu-yang, and Su were incorporated within its jurisdiction. The move was a conscious attempt to strengthen the government's presence in this age-old bandit haven.* The pacification of rebel forts throughout northern Anhwei caused a drastic change in the character of the movement. Cut off from their home base, the remaining Nien forces—in concert with remnant Taipings—began a four-year period as roving bandits. Having lost their role as a family and community enterprise, the Nien soldiers became a mobile bandit army. The discipline of the movement—never good—deteriorated rapidly in unfamiliar territory. Deprived of any secure base of operations, their lightning-like cavalry dashed across the North China Plain in a desperate bid to garner resources and evade capture. Like any bandit army, the Nien momentarily attracted to their ranks impoverished peasants in the areas they visited. The hungry flocked to their side in hopes of seizing something for themselves. As an American missionary reported in 1868, only a few months before the suppression of the Nien: "It is not a rebellion but an enormous corn riot. Driven by want . . . these wretches run riot through the land. No word can describe their barbarities. They are not . . . at all connected with the Old Taipings, who were a very respectable body of insurgents. These are mere robbers who could not behave worse if they fought under the black flag of piracy."[88]

Elements of the Nien were, we know, closely connected to the Taipings and influenced by their rebelliousness, though not their eschatology. Even so, the Nien were in the end an army of

---

*Kuo-yang-hsien chih, 1924, 1/1. A former resident of Kuo-yang has written an interesting account of the county's creation. According to his report, when construction on the new city wall and moat had just been completed, routed Nien diehards returned en masse and drove out the government authorities. Although the Nien occupied the city only briefly, the superstitious officials interpreted the take-over as a highly inauspicious beginning. Thus they decided to move the site for the new city west half a li and to build another wall and moat. To this day, the original wall is said to stand to the east of the city. (Wang Fant'ing, 1970, p. 38.)

predators attempting to seize scarce resources at the expense of others. They shared the limitations of predatory movements the world over. Eric Hobsbawm has summarized the plight of banditry as "inefficient in every way."[89] Its very structure —an association of small, segmented gangs—precluded well-coordinated activity. Its ideology—at best a yearning for a more just society—was a traditionalist ethos unsuited to modern revolution. Anton Blok has pointed out that banditry may impede social transformation both directly, by means of terrorist tactics, and indirectly, by providing channels of upward mobility that tend to weaken class solidarity.[90] In these respects the Nien were in the end little different from other bandit movements. As Ella Laffey has commented, "In general and in the long run, the Taipings were right: survival as local bandits and rebels produced individuals who were poor material for massive and sustained revolt."[91] Successful adaptation as parochial predators would not ensure a smooth transition to modern revolutionary action.

CONCLUSION

For most participants, the Nien presented a concrete opportunity to garner one's livelihood in a situation of extreme insecurity. The movement began as a series of familiar efforts by impoverished peasants to seize scarce resources from others. The later Nien reflected these origins: plundering forays followed the routes of salt smugglers, community feuds continued to be conducted along previous lines, bandit gangs retained their independence of action, and so on. Although the movement managed to absorb protective institutions and to redirect its aggression against the state, it remained primarily the expression of mundane strategies of survival.

An explanation of the Nien as arising out of a parochial dialectic in the Huai-pei countryside runs counter to conventional interpretations both of Chinese peasant rebellion in general and of the Nien in particular. Rural unrest in China has typically been viewed as an unleashing of "natural" forces against the fetters of Confucian control. Embodied in secret societies, this "little tradition" is seen as lying politically latent until the weakening of the "great tradition" permitted its bursting forth in revolt. As Jean Chesneaux states, "The secret societies throughout modern history have been forces of opposition. Their popular religious beliefs were opposed to the orthodox beliefs, their political efforts directed against a dynasty, their 'social banditry' at the expense of the rich, their economic activities carried out in defiance of the state."[92] A recent book by Fei-ling Davis summarizes the view in somewhat greater detail:

Chinese secret societies were the *organized* expression of a central contradiction in the traditional society. They embodied and identified the area of conflict between the interests of the bureaucratic and/or landowning literati ruling class and those of the other classes in society, namely, the middle and poor merchants, artisans, and peasantry. As such Chinese secret societies played a crucial role: first, in leading, articulating and organizing revolt; second, in contributing to the illegal, anti-bureaucratic "petty bourgeoisie"; and third, in elaborating an unorthodox, un-Confucian form of social organization—the non-familial, "democratic," voluntary association.[93]

Davis goes on to characterize the Nien as having "reactivated secret society ambitions for national power." As Chiang Siangtseh states the common view, "There is no way to distinguish the Nien from ordinary local bandits who likewise engaged in kidnapping and plunder, unless the fact that the Nien were led by an insurgent secret society is counted."[94]

Although these authors have initiated an important shift of scholarly focus from the "Apollonian" world of the ruling elite to the "Dionysian" realm of the masses, the terms of their analysis implicitly accept a Confucian dichotomy of orthodoxy and heterodoxy. If, by contrast, we approach the study of peasant violence from the parochial standpoint of the participants, we find a rather more complicated dynamic in operation. It seems that in traditional Huai-pei, rebellion was largely an extension of ongoing modes of local competition. The role of the secret society in this process was at times negligible and, at other times—as in the case of the Old Cows—associated with a conservative, defensive posture on the part of relatively affluent individuals and communities.*

It was the special historical circumstances of mid-nineteenth-century Huai-pei—crippling natural disasters exacerbated by inefficient government and increased taxes, the entrance of the Taiping rebels, the ambitions of certain bandit chieftains and militia captains—that intensified and transformed everyday means of securing a livelihood into massive rebellion against the state. Since the eventual suppression of this rebellion did not, however, alter the underlying natural and social environment,

---

*To be sure, the Nien were not entirely free of sectarian connections. Elements of that enduring group of "heterodox" sects, the White Lotus, did indeed unite with the Nien on occasion. One instance was the case of Golden Tower Fort in Shang-ch'iu, Honan. The leader of this community, Kao Yung-ch'ing, was a White Lotus practitioner as his ancestors had been for three generations. Although Yung-ch'ing's father and grandfather had both been executed for their beliefs, Yung-ch'ing did not recant. When the Nien developed into a powerful insurrection, some of Kao's followers joined the movement in Anhwei. Clearly they did not feel entirely secure from the possibility of plunder, however, for they erected a strong wall and moat in self-defense. In 1861, Nien leader Liu Kou was courteously hosted by the fort and agreed to spare it from Nien attack. With this guarantee of safety, the local populace thronged to Golden Tower Fort for protection. Emboldened by the massive increase in membership, Kao decided to stage an uprising timed to coincide with an imminent lunar eclipse. After consulting with various Nien leaders, he planned a joint attack on the district government offices. The news leaked out, however, and the would-be rebels were forced to retreat. (NC, vol. 2, pp. 189–90.) Like all Nien alliances, cooperation with Golden Tower Fort was fragile and temporary. In 1862, Chang Lo-hsing led a plundering expedition against the fort. Although the fort itself was sturdy enough to withstand the attack, the Nien succeeded in harvesting and making off with all the ripe grain from the surrounding fields. (NC, vol. 3, p. 25.) For further information on the history of the White Lotus of Shang-ch'iu, see Naquin, 1976, pp. 55–56.

Another instance of Nien–White Lotus cooperation occurred in early 1858, when several secret-society leaders in Fu-yang invited Nien participation in a joint uprising. The revolt, carried out from a base of five walled fortresses, lasted some two months before being crushed. Although Nien and White Lotus members fought side by side, they are clearly differentiated in the official account of the incident (NC, vol. 2, pp. 183–87). The same holds for the case of Chang Chieh-san, a White Lotus leader in I-men-chi who in 1854 effected a short-lived alliance with the Nien (Kuo-yang-hsien chih, 1924, 15/10). Some White Lotus communities constituted useful allies for the Nien; however, the two groups were clearly not identical.

predation continued as an adaptive survival strategy, outliving the imperial system itself. The defeat in 1868 of roving Nien forces by no means signaled the demise of the predatory strategy.* Smuggling, feuds, and organized banditry persisted as regular modes of Huai-pei peasant behavior well into the Republican period.

*In 1872, former Nien attempted an uprising along the Honan-Anhwei border. In 1876, they initiated a brief revolt in Kuo-yang. In 1896, Liu Ke-ta and Niu Shih-hsiu led an uprising in Kuo-yang and Meng-ch'eng, Anhwei, which patterned itself on the Nien. In 1900, Yen Te-jen attempted an anti-Ch'ing movement in Ju-nan, Honan—the same location where Nien chieftain Ch'en Ta-hsi had been active. See Chiang Ti, 1959, p. 1.

5. Protectors Turn Rebels:
The Case of the Red Spears

The Ch'ing government's encouragement of local defense measures, although an effective method for subduing the Nien, opened the way to alternative forms of resistance. Mid-nineteenth-century Huai-pei had witnessed a rebellion of predators. In the early twentieth century, by contrast, it was the protective strategy that launched an antigovernment assault. The Red Spear Society (*hung-ch'iang-hui*) was a rural self-defense movement well known for its success in combating bandits, warlords, and tax collectors alike. For virtually the entire Republican period (1911–49), intermittent Red Spear activities posed a major challenge to government control in North China.

Much of the explanation for this turnabout from predatory to protective rebellion lies in the development of local militia, which had mushroomed in response to the Nien and Taipings. The emergence of this institution altered the balance of collective action in Huai-pei, strengthening the hand of the protective strategy. Led for the most part by local notables anxious to defend their resources against outside incursions of any sort, the militia proved effective not only in combating banditry, but in resisting taxes as well. A second and related reason for this change in the form of rebellion was precisely the growing tax burden that accompanied the demise of the Ch'ing. As outside exactions increased in the form of higher land taxes and surcharges, rural property holders were quick to redirect their defensive energies in opposition to these new demands.

The unruly potential of the local militia had already been strikingly demonstrated in the famous Boxer Rebellion of 1899–1900. Prior to that uprising, peasants had been laboring for several years under a tax burden to pay for the indemnities resulting from China's defeat in the Sino-Japanese War.[1] A multitude of smoldering animosities occasioned by the foreign presence in North China burst into flame when a prolonged drought pushed the local inhabitants to the point of resistance. Capturing international attention by their attacks upon foreigners and their fantastic claims to physical invulnerability, the Boxers were rooted organizationally in the village defense forces. Their early struggles against both Western intrusion and Manchu rule were based upon successfully wedding a sectarian tradition of esoteric religious and martial arts practices to the institutional framework of the militia.[2] Ironically, an end result of the Boxer affair was yet another set of indemnities, imposed upon China by the foreign powers, which greatly exacerbated the tax burden of the peasantry. Less than a generation later, the Red Spears, a movement remarkably similar to the Boxers in its combined militia and sectarian composition, arose to carry on the struggle for community protection against outside exactions.

RED SPEAR ORIGINS

The name "Red Spears" referred to the most common weapon of the group: a wooden spear to which was affixed a decorative red tassel. The origins of the movement are shrouded in a veil of mystery hardly less dense than that surrounding the early Nien, but according to some contemporary accounts, the Red Spear Society was a direct descendant of the Boxers. Forced to abandon their forbidden "Boxer" title after the suppression of that uprising, a number of former Boxers are said to have gone underground in the western Shantung area. The growing bandit menace that accompanied the early Republican period once again called forth their reputedly magical talents for self-protection, this time as religious advisors to the burgeoning Red Spear

154 The Red Spears

movement.*[3] Like the Boxers, the Red Spears evidenced a heavy dose of popular religious inspiration, members believing themselves impervious to enemy weapons if they observed the necessary rituals, pronounced the proper incantations, and swallowed the prescribed charms. And, again resembling the Boxers, the Red Spears were heirs to another equally vital legacy: the militia tradition of rural self-defense.[4]

The beginnings of Red Spear activities are not easily dated. Some sources trace their earliest appearance to 1911, a response to the bandit Pai Lang. Others place the beginnings of the Red Spears in 1915–16, a reaction to the rampages of brigand Lao Yang-jen. In any event, all accounts agree that the Red Spears were well underway by the early 1920s, in opposition to a host of bandit armies then plundering across the North China Plain.[5] Regardless of the precise date of its first appearance, it is certain that the movement began as a form of local defense against the rampant brigandage of early Republican China.

The confusion attendant upon the overthrow of the imperial system, followed by the incapacity of the shifting coalitions of new rulers to impose control on the countryside, turned much of the former empire into brigand territory. Driven by a terrible string of natural and social catastrophes to eke out their living by plunder, bandits swarmed like locusts across North China. Throughout the first decade of the Republican period, famine haunted the Huai-pei plain, floods alternating with drought to deny large segments of the population even a meager subsistence. The turmoil of warfare among competing militarists who raged across the region in the early 1920s intensified the difficulties of garnering a livelihood from agriculture. By the mid-1920s, Huai-pei was said to harbor some two to three hundred thousand bandits, clustered along the four provincial borders of Shantung, Honan, Kiangsu, and Anhwei. In 1925, Honan Province alone could claim nearly five hundred thousand brigands, and by 1930 Shantung was said to contain a full million.[6]

*For accounts of the Red Spears' origins, see note 3.

Although virtually no section of Huai-pei was entirely free from the threat of banditry, the situation in Honan was particularly acute. This province was home ground for exceptionally large bandit armies, most notably those of Pai Lang and Lao Yang-jen. The latter brigand, known as the "Old Foreigner" because of his height and curly hair, commanded a force of several thousand followers who scoured the countryside for food, wreaking terrific destruction as they went. Mounted on horseback, his troops were said to be able to travel up to seventy miles overnight between raids. This bandit army consisted of twenty to thirty semi-independent gangs of a hundred men each, which commander Lao Yang-jen dispatched on plundering missions as he deemed fit. For years, his forces pillaged the towns of Honan and Anhwei until Lao Yang-jen was finally "pacified" by the warlord Wu P'ei-fu, who won over the brigand by the offer of an army position.[7]

The absence of effective government control—responsible as it was for the dike disrepair that fostered flooding, for the lack of famine relief, and for the disruptive warlord struggles—contributed directly to the rise of massive banditry. By the same token, this very lack of state power left bandit-threatened areas with no option but to devise some sort of private police response. Building upon the defensive tendencies that had led to the proliferation of crop-watching associations and other protective measures during this period, villagers began to establish Red Spear societies as an extralegal, yet effective, means of local defense. A community-based movement, the Red Spears were most active in places subject to the greatest predatory threat. Red Spear chapters sprang up across Huai-pei, but in the early Republican period they naturally attained their highest organizational development in Honan, home of the most massive bandit armies. Although rural villages constituted the basic organizational unit of the Red Spears, in Honan the movement expanded to encompass a network of village alliances.

The growth of the Red Spears was a part of the process of

village institutionalization underway in North China during the late nineteenth and early twentieth centuries.[8] Whether a cyclical instance of "community closure" or a secular trend reflecting the unprecedented difficulties of the late Ch'ing and early Republican periods, this process apparently resulted in a gradual shift from lineage to settlement as the focal point of rural organization. During the time of the clan-based Nien, lineage and settlement had constituted reinforcing units, inasmuch as many Huai-pei villages were in fact lineage communities. In subsequent years, however, it seems that the strength of the lineage declined, possibly as a result of increased mobility accompanying a deterioration in peasant livelihood during this troubled period.[9] In any case, the Red Spears were an association forged along settlement rather than kinship lines. Although the movement comprised numerous offshoots distinguished by a bewildering variety of disparate names and practices, the branches shared in common the character of a community-rooted reaction to predatory threat.*

Like the Old Cows, which had emerged in response to a similar challenge half a century before, the Red Spears originated as a kind of private militia system. In contrast to the nineteenth century, however, official defense leagues now received relatively little concrete support from the government. Although formally similar to the Ch'ing militia, state-sponsored defense forces during the Republican period in fact lacked the resources or legitimacy of the earlier institution.[10] Religious sects therefore stepped in to fill the gap. What had once constituted a minor form of local defense now became the dominant variety of rural protection.

*I have used the term "Red Spears" to refer broadly to all community-based protective groups adhering to certain beliefs and rituals intended to ensure physical invulnerability. The term was used in this generic fashion by contemporaries, despite the fact that many of the groups did assume different appellations. When referring to specific sects that adopted a variant name, I will identify the name in question.

EARLY RED SPEAR ACTIVITIES

Our earliest substantive account of Red Spear–type activity during the Republican period concerns a group known as the Red Flags (*hung-ch'i-hui*), active in southern Shantung from 1919 to 1921. This sect developed in the area menaced by the Sun brothers' bandit gang and was in fact responsible for beheading bandit chief Sun Mei-chu, elder brother of the mastermind behind the infamous Lin-ch'eng railway holdup of 1923.[11]

If southern Shantung had the distinction of producing the first Red Spear–type unit, the pattern was rapidly transmitted to bordering provinces suffering from similar bandit disturbances. By 1923, villages in neighboring Kiangsu's Hsüchou district had taken up the Red Spear model to compensate for the incompetence of the official militia in their area.[12] The impetus for the new organization came when the captain of the official defense league in the town of Fang-ts'un sent out a requisition for fees from the surrounding countryside. The village elder in the Chao Family Village refused to comply, explaining that the last time the village was attacked by bandits the militia had dispatched not a single man to provide assistance. Rather than continue to pay for a nonexistent service, the village decided to organize its own "Tasseled Spear Society" (*ying-ch'iang-hui*) instead, hiring a teacher who instructed them in reciting incantations and swallowing charms to induce invulnerability. Friction between the regular militia and the Tasseled Spears escalated, with both sides putting on public demonstrations of their military might in classic feud style. Apprised of the situation, the county magistrate sent his security forces to subdue the dissident Chao Family Village Tasseled Spear Society, outlawing it as a transformation of the Boxers. In response, the Tasseled Spears allied with sympathetic groups in neighboring villages, thereby amassing a force of more than a thousand people to resist government suppression. Under a red banner emblazoned with the age-old rebel slogan "Preparing the Way for Heaven" (*t'i-t'ien hsing-tao*), the allied defense force sallied forth to meet the government troops. When the county security forces captured the leader of one of the participating Red Spear groups (the Red Tassels of nearby Tan-chi-shih), the enraged village alliance enlarged its forces to counter the government offensive. Faced with this dangerous situation, the magistrate called a meeting of all the fortress chiefs (*yü-tung*) in the area.

As a legacy of the Nien, the region continued to be organized militarily into fortresses, each of which was intended to provide refuge for several contiguous villages. The Chao Family fort, home of the Tasseled Spears, had been constructed in 1852 to encompass three villages; the Fang-ts'un fort, site of the official militia headquarters, had been established in the same year to provide protection for twelve villages.[13] Not surprisingly, the fortress chief of Chao Family Village refused to comply with the magistrate's instructions, instead summoning a combat force of six to seven thousand Tasseled Spears. Despite this impressive assembly, the government managed to control the ensuing battle, staging a frontal assault on Chao Village, razing its fortress wall, and taking captive its Tasseled Spear teacher. As a last resort, the Tassels attacked the local militia headquarters, which they burned and looted for arms, in the process seizing the militia captain, whose hands they summarily chopped off in revenge. The group was soon quelled by an overwhelming deployment of county security forces and infantry, but in subsequent years the Tassels continued to be active in a number of locations across northern Kiangsu and Anhwei.

Although the scenario of pitched battles among walled fortresses, or *yü-chai*, recalls the drama of the Nien Rebellion, something of a change in cast had occurred over the intervening years. With the state now proving useless in combating the predatory menace, private defense institutions—tainted by a "heterodox" sectarian coloration—found themselves playing the role of opponents to bandits and government alike. As the case of the Chao Family Village illustrates, continuing demands for monetary support of ineffective government services were a key determinant of Red Spear alienation in this early period, presaging their massive antitax rebellion of later years.

At this time, however, the brunt of Red Spear hostilities was directed not against officials, but against the more immediate threat of banditry.* Only insofar as the authorities interfered with this protective activity did they too constitute targets of Red Spear animosity. In places where the government made serious efforts to counter the bandit menace, Red Spears were quite willing to cooperate in the endeavor.† In Kiangsu's Sui-ning County, for example, most Red Spears served as members of the regularly constituted self-defense force. This was because in Sui-ning, peasant households were asked to supply only manpower—not financial support—to the official militia. Leaders of the militia were chosen by the peasants themselves, rather than being imposed by order of the county administration.[14] Viable systems of government-authorized militia were, however, the exception in rural Huai-pei. Thus in most places,

---

*An example of a sectarian group outside Huai-pei that did actually attempt outright rebellion during this early period was the Yellow Way Society (*huang-tao-hui*), active in Honan's An-yang County in 1919–22. A man calling himself "Chu the Ninth" and claiming to be the eighth-generation descendant of the Ming throne was welcomed by the Yellow Way teacher. The two gathered followers on the pretext that only those who joined the sect would be spared the ensuing armageddon. They prepared a yellow banner inscribed with both their names and issued a joint proclamation declaring, "The nation will be united and peace will be restored; again the true dragon [rightful emperor] has appeared. Now we must recruit soldiers and buy horses. Our reign title is Great Brightness [*ta-ming*]. We must have peace. No longer can violations of the Way be permitted." The movement was eventually quelled by local militia and government troops. See Nagano Akira, 1930, pp. 237–38; 1931, p. 251. An-yang had a history of repeated claimants to the Ming throne during the early Republican period. In April 1924, in western An-yang, a man known as Wang the Sixth claimed to have a vermilion sun-moon mark on his hand which certified him as the rightful emperor. Wang mustered three hundred followers before being captured in an attempted raid on the militia armory. See *Shih-pao*, May 20, 1924. Although this particular county spawned a number of overtly rebellious outbreaks, imperial pretensions were rare among Red Spear groups at the time.

†Such was the case in Honan's Kuei-teh district in the fall of 1923. A new magistrate who had just assumed office refused to continue to provide grain rations from the public dole to a local brigand "pacified" the previous winter by the former magistrate. Instead, a combined force of government troops and Red Spears took to arms to eliminate the bandit. See *Shih-pao*, September 6, 1923.

villagers resorted to unlawful means of promoting security. Even an American consul stationed in North China was moved to characterize the "superstitious" Red Spears as "in general, a healthy reaction against the wrongs suffered by the rural population at the hands of bandits and soldiers."[15]

THE MOVE TO REBELLION

Although bandits constituted the principal motivation for Red Spear organization, marauding troops soon came to pose an equally salient reason for self-defense. As warlord soldiers marched across the North China Plain looting from the local populace to more than make up for their inadequate salaries, peasants began to redirect their protective energies against these unwelcome intruders. The locus of Red Spear activities expanded to include centers of military occupation as well as areas suffering from bandit attack.

The first decade of the Republican period, marked by the onset of warlordism, saw a rapid increase in the number of soldiers in Huai-pei. The case of Honan Province is illustrative. In 1911, there were 16,067 soldiers in Honan. The following year the number reached 23,000. By 1915, Honan had 37,600 soldiers, the most of any province in China. Five years later the number was 56,550 and in 1922 it had risen to 78,650. By 1924, there were said to be some 200,000 soldiers in Honan, many of whom were former bandits.[16]

Whereas warlord armies grew by the incorporation of bandits, the Kuomintang (KMT) tried to recruit new troops through household conscription. In fact, however, it was common for richer families to pay poor peasants to take their son's places. The result was anything but a committed force. Often those who accepted the bribe deserted as quickly as possible, joining up again once they had been paid to substitute for someone else. The practice developed into a fairly lucrative profession for poor peasants. In order to prevent desertion, harsh controls were imposed. Like criminals, soldiers were bound together with long ropes and guarded by armed watchmen. When their numbers still proved inadequate, entire villages would be surrounded and all males in sight—including passersby—seized for the army. Living conditions among the troops were grim. Supplies were inadequate and disease rampant. Denied proper food and clothing, soldiers preyed upon the populace to compensate for the deficiencies. The Honan army that pursued Pai Lang in 1914 gained the nickname of "change the shoes army" for its practice of stealing shoes from the villages through which it passed.[17]

As a bandit extermination force, the armies were very nearly worthless. In Honan, the standard practice upon sighting bandits was for the troops to fire blank shots to signal their approach. The advance warning obviated any need for a military confrontation and, by prolonging the bandits' existence, ensured the continued survival of the army as well. When troops from Shensi were sent to Honan, ostensibly to suppress bandits, they were distressed to discover that Red Spears in the area were in fact already conducting an effective antibandit campaign. To prevent these efforts from going too far, the Shensi army ambushed a large Red Spear force.[18]

The first major confrontation between Red Spears and soldiers took place in 1923 in Honan's Lu-shih County, then under occupation by troops from Shensi Province. The occupying army had imposed numerous surtaxes and made heavy labor demands as well. A poor harvest brought the peasants to the boiling point in August 1923. A united force of some one hundred thousand Red Spears and allied self-defense groups surrounded the county seat in a show of strength intended to dispel the unwelcome soldiers. Cooperating groups included the county militia, private vigilantes, and members of the "Hard Stomachs" (ying-tu-tui), a western Honan sect which, like the Red Spears, claimed physical invulnerability. Negotiations with the city officials resulted in an agreement that most of the soldiers would be transferred, and the one remaining division would be prohibited from levying surcharges or seizing people

Map 3. Red Spear Headquarters in Honan, 1927. (Source: Chen, 1927: 3; Hsiang, 1927: 38.)

at will. Having gained these concessions, the local alliance was soon aroused to further action. Now the goal was to expel the one remaining division of soldiers, on the grounds that this unit had never attacked bandits, but had on the contrary repeatedly sold out to them. When it became clear, moreover, that the remaining troops were not abiding by the previous agreement, but were instead continuing their plunder, rape, and conscription, the people refused to pay any more taxes and undertook a full-scale siege of the city.[19]

Tax resistance was a natural outcome for a movement aimed at community defense against threats to property. Although early Red Spear activities focused primarily on bandits and unruly soldiers, by 1925 the center of concern had shifted to tax rebellion. The transition was directly connected to the ascendancy of several warlords whose enormous military expenditures were underwritten by the imposition of onerous taxes. The problem of payment was made more difficult by the irresponsible fiscal policy of these warlords. Taxes had to be paid in officially recognized currency, often gold or silver, but mountains of paper bills were printed up for the exclusive use of the warlord armies. Peasants were thus forced to accept payment for their produce in what was, for their purposes, a useless currency.[20]

As tax-hungry warlords extended their satrapies over large geographical expanses, peasants in the subjugated areas began to unite in opposition, forging progressively wider networks of cooperation to meet the growing threat. Red Spear units developed from simple village chapters to alliances encompassing regions of considerable size. Honan was the home of most of these large-scale networks, their headquarters usually situated along the same railway lines by which warlord troops moved to occupy new territory (see Map 3).*

*The Peking-Hankow line had been completed by 1906; the Lung-hai railway extended from Hsüchou all across Honan Province in 1916. The link between railroad construction and agrarian protest, albeit with rather different intervening causes, has been noted in other societies. See, for example, John Coatsworth, "Railroads, Landholdings, and Agrarian Protest in the Early Porfiriato," *Hispanic American Historical Review*, 54, no. 1 (1974): 48–71.

The most famous Red Spear battles against warlords and their taxes occurred in opposition to the repressive regimes of Honan military governor Yüeh Wei-chün and his successor Wu P'ei-fu. Yüeh, a subordinate of the warlord Feng Yü-hsiang, had made numerous demands on the peasantry, especially those living along railway lines, where imposition of military control was least difficult.[21] In response, a Red Spear headquarters was founded in Ying-yang, a county located near the junction of the Peking-Hankow and Lung-hai railways. Ying-yang had first established a Red Spear chapter in the summer of 1925 at the prompting of several representatives from the Red Spears of Hsin-yang County. In less than three months, some fifty Red Spear branches had been formed in the Ying-yang area, food supplies gathered, and armaments fashioned. Most important, tax collection was entirely assumed by the Red Spear Society, the father of the Red Spear leader in nearby Ying-tse County having been appointed director of the treasury. When a new county magistrate learned upon taking office of this unusual situation, he immediately imprisoned the treasury director. The act provoked a violent confrontation on January 1, 1926, in which some thirteen thousand Red Spears attacked the county seat. Drawing supporters from neighboring counties, the rebels managed to confiscate all weapons from the arsenal and to open the county prison, releasing the detained treasury director and a number of other prisoners. In keeping with the movement's limited aims, the only severe damage inflicted was to the home of the magistrate, which was burned to the ground. Government troops had to be called in to suppress the rebellion.[22]

Opposition to Yüeh's regime was not limited to Ying-yang. In Ch'i County, located about 120 kilometers to the east, Red Spear resistance was even more pronounced. There a leader by the name of Lou Pai-hsün had command of some three hundred thousand Red Spears from throughout the neighboring three or four counties. This formidable force was able to prevent Yüeh from collecting any taxes in the area.[23] The richest county in Honan, Ch'i had a long history of tax resistance. Since the development of the militia in 1853, local defense leagues had played an effective role in blocking efforts at tax collection in the county.[24] Red Spear leader Lou Pai-hsün was able to perpetuate this tradition, thereby denying the provincial government a major source of revenue. The significance of this show of strength was not lost on outside observers of the Honan scene. In early 1926, warlord Wu P'ei-fu saw an alliance with the Red Spears of Ch'i County as his key to a take-over of the province. Promising high military rank to Lou Pai-hsün and a three-year tax holiday to Lou's followers, Wu was able to obtain crucial Red Spear assistance in defeating the forces of Yüeh Wei-chün and assuming control of the Honan government himself.[25] Red Spear elation at the ouster of Yüeh Wei-chün was short-lived, however, as Wu P'ei-fu soon proved a more demanding overlord than his predecessor. Having taken power, Wu turned against his former allies. Fourteen Red Spear leaders were shot to death and the society was ordered to disarm. Unwilling to forgo revenue from the wealthiest county in the province, Wu also immediately reinstated a heavy tax quota on Ch'i County. Rather than abide by the order to disarm, Lou Pai-hsün responded to the challenge by instructing his followers to continue their tax boycott.[26]

Hoping to expand the struggle against Wu P'ei-fu throughout the province, the Red Spears now issued pleas for support to other areas. One of the few surviving Red Spear documents—addressed to the inhabitants of K'ai-feng city—dates from this time. The proclamation provides vivid evidence of the essentially defensive motivation behind Red Spear resistance to warlord demands:

Brethren of K'ai-feng city, last year Wu P'ei-fu entered Honan because he agreed to three years without taxes and to the abolition of oppressive surtaxes. Now that he is in Honan, not only has he not abolished taxes, the situation is ten times worse than before. Think of how we raised our swords and rushed to the line of fire on his behalf so that we might pass our days in peace. Now that he has arrived he proves even more ferocious than his predecessor. Here a surcharge, there a surtax. Today it is requested, tomorrow it is demanded. Sell your grain and pawn your clothing—still you haven't enough to pay his cursed taxes. See how his army is even more vicious than bandits. He watches bandits running rampant everywhere but does nothing to interfere. No longer can we stand for this. Our brothers in western Honan have already begun to act. In Hsin-an, I-yang, Lo-ning, Teng-feng, and Yen-shih our brothers have started tax resistance. In every county of the province our brothers are preparing to rise up in response. Brethren! The scourge of Wu P'ei-fu is no less terrible for you than for the countryside. Seizing one month of rent, imposing taxes on cooking oil, auctioning off the public lands, issuing five million bank notes, imposing interest bonds—all these are conscious efforts to deprive you of your very lives. Large businesses and small shops alike have been driven to bankruptcy. Will you stand for this? Will you be content to let the businesses you have managed for so many years come to ruin? If you can muster the courage—if you dare to resist—we your brothers in the countryside swear to be your helpmates. Brethren of K'ai-feng city, to die is to die. Rather than expire at the hands of the police and yamen clerks while trying to pay taxes, it is much more glorious to die in resisting them. In the future we will not listen to the soldiers or officials with their sweet words, for behind their smiles lie hidden daggers. As long as we unite we are strong and need have no fear. To action, brethren! We your country brothers swear to be your helpers; to oppose the rents, the oil taxes, the auctioning of public lands, the issuing of interest-laden bonds. Burn their banks! Down with Wu P'ei-fu! Everyone, unite with one mind! To action![27]

In March and April, thousands of indignant peasants in Ch'i County gathered for a tax resistance demonstration in front of the county offices. The protest succeeded in reshuffling the personnel in the tax bureau, thereby returning financial control to the Red Spears. With the county magistrate incapable of containing the rebellion, Wu P'ei-fu's reply was to dispatch on May 6 a large armed force ordered to destroy White Tower Fort, the home village of Lou Pai-hsün. Lou himself managed to escape before the attack, but not one of the remaining five thousand inhabitants is said to have survived the assault. Having annihilated the population, the army proceeded to occupy the fortress. Determined to avenge, Lou Pai-hsün managed by May 15 to amass more than ten thousand sympathetic Red Spears from neighboring villages. The group staged a frontal assault on

White Tower Fort, but after a week's siege was forced to retreat. Pursuing with cavalry, the army burned any village through which the Red Spears had passed. In this way more than twenty villages were razed and thousands of innocent people killed. Lou Pai-hsün having escaped once again, a large contingent of remnant Red Spears decided to vent their fury on nearby Sui County. Equipped with cannon, rifles, and ladders, the group moved to surround the county seat. A foreign missionary was sent forth to negotiate, pledging that the city would pay a goodly sum of money should the Red Spears agree to desist from the planned attack. When the angry crowd refused to be placated, the armed forces occupying Ch'i were called in to break the siege.[28]

Meanwhile Lou Pai-hsün had linked up with over a thousand bandits across the border in Anhwei's Po and Kuo-yang counties, the old home base of Chang Lo-hsing's Nien. On May 20 the group crossed from Anhwei back into Honan, attempting an assault on the Huai-yang county seat. Finding the city already locked up and well defended, Lou turned to the surrounding countryside instead. At first the villagers, being on bad terms with the county administration themselves, welcomed Lou with generous contributions of tea and food. However, when it became clear that the group was in fact intent on plunder, the peasants sealed their communities in self-defense. Although more than thirty villages were severely damaged, those equipped with strong walls and moats managed to survive the attack relatively unscathed. Finally, a combined militia and army force succeeded in dispelling the unwelcome Red Spear and bandit intrusion.[29]

Predatory-Protective Synthesis

The case of Lou Pai-hsün demonstrates the rapidity with which protectors could turn to predators once their property base had been destroyed. Originally a Red Spear leader defending his community against intrusion by tax collectors, Lou moved to a predatory strategy after the loss of his home village. The line between propertied and destitute was thin in Huai-pei. Whether from natural or social causes, threat to one's land was ever present.

As the first decade of the Republican era gave way to a second, the scourge of natural catastrophe continued to bring year after year of hardship. In 1920–21 an extremely severe famine affected the entire North China Plain. In late 1921 massive floods occurred. These were followed by a drought in 1923 and yet another major inundation in 1925. The effects were disastrous. In Kiangsu's Hsüchou district, some 450 villages in 1925 were unable to harvest any crops at all. Seven to eight thousand of the inhabitants left as soldiers; another ten thousand migrated out as refugees.[30] In 1926 an American visitor to Yung-ch'eng, Honan, reported: "There was not a single time or place, when I was on the major road, that I was out of the sight of refugees. They have been passing all the fall, and conditions grow worse and will continue to do so till a wheat harvest is gathered."[31]

The distress gave rise, as we have seen, to bandit armies that scoured the countryside for food, wreaking terrific destruction as they went. An example of the suffering that such attacks brought to the victimized areas is seen in the case of Hsiang-ch'eng, Honan. In 1926 the county was twice attacked by the bandit "Old Chicken," whose followers occupied the county seat for over a month, burned down some twenty thousand dwellings, and inflicted ten million yüan in property damage. The following year the county was again harassed by bandits for two months. This time more than three thousand people lost their lives, thirty thousand houses were burned, and twenty million yüan of damage was incurred. Throughout most of 1928 the county seat was occupied by yet another contingent of bandits, and the surrounding area for several dozen li was devastated as a result.[32] In January 1926, a foreigner who had witnessed a bandit attack on Po, Anhwei, reported: "From all I have seen in the city and suburbs of burned houses I should think that not less than 25,000 people are without any kind of a roof over them in this the coldest weather we have had this winter. The burnt streets, counting both sides, I should think would make a stretch of at least 20 miles."[33] It was to prevent just such bandit attacks as these that the Red Spears had first come into existence, but the destruction wrought by combined natural and social disaster deprived numerous inhabitants of their belongings, thereby undercutting the rationale for self-defense.

To blur the distinction between predation and protection further, the launching of the Kuomintang's Northern Expedition in the summer of 1926 met opposition from Huai-pei bandits and Red Spears alike, both of whom resented the encroachment of Nationalist troops upon their home territory. Instances of cooperative ventures against the Expeditionary forces grew increasingly common. In Honan's Nan-yang County, for example, Red Spear units were said to have made contact with some fifty thousand bandits, engaging in joint attacks on county seats and severing the Peking-Hankow railway at several points to deter the KMT advance.[34]

The fusing of strategies could work in both directions. While Red Spear groups frequently turned to banditry in the wake of the Northern Expedition, it also became common for initially predatory outfits to adopt aspects of the protective tradition. For example, in 1928, after a Red Spear force succeeded in routing bandits from Anhwei's Hsü-i and Ting-yüan counties, the brigands regrouped in nearby Hsüchou. Frightened by the massive incursion, peasants in the Hsüchou countryside rushed to seek refuge behind the city walls. The bandits then moved into the abandoned villages, ensconcing themselves within the *yü-chai* fortifications where they raised red flags, donned red turbans, and proclaimed themselves friends of the poor peasants.[35] Not only did twentieth-century brigands borrow the Nien precedent of occupying fortifications, they also continued the practice of masquerading as self-defense forces. With the ascendancy of the Red Spears, bandit groups began to assume the name, and sometimes the rituals, of the growing secret-society movement. More than a few "Red Spear" chapters were in reality bandit outfits, using their cover as a license to plunder and kidnap for ransom.[36] As an American missionary described a group operating in north Anhwei: "Men were sitting on the bank blowing cows' horns. They had big spears with red tassels on them stuck in the ground at their sides. 'Cows' horns and red-tasseled spears,' I commented. 'It looks like the Red Spear Society. We probably shall have a bandit raid tonight. They are the worst robbers in the country around here.'"[37]

Along with the trend toward banditry went another feature of the predatory strategy, a propensity toward feuding. As Red Spear–type groups proliferated, conflicts among them over territorial control became commonplace. One of the more vicious disputes occurred in the area of Ying-yang, site of the large allied headquarters which had been formed in 1925 to incorporate some fifty Red Spear branches. On January 3, 1926, a battle was initiated by more than ten thousand members of the Small Red School sect against several tens of thousands of the rival Big School and their three thousand allies among the Yellow Spear Society. The result of five hours of fierce fighting was a decisive victory for the Small School. The Yellow Spears subsequently were completely dissolved and their weapons confiscated by the victors. The leader of the Big School was forced to pay 50,000 yüan in cash, and his subordinates were reorganized into the Small Red School.[38]

Perhaps the most famous feuding was that between the Heavenly Gate Society (t'ien-men-hui) and neighboring Red and White Spear associations. The Heavenly Gate Society was founded in early 1926 by a stonemason who claimed to have discovered inside one of his stones a magical engraving with a formula for physical invulnerability. Impressive victories against bandits and soldiers swelled the ranks of the Heavenly Gate Society and permitted it to gain hegemony in some twenty counties. Unlike most Red Spear groups, however, the Heavenly Gate Society was notably hostile to landlords. Led by poor peasants, it gained a reputation for liquidating more than a few members of the local elite. Not surprisingly, such actions evoked an unfriendly reaction from nearby Red Spear associations whose leadership was drawn primarily from the upper sectors of rural society. Although such groups managed to cooperate with the Heavenly Gates in 1926–27 to resist the advance of the Feng-t'ien Army, they turned openly hostile once the outside threat was eliminated.[39] In 1928, animosities reached the boiling point in Yung-nien, Hopei, when a Heavenly Gate member killed the White Spear leader. The White Spears retaliated by murdering twenty or thirty Heavenly Gate members. In return, the Heavenly Gates burned down the house of the slain White Spear leader, killing his son in the flames. Acts of revenge between the two groups persisted for some time. Similarly, in nearby Ts'u-chou, the Red Spears waged an all-out battle against the local Heavenly Gate Society, mercilessly slaughtering the families of Heavenly Gate members.[40]

Another lingering resentment that came alive once again in Red Spear feuding was the ethnic prejudice against Muslims. Using Muslim reluctance to observe Red Spear rituals as a pretext for persecution, the Red Spears are said to have pillaged numerous Muslim homes, killing many family members and burning their houses. Mosques were also set on fire, or converted into pigsties in the ultimate insult to Muslim religious beliefs.[41] Inasmuch as the Red Spears were remarkably tolerant of other faiths, most notably Christianity, we are probably safe in interpreting their assaults on Muslims as the rekindling of age-old animosity, rather than an expression of religious zeal.

Hostilities among protective groups were often rooted in the ongoing competition for scarce resources. A telling example was the conflict between two Red Spear–type units in Kiangsu known as the Big Swords and Small Swords. This dispute stemmed from hostilities generated when large numbers of peasants from the Huai-pei region of Kiangsu emigrated south in search of a more dependable livelihood. The migrants took with them their own standard of living, which was considerably more austere than that of the southern peasantry. Whereas the natives lived in brick-walled houses with tiled roofs, the Huai-pei peasants continued to build their thatched earthen huts. The economic competition was strongly resented, and the immigrants were looked down upon for their "primitive" ways; intermarriage between the two groups was rare. Hostilities sharpened in 1927 when bandits became a serious menace in the countryside. Because the Huai-pei immigrants were almost never robbed, the local inhabitants suspected the newcomers of bandit connections. As repayment, they burned down thousands of immigrant huts. In response, the peasants from Huai-pei organized a branch of the Small Swords, a secret society active in the Huai-pei area. Thereupon the natives formed a chapter of the Big Sword Society. Sporadic fighting between the two groups continued until an uneasy truce was concluded in February 1928. This agreement was short-lived, however. Joined by bandits, on September 10–11 two thousand Small Swords moved from village to village, demanding firearms, pork and chicken, prepared food, and money. Six villages that either refused or were unable to meet the demands were burned and many inhabitants killed.*

Although the banditry and feuding of Red Spear groups in the late 1920s indicated the absorption of predatory impulses, the movement as a whole did not thereby shed its basically protective purpose. Just as the Nien had continued to reflect their origins throughout the duration of that rebellion, so too the Red Spears retained an identifiable character. As defenders of propertied interests, Red Spear groups continued to conflict with local predators in a way strikingly reminiscent of Old Cow hostilities against the Nien.

Group conflict generally operated on an intervillage level, but within villages the population also sometimes divided into warring factions organized in part along economic lines. A telling illustration of this process occurred in Kao-t'ou village in west-

---

*J. L. Buck, 1927; Wu Shou-p'eng, 1930, pp. 66–67. Villages that had not formed Big Sword societies were spared attack in this encounter. One of these more fortunate villages had refused to join the Big Swords because the village headman, a Christian, expressed an unwillingness to worship idols and a disbelief in the society's claim of invulnerability.

ern Hsin-yang, Honan, during the late 1920s.[42] The village contained many unemployed people, one of whom—a bachelor by the name of Wang Erh—had attempted to rob a certain rich household in the community. Captured in the act, Wang was threatened with the power of the Red Spears should he commit any more robberies, and then released. Rather than heed the warning, Wang went home and gathered together the other bare sticks in the village to plot revenge. The group decided to purchase weapons and form their own society in opposition to the Red Spears. As leader, Wang pretended that the motley association was a local militia. He established their headquarters at an ancestral temple in the north corner of the village and took the name "Bare Egg Society" (kuang-tan-hui), attracting numerous followers from among the unemployed yu-min of the area. Members were divided into seven functional units, with some 2,650 people.* On the first and fifteenth of each month, Wang called together his seven division chiefs to prepare for regular plundering forays. Despite the success of these expeditions, old animosities were not forgotten. One night several dozen Bare Eggs killed the Red Spear member who had humiliated Wang Erh. The following day a large Red Spear contingent showed up to exact revenge. Wang, however, had trained his group well. The Bare Eggs delivered an impressive defeat.

Throughout the Hsin-yang area, in 1928 peasants were divided into the two groups, Red Spears or Bare Eggs, competing among themselves as ferociously as against outside incursion.[43] Although loyalties were sometimes blurred, the basic lines of conflict seem clear enough. The Bare Eggs, like the early Nien, were an association of local desperadoes, struggling to survive. The *North China Herald* described them as peasants "who see no

---

*The seven functional units had the following breakdown. The first division, consisting of 36 people, was in charge of rewards and punishments for Bare Egg members. (The expression "bare eggs" was Huai-pei slang for "poor folk." The term appears repeatedly in folk tales and songs about the Nien, where those who joined the movement were referred to as "we bare eggs.") The second unit, of 90 people, was responsible for securing weapons. The third unit (64 people) had charge of food provisions and was composed of affluent people who had been coerced into lending their assistance. The fourth division, of 180 people,

hope except to take to brigandage of the most ferocious type."*
The Red Spear Society, by contrast, developed and flourished in
opposition to just such threats, whether of the small-scale variety represented by the Bare Eggs or the massive bandit armies
and marauding troops that ravaged the area at this time.

The Height of Red Spear Rebelliousness

It was the defensive stance of the Red Spears, tinged by an increasingly aggressive thrust as time wore on, that underlay their
impressive resistance to outside forces. As the society grew to
include some three million followers, it constituted a pivotal
element in the balance of power in North China. In the spring of
1927, Red Spears waged major battles against the forces of warlord Wei I-san in southern Honan and against Chang Chih-kung
in Lo-yang. They were instrumental in expelling the Feng-t'ien
Army from northern Honan and in staging a decisive victory
over the Chih-li–Shantung forces at Pang-p'u, Anhwei.[44]

The demonstrated strength of the Red Spear Society, which
reached its zenith in the immediate aftermath of the Northern
Expedition, prompted the group to attempt take-overs of entire
county administrations. When the Expeditionary forces reached
Honan, Red Spears again arose against the oppressive regime of

---

was charged with recruiting new members. The fifth unit, of 120 people, was
responsible for gathering military intelligence. The sixth division, of 215 people,
was in charge of military training. The seventh and largest unit, of 1,943 people, was in control of military strategy and orders.

According to the group's regulations, members were not permitted to steal
items of worship (such as incense or candles), pork, lamb, or hats. The death
penalty awaited anyone who violated the prohibition.

*NCH, June 30, 1928, p. 553. According to the *North China Herald* report, the
Bare Eggs—realizing that their unlawful predatory behavior would endanger
the lives of their relatives—killed all their aged kinsmen and little children and
burned down their villages. Some twenty-seven villages were said to have been
destroyed in this way. The remaining active men and women then formed the
nucleus of the Bare Egg band. It should be noted, however, that it was common
for Chinese officials to discredit rebel groups by accusing them of killing off their
old and weak so as to facilitate a strong fighting force. The Nien were often
accused of this crime in official documents, although there was no factual basis
for the accusation. See, for example, FL 88/12–14. The *Herald* report was quite
likely a repetition of official slander, rather than an accurate representation of
the situation.

Wu P'ei-fu. This time the warlord was finally routed. Red Spear leader Lou Pai-hsün then avenged his earlier losses by occupying the city of K'ai-feng and setting up an independent government of which he assumed for a time the position of commander.[45]

Similarly, in Honan's Ch'üeh-shan several local Red Spear chapters joined forces to occupy the county seat in March 1927. After imprisoning the magistrate, the group established a seven-person committee which governed the county for three months. In June 1927, Red Spears posing as official militia entered Hua County, Honan, and proceeded to steal arms from the police station, military headquarters, and antismugglers bureau as well as to plunder the treasury and salt office.[46] The same month, an official in Yung-nien, Hopei, described a similar attack in that county:

At 11 P.M. on June 2, I was in the Wine and Tobacco Office enjoying the cool evening with a colleague. Suddenly we heard shouts and gunfire. My colleague hurriedly opened the door to see what was happening. They had already entered the city. We officials are the objects of their fury, and we were frightened beyond words. We fled to the back yard of landlord Hu to hide, locking the gate. Before long, thirty to forty of them were at the gate, demanding entry. They were delayed by Hu's aged mother, who told them that all the officials had already fled. Then they went to the east courtyard and cut the wires to the telegraph and telephone office. Shortly we heard a commotion in front of the county offices and we knew they had already seized the rifles of the police. The next morning all shops were closed and the streets saw only Red Spears. Some of the elder gentry and merchants decided that a compromise had to be negotiated. The magistrate was called out of hiding and agreed to all Red Spear demands. Control of the city was essentially taken over by the Red Spears.[47]

As this eyewitness account suggests, Red Spear wrath came to be directed with full force against government officials, who were seen as representatives of the policies and taxes that threatened the precarious existence of rural property holders. Railroads, armies, schools—and the taxes and personnel that supported them—constituted targets of increasing resentment.

In the fight against such features of the new Republican administration, Red Spear–type activities often assumed a reactionary posture. On February 13, 1929, for example, Small Sword members in northern Anhwei and northern Kiangsu carried out a joint uprising to protest a Kuomintang campaign against superstition in the countryside. Led by a lower degree holder, the protesters inflicted damage on the new schools in the area as well as the KMT headquarters.* Likewise, a Small Sword group in Kiangsu's Lien-shui County, having confiscated weapons from the village security offices, marched on the county seat with the aim of killing all KMT members and reinstating imperial rule. Although that disturbance was suppressed, with more than one hundred Small Sword rebels losing their lives, in 1929 other Small Sword uprisings in nearby counties succeeded in killing numerous Kuomintang members, government soldiers, and students.[48] The protests were a reaction, led by the rural elite but supported by many elements of village society, against the fiscal and cultural demands of the new, urban-based Republican regime.

It was in this state of alienation from the post-imperial scene that many Red Spear–type groups adopted what came close to being a political platform. Heavy with nostalgic yearning for the past, the common platform was distinctly messianic, if not millenarian:

We can no longer endure the scourge of bandits, soldiers, and evil government. The present warlords and politicians are not the rightful rulers of China; we wait expectantly for the true Yellow Emperor to appear. We will only honor the Emperor himself as the rightful ruler; until his appearance there is no one fit to govern us. In our eyes, the current officials and warlords are the same as bandits; we do not recognize their authority. Because our bodies are protected by the Yellow Emperor, we are impervious to weapons.[49]

Few Red Spear groups took the next step in proclaiming their leader the rightful occupant of the throne. Although their plat-

*Tai Hsüan-chih, 1973, p. 183. The slogans of the movement included: "Destroy the Three Principles of the People," "Eliminate the Party Headquarters," "Use the Lunar Calendar," "Root Out the New Schools," and "Repair the Temples."

form was chiliastic in tone, it lacked the millenarian belief in cataclysmic kalpas and in the return of the Maitreya Buddha that had fueled White Lotus rebels for generations. With the rural elite in command of the movement, the Red Spears were more willing to react against government initiative than to embark on a full-scale rebellion of their own. The harking back to halcyon days of imperial rule was natural for local notables who had in fact enjoyed prestige and security in the bygone era. To the extent that such things could be ensured under the new regime, the motive for resistance was substantially reduced.

RELATIONS WITH THE GOVERNMENT

Red Spear relations with official authorities were a revealing barometer of the Kuomintang's level of success or failure in the countryside. Although, as we have seen, the Red Spears turned increasingly rebellious in the immediate aftermath of the Northern Expedition, in subsequent years their sympathies oscillated between outright antagonism and a kind of uneasy cooperation. The fluctuations reflected shifts in government policy and presence, rather than any basic change in the Red Spears themselves.

The Kuomintang entry into Huai-pei in the late 1920s was accompanied by government attempts to extract higher taxes and to root out remnants of "backward" social and cultural practices. It was this initial effort at state penetration that aroused strong Red Spear antipathy toward the officials. Subsequently, as the government was forced to compromise its demands on the countryside, a modus vivendi with the local protectors developed. Thus, for nearly a decade Red Spear units were incorporated within the official defense system. However, after the outbreak of war with Japan, the Kuomintang's retreat from the rural areas occasioned a resurgence of the Red Spear Society. Once again the groups arose to defend their home communities in the face of a chaotic and threatening environment.

To trace this shifting pattern of Red Spear–government relations, it is first necessary to sort out the confusing array of official and unofficial defense forces then operating in the Huai-pei countryside. Very roughly, three categories of local protective groups can be identified in the early Republican period: *min-t'uan, lien-chuang-hui,* and Red Spears. The term *min-t'uan* covered a wide variety of indigenous paramilitary units organized by communities for self-defense. Led by local notables, these groups often constituted the organizational foundation for the Red Spear societies that mushroomed during the 1920s. As village after village invited Red Spear teachers to establish altars and to instruct inhabitants in magical martial arts routines, the *min-t'uan* as such tended to disappear through absorption into the new movement.[50] Although the *min-t'uan* were not direct creations of government edict, they had been condoned by the authorities from the late Ch'ing period on as an inexpensive means of keeping the peace in rural areas. Their replacement by "heterodox" Red Spear chapters, however, signaled a challenge to government control.

Unlike the *min-t'uan* and Red Spears, the *lien-chuang-hui* were primarily a product of government initiative. As a system of intervillage defense, the concept had been born under the impact of the Nien threat to Shantung. During the Republican period, the institution was revived by provincial directives that instructed every county to establish *lien-chuang-hui*. Since this defense corps was decreed from above and was to be financed by a heavy land surcharge that affected both rich and poor landholders, its imposition aroused a certain amount of popular opposition. A common response was for communities to establish their own Red Spear chapters, yet call them *lien-chuang-hui* so as to comply with official regulations. Kiangsu's Sui-ning County, for example, in 1925 had a so-called *lien-chuang-hui* composed almost entirely of Red Spear members. Despite its orthodox name, the group managed to mobilize twenty or thirty thousand peasants in a successful tax protest. Where Red Spear chapters were able to forge intervillage links, they often simply dubbed these large-scale alliances *lien-chuang-hui*. In actuality, however, such networks were organized according to Red Spear principles and were referred to as Red Spears by the local people.[51]

Attempts by county officials to undermine Red Spear popularity at this time were notably unsuccessful. In 1926, when the magistrate of T'ung-hsü ventured into the countryside in an effort to dissuade the elite from participation in the Red Spears, his sedan chair was stoned. The local notables are said to have responded to his visit by charging that "if there were no bandits, no ill-behaved troops, no oppressive surcharges, and if taxes were paid in paper currency, then we'd have no need to worship with the Red Spears."[52] As it was, the unorthodox association provided one of the few available defenses against unpopular government policies. Even where Red Spears were willing to undergo reorganization into regular militia forces, they frequently continued their previous tax resistance activities. In Lo-yang, for example, five magistrates were appointed and dismissed in the space of less than four months when they proved unable to collect any taxes from Red Spears turned militia.[53]

Thus, although min-t'uan, lien-chuang-hui, and Red Spears had different origins and different status in the eyes of the government, during the late 1920s they tended to merge into a common rebel position, guided by Red Spear initiative.* All three groups were led by local power holders who saw their interests threatened both by the demand for higher taxes and by the state's inability to provide protection against banditry and unruly soldiers.

Over time, however, changes in the nature of the Kuomintang presence in Huai-pei resulted in a marked shift in the response of protective associations. Probably the principal reason for this shift was the accommodation the Kuomintang proved willing to make with the local elite.[54] Whether by a simple reduction in

---

*Baba Takeshi (1976, pp. 72–75) suggests that the official origins of the lien-chuang-hui distinguished them markedly from the Red Spears. He argues that although both groups opposed bandits, the lien-chuang-hui almost never challenged the government authorities. During the confused period of the 1920s, however, in many areas this distinction was not always clear. Government control was simply not strong enough to guarantee that lien-chuang-hui groups retained a strict allegiance. The close identity of the lien-chuang-hui and Red Spear activities is pointed out in Mitani Takashi, 1974 and 1978.

extractive demands, or by the provision of concrete remunerative incentives, the government was increasingly able to win a degree of cooperation from the indigenous power holders. By the early 1930s, the process of accommodation had progressed to the point where very few protective groups retained the Red Spear appellation. Instead, the vast majority of local defense units now formally enlisted within an officially sponsored system of government militia. According to directives issued in 1930 and 1931, all preexisting self-defense groups were required either to dissolve or to reorganize as government militia. Although the names for the officially sanctioned units varied—in Shantung they were termed *lien-chuang-hui;* in Honan, *pao-wei-t'uan,* for example—the general policy was uniform. Headquarters of the defense corps were to be centered in county seats, with the county magistrate designated as commander of the village chapters within his jurisdiction. According to the printed regulations, any unofficial self-defense group that refused to reorganize would be subject to severe reprisals.[55]

Although it is unclear to what degree the Republican government could actually coerce compliance with its directives, the issuing of the regulations did certainly coincide with a dramatic disappearance of Red Spear organizations. At least to some extent, the process was quite likely the product not just of a compromise with local notables, but also of growing Kuomintang strength in the countryside. It was only after their victory over warlord Feng Yü-hsiang in 1930 that the Nationalists were able to disband the Red Spears and convert them into official militia. A few years later, the government exercised enough control to establish self-defense schools in certain counties and prefectures which offered three-month training sessions for militiamen from neighboring villages.[56]

The decline of the Red Spears did not usher in a period of great harmony in Huai-pei. Much of the rural elite may have been satisfied with the new modus vivendi, but large segments of the ordinary peasantry continued to have grounds for protest. Probably the greatest single cause of rural unrest in Huai-pei at this time was the opium tax. As early as 1923, the promise of lucrative revenue had led to a removal of the ban on opium production. Land that had previously been taxed at the rate of twenty-five or fifty cents a *mou* was subject to taxes of five to eight dollars (yüan) as soon as opium was planted. The dramatic increase prompted county magistrates to press village headmen to guarantee a definite number of *mou* for opium cultivation.[57] Peasants who might otherwise have chosen to stick with safe food crops were now often forced into growing opium on their land. The resentment sparked a number of large-scale riots. In northern Anhwei's Su County, thousands joined a two-month struggle during the summer of 1932 to protest the imposition of opium cultivation and its attendant registration fees, inspection fees, measurement fees, committee fees, reinvestigation fees, and the like. The affair ended with dismissal of the magistrate and accession to all of the protesters' demands. The following month, in nearby Ling-pi County, peasants demanding the return of previously paid opium taxes occupied government offices and confiscated weapons from the armory. The uprising was quelled only after the army had been called in to remove the demonstrators by force.[58]

Unlike the tax riots led by Red Spear groups just a few years earlier, the protests of the 1930s seem to have been distinguished by an absence of local elite involvement. In fact, some of the struggles were against affluent landlords as well as officials. In June and July 1931, for example, hundreds of peasants in Hsüchou participated in demonstrations against the neglect of dike repair by both the government and the local elite. Under the slogan of "Down with Kuomintang Control," peasants protested an alleged conspiracy by county officials and landlords to abdicate their traditional responsibility for dike maintenance.[59]

It was only in those rare cases where government initiatives directly threatened the well-to-do that struggles reminiscent of the late 1920s erupted once again. In April 1935, one of the very few instances of Red Spear resurgence during this period was reported in parts of northern Kiangsu. The precipitating factor in this comeback was an official land registration drive then being attempted in the area. The registration effort was aimed at adding to the tax rolls those lands which had been seized and occupied by lake associations (*hu-t'uan*) in the aftermath of the northern shift of the Yellow River some eighty years before. Located in what was once the old channel of the river, the land had never been entered in the registers. In Kiangsu's P'ei County, only one-quarter of the cultivated land, and the least fertile at that, was actually subject to taxation. The remaining fields, lying in the old Yellow River bed, could be sold for high prices because of their special tax-free status. Naturally fearful that registration would be followed by the imposition of taxes, the occupants of the land revived their Red Spear Society to protest the move. Armed with guns and red-tasseled spears, they attacked the police station and destroyed the government offices.[60]

Although such cases of Red Spear activity were rare during this interlude of cooperation between the Kuomintang and the local elite, it was not long before they were to become a general pattern once more. After years of dormancy, the Red Spears again blossomed into life in the wake of the Japanese invasion of North China. Subjected to the ravages of warfare and denied effective protection by the retreating Nationalist forces, the local inhabitants were compelled to mount their own resistance. By the summer of 1938, hardly a village in Huai-pei was without a Red Spear chapter to provide defense.[61]

The situation in Kuo-yang County was fairly representative. On May 11 the Japanese had launched a surprise attack, occupying much of the eastern portion of the county. Five days later, the as yet unoccupied parts of the countryside were bombed. As the official Kuomintang provincial newspaper reported the incident: "Fortunately all the officials had already followed the lead of the magistrate in deserting the city, and except for the death of thirteen inhabitants, injury of twenty, and destruction of more than one hundred homes, there were no losses."[62] Aerial bombardment continued for several days, wreaking tremendous casualties on the remaining populace. On May 31, the Kuo-yang county seat was taken without firing a shot. After the fall of the city, the Japanese set up their own puppet administration, appointing three local inhabitants—a member of the gentry, a merchant, and a "local bully"—to assume control. In the meantime, the Kuomintang officials established a government in exile to the south of the now occupied city. While peasants under Japanese control were subjected to heavy corvée labor demands, those under Kuomintang rule were no less pressed. With fewer than two thousand government soldiers and no provisions, the KMT magistrate levied heavy taxes in an effort to beef up his forces. The result was a serious tax riot involving three or four thousand people, followed by a mutiny among the disgruntled government soldiers who had been denied salaries for several months.[63]

Under these conditions, the struggle against the Japanese invaders was left largely to the Red Spears. On July 12, 1938, as a large Japanese force was moving from Kuo-yang to neighboring Su, sixteen Red Spears ambushed the enemy and were credited with the miraculous feat of killing more than eighty Japanese soldiers. Even the government was compelled to admit that the Red Spear group should be treated as national heroes. Possessed of geographical familiarity and popular support, the indigenous organization was clearly a formidable force. "If only they could be brought under government direction," editorialized the Nationalists, "they would be far more effective than the regular troops in fighting the enemy."[64]

The chaos that followed the Japanese invasion returned Huai-pei to a state of anarchy reminiscent of the warlord period. Again, natural disaster combined with social catastrophe to plunge the region into a severe agrarian depression. In June 1938, after the fall of K'ai-feng to the Japanese, General Chiang Kai-shek issued his famous order to blast the Yellow River dikes in an effort to stem the Japanese advance. The river moved southward to reclaim its pre-1855 channel, bringing untold suffering to millions of peasants. In 1938, flood damage in northern

Anhwei alone affected some two and a half million people and inundated more than twenty million *mou* of farmland. In its restless search for a new course, the river submerged eleven cities and four thousand villages in the Huai-pei region.[65] Inadequate control over the river meant continuing disaster for the area. As a missionary in northern Anhwei reported in 1947:

For eight years now, the muddy waters of the Yellow River have been pouring through the Cheng-meo breach and flowing sluggishly over the vast Honan plain, to enter the tiny Sha River near the Honan-Anhwei border. . . . Every year dykes are built on both sides of the Sha, and every year they collapse, spilling death and destruction over thousands of square miles of fertile farm land. Commonly called "China's Sorrow," the Yellow River of recent years has lived up to its reputation. The old bed is now as dry as the Sahara, while the great wheat fields of North Anhwei have been converted into a veritable wilderness of water.[66]

Once again banditry haunted the Huai-pei plain. And once again those with the resources to maintain themselves took up arms to safeguard their fragile margin of subsistence against brigand and invading soldier alike. From the spring of 1938 until the conclusion of the War of Resistance in 1945, Red Spear outfits were credited with repeated victories against both local bandits and the Japanese Army.*

On rare occasions, the Japanese were apparently able to neutralize Red Spear opposition. In August 1938, for example, the

---

*See Tai Hsüan-chih (1973, pp. 97–98) for a discussion of several impressive Red Spear assaults on Japanese forces during the period. According to Tai, the Japanese religious belief in an afterlife instilled a great fear of the Red Spears. Apparently the Red Spears delighted in wielding their big swords to behead the Japanese soldiers, regarding the severed heads as desirable war trophies. Although willing to sacrifice their lives in battle, the Japanese troops were much afraid of being beheaded, since without a head they could not pass into the next life, but would remain forever as wandering spirits. For this reason, Tai suggests, the Japanese were reluctant to venture out of the cities to battle the Red Spear forces.

The Red Spears' invulnerability belief probably also contributed to their bravery in combating the Japanese. As John Keegan has noted, the most dangerous act in warfare is to run from battle. Thus a belief that causes men to face battle bravely may well enhance their performance. See John Keegan, *The Face of Battle* (New York, 1976).

Peking Chronicle reported that Japanese bribes had persuaded twelve Red Spear leaders to sign over to the Japanese a document of consignment for fifteen hundred Red Spear partisans.[67] Since initial Japanese overtures were rather piecemeal, in 1942 an attempt was made to systematize the mobilization work. An article in *Shimmin Undō*, journal of the Japanese-directed "new people's movement" in China, set forth details on the recommended procedures for work among the Red Spears. While stressing that the group was a formidable association of peasant producers anxious to defend their property and livelihood, the article emphasized that it would be foolish to try simply to take advantage of their military potential. Rather, new ideals and leadership were required to dissipate Red Spear superstition and permit the gradual supplanting of the society by Japanese-sponsored "new people's associations."[68]

For all these ambitious plans, there is little evidence that the Japanese were successful in converting many Red Spears to their side. As a Kuomintang army official reported:

During the past seven to eight months, as we have been working and fighting [the Japanese] in north Kiangsu, north Anhwei, south Shantung, and east Honan, the people who have helped the most—who deserve to be called our friends—are the members of the enormous self-defense group: the Red Spear Society. Their courage and enthusiasm deserve our admiration and even our imitation. It is essential that they be organized and educated.[69]

Determined opposition to the Japanese did not make the Red Spears especially hospitable to the government forces, however. The Kuomintang tendency to desert the rural areas in favor of the protection of the cities hardly endeared them to the village-based Red Spears. To the extent that the government was willing to fight the enemy, temporary alliances against the foreign invaders could be forged. No lasting peace was concluded, however. Even as late as 1948, Red Spear–type units were carrying out armed struggles against the Kuomintang. Under the name of the White Spears, the group was said to be active all across northern and eastern Honan. Although members had once resisted Japanese, bandits, and Communists in the area, after the war they redirected their opposition toward government efforts at tax collection. Led by the so-called natural elite of the region, the White Spears were described in local Kuomintang newspapers as a major barrier to government control in Huai-pei.[70]

Red Spear–type groups remained, to the end of the Republican period, associations of parochial protectors. Their relationship to the government varied in direct response to the Kuomintang's capacity and willingness to promote local security. When threatened by bandits, warlords, government soldiers, foreign troops, or KMT officials, the movement evidenced a predictably defensive response. Although periodic opposition to government authorities lent the Red Spears a rebellious tone, in fact the underlying motivation for such action was a simple desire for noninterference and the maintenance of threatened resources.

BELIEFS AND RITUALS

What noticeably distinguished the Red Spears from such groups as *min-t'uan* or *lien-chuang-hui* was, of course, their religious coloration. Drawing upon a long tradition of popular religion, the Red Spears conducted elaborate ceremonies intended to capture divine favor for their activities. The most striking aspect of these rituals was their reputed power to induce physical invulnerability. Members who underwent the Red Spear ceremony of consecration and who thenceforth observed certain taboos were deemed immune from battle injury. The belief in invulnerability, a familiar theme in cargo cults, millenarian uprisings, and other "revitalization" movements that have thrived in the wake of the West's global expansion, was not a new idea among the peasants of North China. Well before the Boxer Rebellion, White Lotus sects claiming imperviousness to weapons were active on the North China Plain.[71] The Red Spears picked up this longstanding sectarian tradition, elaborating and adapting its practices for use in modern warfare.

As in similar movements the world over, Red Spear invulnerability was believed to depend upon the performance of complicated initiation rites, followed by regular ritualistic exercises. New members were generally subjected to a rigorous induction process which required at least several weeks, and often as long as three months, to complete. The duration and complexity of the ordeal varied from place to place, probably according to the immediacy of a village's need for Red Spear protection. The simplest procedure, common in Honan at the height of the warlord era, lasted three to four weeks. By this method, the new initiate, after performing a hundred kowtows and swearing an oath of obedience before the teacher, would be taught efficacious incantations and presented with a magical paper charm to swallow. He then would embark upon several weeks of military training, steeling his body to receive first hand punches, then blows using bricks, next sword slashes, and finally rifle fire.[72]

The military training, which closely resembled traditional Chinese martial arts performances, was usually held outdoors in some empty field, with only Red Spear members permitted to observe. Typically, a table was set up in the middle of the field, in front of which the initiates lined up. The teacher would wash his hands, burn incense, and kneel in prayer. After invoking divine aid, he burned a paper charm, the ashes from which were put in water and given to the new members to drink. Several bricks were then placed on each disciple's head. The idea was for the teacher to strike the bricks, breaking them without hurting the new initiate. Should the bricks not break and the disciple cry out in anguish, he would be reprimanded as impure in thought or deed. Only those who exhibited no pain were permitted to proceed to sword practice. In this more dangerous stage of training, after incense had been burned the disciples knelt down before the table while the teacher slashed at their bare chests with a sword. The places which had been stabbed could show no mark, or at most a plain white scar, if the novitiate were to graduate to rifle or cannon practice. In this highest stage of training, the teacher would fire at the assembled inductees from a distance of about fifteen paces. Those who perished in the final round of testing were condemned as having harbored insincere thoughts.

The risks in this procedure were, of course, immense, and sometimes touched teachers as well as disciples. In one village, for example, a Red Spear teacher was beaten to death after ten of his initiates were injured in rifle practice. A teacher anxious to preserve the size and support of his following might substitute blanks for real bullets, or dispense with the procedure altogether. Some Red Spear chapters adopted additional charms and incantations in lieu of the dangerous trial by fire.[73]

In northern Anhwei, where many Red Spear units did manage to eliminate the rifle practice, a new initiate was required upon entering the Red Spear hall to kneel before the teacher and swear an oath of secrecy. He was then instructed in the regulations prohibiting adultery, killing of the innocent, wanton plunder, and the like. For the next week the novice went twice daily to the hall to burn incense and kneel before an image of Kuan Yü, the god of war. Having successfully completed this first phase of the process, he would be taught a magical incantation designed to induce invulnerability:

> When one shoots you in the front,
>   Keep your breast stiff;
> When one shoots you from behind,
>   Keep your back straight.
> Shooting your two shoulders is
>   Like shooting at iron and steel.
> In the foreground stand the two generals,
>   The turtle and the snake;
> In the background the peach-fairies
>   Give you their aid.

In addition to frequently repeating the incantation, new members were expected to participate in "night kneeling" (yeh-kuei) ceremonies. In the dead of night, the initiates would be led by the teacher to some deserted field where they were required to kneel silently with closed eyes for two to three hours. After several weeks of this routine, the novice was expected to submit to a series of beatings by the master from which he could show no feeling of pain. Having passed these ordeals, he would be presented with three magical formulas written on paper: one to be burned, a second to be kept on his person, and a third to be swallowed.*

In other northern Anhwei villages, the first day's ceremony consisted of burning paper money, offering sacrifices, and performing numerous kowtows before sacred plaques, teacher, and chapter leader. At the conclusion of the ritual the initiate was sprinkled with holy water by the leader. Then he was taught to recite four phrases of reputedly magical power:

> I hold in my hand a red spear;
> Filled with the power of the ancestors,
>   I challenge Heaven.
> Fearing neither Heaven nor Earth,
> The brave man does what he must.

From the second day, all new members were required to report to the hall each evening to burn incense and kneel stiffly for long periods. This routine continued for forty-nine nights to complete the initiate's purity. Only then was he instructed in a repertoire of simple martial arts. This training also lasted for forty-nine days, after which the new member was presented with the three charms. The first and last days, plus the kneeling and fighting periods, totaled one hundred days of initiation.[74]

As a rule, new members were required to observe certain taboos in order to render themselves receptive to the power of the initiation rites. Since women were believed to vitiate the Red Spear magic, initiates were enjoined to refrain from sexual relations for the duration of the initiation period. Dietary proscriptions were also common. Many chapters forbade consumption of meat during the initiation period. Others enforced a permanent injunction against eating the "three uncleans of the sky"

---

*"Initiation Ceremonies," 1934, pp. 147–51. Sometimes the charm to be kept on one's person was written on a square piece of cloth which was then worn on the front of the chest to ward off enemy bullets. See Chang Chen-chih, 1929, p. 136.

(wild goose, quail, and pigeon), the "three uncleans of the land" (dog, horse, and cow), and the "three uncleans of the sea" (shrimp, turtle, and bullhead). On the day of initiation, new members were usually required to bathe themselves as a sign of purification. An infrequent luxury for Huai-pei peasants, the bath symbolized entry into a new way of life.*

In some instances, spirit possession was a feature of the initiation ceremony. After burning incense, the teacher would kneel and, on behalf of the new initiate, call upon various deities to appear, intoning phrases such as: "Disciple so and so requests the Jade Emperor to come forth from his palace and sniff the incense." A host of heavenly spirits ranging from the Goddess of Mercy to the Duke of Chou might be summoned in this way to possess the new believer and endow him with supernatural powers.[75]

Regardless of particular variations, the ceremonies were all directed to the same purpose: cultivation of physical invulnerability. As long as the new members were properly initiated and refrained from violating any taboos, they were supposed to be impervious to weapons of any kind. Whether religious masters genuinely believed in the efficacy of their teachings is an open question. In any case, most followers were apparently convinced of their newly acquired powers and anxious to demonstrate their invulnerability to others. A *North China Herald* reporter who witnessed such a demonstration observed:

One of the interesting events of the siege was the coming to the front of two men to a place near the city wall where they invited the soldiers to have free shots at them to their hearts' content. These men had some

*Chang Chen-chih, 1929, p. 136; *Ho-nan nung-nin*, 1927, p. 5; "Hung-ch'iang shih-hsi-chi," 1928, p. 2; Li Ying-chou, 1926; Nagano Akira, 1931, pp. 290–91. Tai Hsüan-chih has pointed out the rationality behind the dietary proscriptions—some for health reasons, others for moral purposes, and yet others to curb sexual appetite. See Tai Hsüan-chih, 1973, p. 103. Mary Douglas, *Purity and Danger: An Analysis of Concepts of Pollution and Taboo* (New York, 1966), discusses the importance of bathing as a ritualistic purification in secret societies. One informant who was a former Red Spear member in Shantung recalled that his chapter lost members during the winter months, since a daily bath in the icy streams was required of all Red Spears.

Buddhist insignia in a circle on their chests and one of them had a small Buddha in his hand and the other a fan only with which he waved off the bullets. There are many witnesses to this incident and in spite of several scores of bullets being directed at them they were unhurt. Whether this is a triumph of the magical rites these men go through or merely another example of wonderful marksmanship from the wall each man must judge for himself.[76]

A more convinced firsthand observer of Red Spear powers was Wu Ping-jo, a Kuomintang cadre sent to Huai-pei to organize peasant associations and self-defense forces. After numerous requests, Wu was finally invited to a Red Spear demonstration. The performance was conducted in a small empty field in which an altar had been set up, in front of which were placed eight rifles and a sword. The teacher, accompanied by his followers, kowtowed sixteen times before the altar in a ceremony known as "summoning the deity" (ch'ing-shen). Suddenly the incense burning on the altar let off an exploding noise like a firecracker. The teacher then kowtowed sixteen more times, stood up, and announced that the deity was approaching. Hearing this, the followers all rushed to the center of the field, thrust out their fists, and tightened their stomachs like soldiers nearing battle. The teacher then addressed them, "If any of you has recently done anything shameful—if in the last three days you have committed any impurity—speak up quickly, for when the rifle sounds, regret will be too late." The appeal was repeated solemnly. When no one responded, the teacher called eight students to his side and gave them each a rifle and ammunition. The guns were fired and the teacher slashed with the sword at the bare chests of those lined up in formation, but no one was injured. Wu inspected the weapons and found to his amazement that they were genuine. He concluded, "I who was once highly suspicious of Red Spear claims to invulnerability, now believe that they undergo a physiological change which renders them resistant to bullets and sword wounds."[77]

Not all members carried out their public demonstrations so successfully. In February 1927, two Red Spears were taken prisoner by the authorities in Honan. Upon interrogation, both professed imperviousness to weapons and a readiness to submit to a test of their claim. When a sharp sword was brought forth, the first man thrust out his neck defiantly and had his head promptly chopped off. Seeing the demise of his comrade, the second man dropped to his knees and pleaded for his life, explaining that he had been deceived by his Red Spear teacher. His plea was granted on the condition that he return and inform the other members of his village about the incident, in an effort to dissolve the organization.[78] In instances where harsh reality managed to disprove claims of invulnerability, the usual rationalization proffered by the teacher was that the victim had committed some impure act which had vitiated his magical protection. When an encounter with bandits left five Red Spears killed and twenty-nine wounded in a Shantung chapter, the tragedy was attributed to someone's having thrown shrimp skins into the village well.[79]

Despite repeated disconfirmation, the belief in invulnerability persisted and proved highly adaptable to new conditions. Just as the Boxers had extended traditional sword-fighting techniques to counter the threat of modern firearms, so the Red Spears now carried the extension a step further in battling the military might of the Japanese army. A government soldier who witnessed Red Spear maneuvers in northern Anhwei during the spring of 1938 described his experience:

As one of their teachers was in the middle of his talk, suddenly the sound of enemy planes could be heard overhead. Hearing the noise, the peasants showed signs of discomfort. However, one of their chiefs immediately jumped onto the speaker's platform yelling "Holy water! Holy water!" Someone who had already been stationed in front of the platform with a bucket of drinking water now knelt down and offered a bowl of water to the chief. Simultaneously, a representative from each of the dozen or so chapters rushed forward to take a bowl back to his respective group. Under instructions from the chief, each person drank a sip of the "holy water." Then all three to four thousand of them knelt, closed their eyes, and began to mumble their magical phrases. When the incantation was over, they jumped up as if awaking from a dream.

Their breathing was forced, their eyes bloodshot, their gaze unswerving, and their muscles tense—as though gripped by madness.
The silence was deafening. Each member grasped his red-tasseled spear, firmly planted like a tree. The light breeze set the tassles to fluttering, creating an even more awesome spectacle.
Fortunately the enemy planes seemed to have had some other destination in mind. Nine in a row, they flew off toward the northeast in apparent oblivion of the red glow beneath. The danger over, one of the teachers happily explained that they had been chanting a "block hole charm" which had worked to stop up the barrels of the Japanese guns, ensuring that no bullets could shoot forth.[80]

To guarantee continued efficacy of their magical powers, Red Spear members were expected to abide by certain regulations. The most important rule was that which demanded strict secrecy about the operations of the society. The pledge to silence served both a strategic purpose, by reducing the intelligence available to hostile bandits or government officials, and a sociological purpose, imbuing members with a sense of separateness. In addition to the commitment to secrecy, members were generally required to adhere to a code of discipline. Although the particulars of the codes varied from chapter to chapter, most included injunctions against rape, plunder, wanton arson or murder, and temple desecration. Rape was believed especially liable to undermine one's supernatural powers, inviting death on the battlefield for the culprit. Known violations of any of the prohibitions were punishable by execution.[81] No doubt a creation of their elite leadership, regulations of most Red Spear chapters included exhortations to filial piety toward parents and respect toward elders. Members were expected to exhibit a Confucian sense of "propriety, justice, honesty, and shame."[82]
In addition to maintaining a high standard of personal morality, Red Spears were required to participate in regular martial arts practice and religious worship. Military routines were generally an elaboration of the brick, sword, and rifle demonstrations that had formed the final stages of the initiation process. The performances were invariably conducted within the

context of a religious ceremony which invoked other-worldly aid for their success. Worship itself usually consisted simply of kneeling for long periods, burning incense, and repeating esoteric incantations intended to communicate with the patron spirits of the Red Spear chapter. The gods so worshiped encompassed a whole pantheon of popular deities: the God of War Kuan Yü, the Goddess of Mercy Kuan Yin, the Buddha of Western Heaven, the Peach Fairies, the Duke of Chou, Lao-tzu, Confucius, and dozens of others.* No potential source of power was to be overlooked in the quest for supernatural assistance.

Charms, both written and spoken, were a key element in the religious regimen. There were more than three hundred of these in the repertoire of some Red Spear groups. Ordinary members were often expected to master as many as one hundred. In some instances, the charms were used for healing. After examining a patient, the religious teacher would write a curing formula on a piece of paper that the patient was to swallow. More commonly, of course, the charms were intended to induce invulnerability. Before entering battle, charms were used in a variety of ways: written directly on one's body, worn in pouches on the head or around the neck, chanted incessantly, and swallowed. It has been suggested that there was actually some physiological basis for the martial bravery that such consumption of charms seemed to induce. The charms were often written with cinnabar on thin yellow slips of paper made mainly of saltpeter. Whereas cinnabar was traditionally used to calm the nerves, saltpeter had a stimulating effect. The combination of drugs may have helped to create a bold frame of mind. According to some accounts, the magical concoction induced a hallucinogenic delusion of invulnerability that lasted for about two hours, ample time to cover most skirmishes with bandits and soldiers. Whatever its chemi-

*Chieh Ch'en-shih, p. 13; Li Ying-chou, 1926, p. 4. Many of the deities were taken from characters in the novel *Feng-shen yen-i*. The fact that these figures had been portrayed as warring against one another in the novel did not inhibit their all being happily incorporated as equally worthy of worship.

cal effects, the practice of swallowing charms certainly exerted a powerful psychological influence on Red Spear participants.[83]

Breath control was another important part of the religious routine. Deeply rooted in popular Taoist tradition, the breathing exercises probably also brought both physical and emotional results. In any case, the practice was claimed to have certain magical properties. A Chinese journalist who witnessed a demonstration of one such exercise reported that a Red Spear teacher had managed to control the flame of a lantern some distance away, first extinguishing and then reigniting it. The teacher explained that in the event bandits attacked and burned a village, this method could be put to good use in controlling the conflagration.[84]

Red Spear rituals and beliefs, bizarre as many of them may seem, were directed principally at bolstering community defense. The assertion of invulnerability had obvious utility for a movement attempting to provide protection in the face of overwhelming threat. Like the Boxers, who had also combined supernatural claims with the concrete institution of the local militia, the Red Spears were organizing to resist intrusion. Against bandits, missionaries, warlords, and soldiers alike, a belief in physical invulnerability was a powerful weapon for bolstering the resolve of people who possessed few alternative resources with which to defend their meager holdings.

In view of the close similarities between the Boxers and Red Spears, it is interesting that the latter group did not evidence much hostility toward Christianity or, with the important exception of the Japanese invaders, toward foreigners in general. As a newspaper reported about the Red Spears, "Unlike those of 1900, the 'new Boxers' are not at all anti-foreign. In fact they have accorded the fullest protection to the few missionaries who happen to be in their midst."[85] Another contemporary news report noted that Christian converts were not required to participate in Red Spear idol worship and were in fact sometimes invited to exhort the Red Spears to observance of the Ten Com-

mandments.[86] Similarly, during a series of Christian evangelical
tent meetings in Shantung, village elders—grateful for missionary involvement in famine relief—insisted that Red Spears be
present at the meetings to provide protection.*

If the Red Spear belief in invulnerability was not primarily a
response to culture conflict, it did nevertheless prove useful in
generating determined opposition to a variety of outside intruders, both Chinese and foreign. It is commonplace to attribute a
cult of invulnerability to military weakness: lacking material
weapons, the peasants are said to turn instead to spiritual defenses. In the case of the Red Spears, however, there are some
problems with this conventional explanation. As Japanese
scholar Baba Takeshi has pointed out, the gradual acquisition of
modern weapons by Red Spear units was not accompanied by
any diminution or disappearance of the invulnerability cult.
Baba interprets the belief, not as a rationalization for military
weakness, but as a powerful ideology capable of overcoming village parochialism and imbuing peasants with the sense of entering a new life.[87]

It is clear that Red Spear religious beliefs had great importance
for building group solidarity. The rituals were especially useful
for a movement whose membership was drawn so markedly
from across class lines. Although leadership rested primarily in
the hands of the rural elite, manpower came largely from the
ranks of ordinary peasants. Presumably the elaborate cere-

*NCH, December 24, 1927, p. 524. The picture was not unmixed, however.
An American-sponsored church in T'ai-shan, Shantung, was robbed by Red
Spears (STSP, May 23, 1926, p. 7). Several Christian converts in Cheng-chou,
Honan, were captured and beaten until they consented to contribute money to
the Red Spears (NCH, February 6, 1926, p. 299). In Shensi one missionary narrowly escaped execution after falling into Red Spear hands (NCS, June 18, 1927,
p. 1). Such cases seem, however, to have been exceptions in a movement that
was generally described as neutral toward Christianity. The U.S. consul in Shantung saw little need for concern on this score. As the consul reported in a
dispatch, although some missionary faculty members of Shantung Christian
University had been captured by Red Spears while on an Easter hike in the
mountains south of Tsinan, they were released when their identity was established. The Red Spears had explained that they were simply antibandit. See
Decimal File on China, 893.43, September 7, 1927.

monies and fantastic claims to magical prowess helped convince peasants of the benefits to be gained by lending their support. Whether in the confused Republican period it was in the "objective" interest of poor peasants to join Red Spear chapters rather than bandit gangs is an open question. The supernatural authority exercised by Red Spear leaders may have made the choice less difficult for some.

ORGANIZATION

If religious beliefs and practices helped attract members, how did the new adherents coordinate their activities? At its height, the Red Spear Society boasted some three million members, about half of whom lived in Honan Province alone.[88] How were these enormous numbers of people organized?

As a community protection association, the Red Spears were based upon the village as the primary unit of organization. Known variously as "incense halls" (hsiang-t'ang) or "meeting halls" (hui-t'ang), the basic headquarters were usually located in a village temple or shrine. Their outside appearance was forbidding, modeled on the order of an army command post. In front of the temple gate would be hung a distinctive three-foot-square yellow dragon banner, by the side of which was written the name of the particular chapter. Guards equipped with red spears, swords, or pistols stood watch. In counties where the Red Spear Society was officially prohibited because of its alleged subversive potential, the group often reorganized under the name of "Red Schools" (hung-hsüeh). In these cases, the local centers were known as "schools" and might indeed be lodged in the community schoolhouse. Wherever situated, the local headquarters were quite plain on the interior. In the worship room, the altar often consisted simply of a suspended piece of yellow paper upon which were inscribed the names of the patron deities. A tile pot served as an incense burner, on both sides of which oil lamps might be placed to provide some illumination for night worship services.[89]

The establishment of these local chapters was almost always at the initiative of village notables. Looking for a means of coping with the threat of bandits and soldiers, a village leader would invite a Red Spear teacher into his community to provide training in the martial arts and magical charms for which the society was known. Hiring such a teacher was not expensive, the usual arrangement being simply to provide room and board for the duration of the stay. After a welcoming feast, the teacher would consecrate the village altar and set about instructing eligible members in the esoteric ways of the society.[90]

The membership of local units numbered from a few dozen to several hundred, depending upon the size of the village and the level of predatory threat. In many villages virtually every household—landlords included—contributed at least one son to the organization. Participation was still somewhat restricted, however, inasmuch as units often limited membership to males over eighteen years of age from landowning families. Although the property requirement excluded only a small fraction of the rural population in Huai-pei, it was a clear effort to guarantee a protective orientation on the part of all Red Spear members. Once the chapter was established, new initiates had to be sponsored by two members, an additional check on their background and character.[91]

Financial arrangements of Red Spear units varied from place to place. Sometimes the treasury was drawn from an initiation fee required of all new members. More often, villagers were assessed according to their landholdings. Combinations of the two methods were also common. In some villages, one dollar (yüan) and thirty cents was charged as an initiation fee, in addition to twenty cents per ten *mou* of land for a year's protection. Nonmembers were charged double rates, a powerful incentive for participation. In a few cases, a head tax was imposed upon all adult males. Where participation in the Red Spears was compulsory, absences were punishable by fines levied upon the families of the absentees. The fines might be as high as several times the basic head tax, and were put into a group fund for the purchase of military equipment.[92]

Like crop-watching associations, Red Spear societies were a cooperative response to a degree of threat too severe for solution by individual households. The form of the cooperation varied considerably, depending upon the composition of the village. In the relatively rare cases where the village was a community of one landlord and his tenants, the landlord might assume the leadership role. Furnishing weapons for the group, he demanded participation from his tenants as part of their contract, in classic patron-client style. Alternatively, villages with one or more affluent households might hire full-time Red Spear mercenaries to provide constant protection. Since mercenaries were costly and unreliable, however, this arrangement was also atypical. By far the most prevalent type of Red Spear Society was common in freeholding villages, where residents participated voluntarily. Although leadership still rested in the hands of local notables, the membership was largely ordinary peasants who normally engaged in farming, taking up arms only when threatened by bandit or troop incursions. Their leaders might even be elected, and a rough equality obtained among all members.[93] In this freeholder situation, members were expected to equip themselves. Those able to afford them used Mauser rifles; poorer participants came armed with simple red-tasseled spears.*

Organizationally, Red Spear chapters were divided into two sections: a "civil" (*wen*) bureau in charge of records, finance, and judicial rewards and punishments; and a "military" (*wu*) bureau responsible for training in martial arts, amulets, and the like.[94] This functional division was also reflected in two types of Red Spear leadership. The civil leader, known as *hui-chang* or *hsüeh-chang*, held the real decision-making power over chapter operations. Such figures were drawn overwhelmingly from among the rural elite: landlords, rich peasants, even degree hold-

---

*According to some sources, the number of red tassels wound around the handle of one's spear was an identification of rank (NCS, May 6, 1926, p. 8). Five tassels, for example, was the insignia for a commander of five hundred men (Chieh Ch'en-shih, p. 15). Another version holds that a tassel was added for every battle fought. The spears were usually about ten feet in length: one foot for the top and nine for the handle ("Genzai Shina," 1927, p. 61).

ers from the earlier era.* In many cases, the Red Spear chief and village headman (*pao-chang*) were the same individual.[95] It was at the request of these local notables that the second type of Red Spear leader, the religious teacher (*lao-shih* or *tao-shih*), entered the scene. The teacher established the chapter altar, officiated at worship services, and was responsible for the religious-military training of members. Perhaps a remnant of the Boxer uprising, most teachers hailed from western Shantung, traveling across the North China Plain to spread their esoteric regimen. Although little is known about the background of these people, it is apparent that they were perpetuating an ancient missionary tradition of sectarian masters.†

The contrast with imperial days was striking, however. Whereas earlier White Lotus sects had recruited clandestinely, on the basis of individual pupil-teacher ties, now conversion occurred openly, and by entire villages at a time. The initiative rested with the rural elite, who saw the sectarian practices as a useful way of coping with the overwhelming problems of banditry and marauding troops. It was natural that the well-to-do would be attracted to a movement whose raison d'être lay in the protection of property, but it is nevertheless curious that rural power holders were willing to be associated with a "heterodox" secret-society operation. Much of the explanation for this phenomenon must lie with the collapse of the imperial state in 1911. The demise of the bureaucratic system gave the local elite less reason to identify their own interests with those of the gov-

---

*Chi Fan, 1927, p. 12; *Ho-nan nung-min*, 1927, p. 7; I Shih, 1960, p. 21. Interviews I conducted with eleven former residents of Honan, Anhwei, and Shantung confirmed that leaders of their village Red Spear societies, without exception, were the most prestigious individuals in the village. In one case, the informant's uncle had served as Red Spear leader. A resident of T'eng County in southwest Shantung, the uncle was a warlord with more than one hundred *mou* of land. He had been educated in the Confucian classics and exposed to no Western learning.

†Although the teachers initially came from western Shantung, as the movement gained popularity it began to recruit local personnel as teachers. When the original teacher moved away to proselytize elsewhere, a faithful disciple among the new members—usually from an affluent local family—might be appointed to serve as religious teacher in his stead. (Chang Chen-chih, 1929, p. 139.)

ernment. Moreover, loss of an emperor meant the end of an orthodox Confucian state creed. The Republican revolution produced no institutional or ideological vehicle for recapturing the lost allegiance. Rather, as the government proved incapable of protecting the populace from the scourge of banditry and warfare, disillusionment grew apace. If the rural elite had once been deterred by the official ban on "dangerous" popular religion, such inhibitions dwindled in the chaos of the Republican period.

With little help forthcoming from the government, property holders were forced to devise their own means of collective defense. Although cooperation was most easily effected at the village level, single villages frequently proved inadequate to withstand the onslaught of a massive bandit army. For this reason, alliances were forged among nearby Red Spear units, each pledging to come to the assistance of its neighbor in an emergency. When the alliance encompassed a number of villages, a joint command post might be set up in the local market town. The post usually coordinated five to thirty village chapters, with a combined membership of several thousand. At the signal of three cannon shots, all members within hearing range were expected to muster for duty. A commander, chosen from among the civil leaders of the cooperating units, had formal authority to coordinate Red Spear military operations in the area.[96] Sometimes, as in the case of Ying-yang County, a head religious teacher and councilor were also appointed to assist the commander, while other participating chapter leaders were assigned the status of "sworn brothers."[97]

To systematize operations and tighten up interchapter coordination, a number of Red Spear associations enacted formal organizational codes. The extent to which such regulations were actually put into practice is difficult to ascertain. Nevertheless, in late 1927 it became common for Red Spear groups to adopt codes, at least on paper. The standard format was devised by a member of the Honan provincial elite, Wang Yin-ch'uan. Wang had originally enjoyed close connections with the Red Spears in his native province. However, when various Red Spear units

refused to follow his advice regarding discipline and organization, Wang terminated his involvement and moved to Peking.
After the Red Spears suffered a series of defeats at the hands of
warlord Feng Yü-hsiang, they began to appreciate the wisdom
of Wang's efforts. Thus in October 1927 representatives of more
than a dozen Red Spear groups in northern Honan traveled to
Peking to meet with Wang to request his aid in reorganizing the
movement. Wang thereupon printed up several tens of
thousands of copies of a set of rules for the representatives to
take back to their respective groups, with the promise that if
they would abide by these regulations Wang himself would return to Honan to help out.[98] Since the copies were widely distributed, the rules have often been cited as a universal Red Spear
code of discipline.[99] The code (included in Appendix B) consisted of twenty points, the first being a clear statement of the
association's purpose as a self-defense force aimed at promoting
local security. Subsequent points stressed commitment to the
values of filial piety, patriotism, mutual aid, and the like. A
complex pattern of military organization was spelled out, and all
members were pledged to strict obedience.

It is doubtful that many Red Spear groups succeeded in observing the code faithfully. The organizational scheme set forth
was based upon the impersonal model of an army, neglecting
the importance of the village as the basic unit. As local defense
leagues, Red Spear chapters were committed to a confined
scope of operations that did not easily lend itself to a mobile
military pattern. To the extent that intervillage cooperation
developed, it usually followed the lines of long-standing friend-
ships among members of the elite, rather than any neat military formula imposed from outside. Although impressive numbers of Red Spears could on occasion be mustered for battle
against threatening bandits or soldiers, the organization behind
these massive mobilizations was a shifting coalition of semiautonomous village chapters, linked by personal contacts
among cooperating leaders. The agreement to merge forces was
always short-lived; before long, the call of family and home was
overpowering for most participating units.

Besides the pull of parochialism, another feature of the movement worked against sustained cooperation: the wide variation among Red Spear–type groups. As we have seen, units differed in their style of religious practice, as well as in membership composition and form of leadership. In addition to groups calling themselves Red Spears, there was a bewildering array of related associations that assumed different appellations. Sharing a claim to physical invulnerability, these associations were also organized at the village level. (Appendix C presents a partial listing of these protective associations, as reported in contemporary accounts.)

In most instances, the establishment of a distinct association seems to have been the product of an enterprising leader who posed as a source of supernatural authority outside, and sometimes in competition with, the Red Spears. Often the groups had rules and rituals that deviated from the prescribed Red Spear pattern; occasionally their leaders assumed messianic or imperial roles. An example was the Fan Society, started in 1928 along the Honan-Anhwei border. The founder of the association, known as "Crazy Chang," claimed to possess magical powers learned from an immortal. His following included three to four thousand people, all of whom were apparently rather affluent, since a hefty fifty yüan was required upon joining the group. Members were presented with a paper fan and several charms to guarantee their immunity to bullets. Calling himself an emperor, Crazy Chang repeatedly led his followers off on expeditions ostensibly in search of an empress, seizing any attractive young woman who met his fancy. The group was finally suppressed by a government-sponsored defense corps in the area.*

*Nagano Akira, 1931, pp. 259–60. A larger messianic movement, located north of Huai-pei in Hopei's Yang-wu County, was the Black Spear Society. The leader of the group, Lu Yen-sha, at age forty claimed to have had a dream in which he became a small boy again. In the dream, while playing with two other lads, Lu was interrupted by an elderly man who descended from heaven with three holy scriptures which he presented to the boy. Admonished the old man, "Carefully remember these writings and you need fear neither gun nor sword, but can help bring about the appearance of the true emperor." When he awoke, Lu reportedly found the three books still in his possession. He followed their prescrip-

Of some interest because of its resemblance to the Old Cow Society of Nien fame was the Mourning Clothes Society. Known also as the White Heads, members of the group wore white turbans and robes and hung amulets on their chests to ward off bullets. Upon meeting the enemy, they performed three kowtows and wept loudly in an effort to unnerve their opponents.[100] Another interesting group was the Flower Basket Society, composed entirely of women. During battle, its members held a basket in one hand and a sword in the other. The sword was, of course, for subduing the enemy; the basket was intended to catch all of the opponent's bullets. Armed with their magical baskets, the women themselves were believed impervious to ammunition. As a women's organization parallel to the all-male Red Spears, the Flower Baskets were comparable to the Red Lantern Societies of the Boxer uprising.[101] It was common for women to play an important role in White Lotus–inspired sects, although this highly segregated form of participation does not appear to have been a traditional feature. Perhaps the separation came with protective movements whose gentry leaders found the intermingling of the sexes a breach of Confucian propriety.

Sometimes these societies cooperated with Red Spear units in the area. An instance of this was the Limitless Way (*wu-chi-tao*), a large secret society with more than fifty branches in twenty-four southern Shantung counties. The founder of the Limitless Way, Li Kuang-yen, swallowed charms to generate invulnerability. In concert with local Red Spears, White Flags, and Small Swords, Li led an effective resistance against bandits and unruly soldiers. One of the leaders of the group, Yang Lao-tao, was head abbot of a Taoist temple in southern Shantung. Attired in the red-tasseled hat and yellow mandarin jacket of a Ch'ing of-

---

tions for inducing invulnerability and proclaimed himself the rightful emperor. A successful battle against bandits, from which Lu's followers emerged unscathed, greatly enhanced the group's popular appeal. By 1930, the Black Spears had attracted several hundred thousand adherents across Hopei, Shantung, and Honan. See Chang Chen-chih, 1929, pp. 134, 146–47; Chieh Ch'en-shih, pp. 16–17; *Shina no dōran*, 1930, p. 117; Tanaka Tadao, 1930.

ficial, Yang led mass attacks on railway lines in protest against the Kuomintang's early antisuperstition campaign.[102]

Such variation among the many component units of the Red Spear movement is not surprising. Form and practice differed in accordance with the needs and tastes of particular villages and regions. Nevertheless, certain common characteristics can be identified. Although the movement opened the door to scattered millenarian cults, the dominant pattern was clearly not that of a coordinated sectarian rebellion against the state. Instead, the picture that emerges is of a series of village defense associations formed around preexisting social structures. Leadership authority was vested in the hands of local notables, and membership was recruited on the basis of residence.

CONCLUSION

In one sense, the rural violence Huai-pei experienced in the Republican period was strikingly similar to that of the mid-nineteenth century. Bandits and defense societies thrived in fierce competition with one another, responding to the acute natural and social crises of the time. In another sense, however, peasant protest had been transformed. Whereas the Nien had evidenced the rebel potential of predators, the Red Spears represented a distinct shift toward protective rebellion. The organizational foundation for such protest had, of course, been laid with the fortification construction and militia development that flourished in opposition to the Nien. The redirection of these defensive energies from opposition to banditry to rebellion against the state was, however, due less to any qualitative changes within Huai-pei itself than to the transformation of the larger political scene and its new impact upon local society. The Republican government's effort to extract more resources, coupled with its blatant incapacity to provide security, moved rural power holders to take administrative control into their own hands.

The process by which Red Spear associations reached the

point of open revolt was, as we have seen, gradual. It was with evident reluctance that the movement turned from fighting bandits to opposing soldiers and, finally, government officials as well. Ecological disaster, warlord oppression, state penetration, and foreign invasion had worked to meld defensive and offensive strategies in joint resistance. Despite the massive confrontations that such combined resistance generated, however, the organizational structure of the movement remained firmly embedded in semiautonomous village chapters. The fact that the Red Spear Society was a reflection of established social patterns lent an inherent conservatism to its activities and objectives.

In these respects the Red Spears invite comparison with another long-lasting protective institution in a quite different cultural setting: the Sicilian Mafia. The Mafia also arose in bandit-infested regions where government power was weak, playing a mediating role between state and peasantry.[103] Constituting a secretive system of law and organized power parallel to and in competition with that of the state, the Mafia too served a protective function for the rural populace. As Eric Hobsbawm has explained, "For the feudal lords it was a means of safeguarding property and authority. . . . For all, it provided a means of defense against the foreign exploiter . . . and a method of national or local self-assertion." The leaders of the Mafia were, like Red Spear chieftains, local notables—men of wealth anxious to defend their holdings. This fact, according to Hobsbawm, rendered the Mafia an essentially conservative force, with limited social aims, not easily adapted to modern protest movements. The tendency to degenerate into crime and gangsterism— analogous to predatory strains within the Red Spears—further militated against any revolutionary potential.[104] In short, there were certain inherent limitations to rural protective movements, just as there were to predatory movements, that undermined the possibility of transition to a more revolutionary mode of collective action.

Religious practices played an important role in maintaining this conservative stance. Although the "heterodox little tradition" has sometimes been credited with an inherently rebellious—or even revolutionary—dynamism, in the case of the Red Spears it is apparent that the tradition had other potential as well. Local power holders, if alienated from government initiatives, could draw on the sectarian legacy to buttress their own positions in defiance of central control. In such circumstances, the secret society was much less a vehicle for the expression of poor peasant demands than a meeting place for cross-class participation. Missing from the Red Spears was the egalitarian flavor of social banditry exhibited by some Nien groups. Clearly the sectarian, or "heterodox," character of Red Spear beliefs did not ensure a progressive social content.

The Red Spears were rebellious to the extent that they challenged government directives, but their underlying aim was to maintain existing power relations in the countryside. Although a few groups took advantage of the opportunity to mount separate millenarian uprisings complete with imperial pretensions, for the great majority of Red Spear units, religious inspiration was subordinated to entrenched local interests. Thus when the Kuomintang demonstrated during the Nanking decade its willingness to seek an accommodation with rural notables, most Red Spear chapters quickly dispensed with their religious coloration and enlisted in the officially approved militia system.

Paradoxically, the very limitations of the Red Spears were telling evidence of their strength as a local survival strategy. The fact that the movement was organized along communal lines, directed by the indigenous elite, and staffed by fellow villagers lent it a persistence and resilience not easily eroded by outside forces. Like the Nien before them, the Red Spears were an outgrowth of ongoing survival strategies that were intimately linked to social structure. It was precisely the adaptive value of these forms of collective violence in the context of traditional village life that would make their eventual supplanting so problematic.

6. Rebels Meet Revolutionaries: The Communist Movement in Huai-pei

When Communist cadres first penetrated the Huai-pei area, they encountered a peasantry well schooled in the art of collective violence. Banditry was rife, underground religious sects plentiful, and memories of massive rebellions fresh and vivid. Brigands and sectarians alike were skilled practitioners of collective warfare, tempered by the hard-won wisdom of generations of peasant rebels before them. Clearly, however, the underlying motivation for this impressive experience in peasant protest was pragmatic and parochially specific. How then would these battle-wise peasants, masterly in fighting for their own local interests, greet the advent of outside revolutionaries? How too would the revolutionaries, for their part, choose to deal with the myriad of armed and organized units that predated their arrival? Would existing patterns of rural violence constitute building blocks or barriers to revolutionary change?

The answers to these questions, we will discover, are complex. In the first place, there were of course two distinct strategies of peasant violence in Huai-pei, each with its own rationale, organization, and limitations. Furthermore, the Chinese Communist revolution itself passed through a series of distinct phases: from peasant movement, to soviets, to war of resistance, to civil war. Each period was marked by somewhat different problems and priorities, calling for changing relations with both types of local rebels.

OVERVIEW OF COMMUNIST ACTIVITIES IN HUAI-PEI

The early history of the Communist movement in Huai-pei is a discontinuous record of fits and starts. Although the Chinese Communist Party (CCP) actively sought to establish a foothold among the peasantry as early as 1925, it was not until several years later that these efforts yielded any success in the form of newly organized bases of popular support. Even then, the results were short-lived.

Initial CCP penetration of the Huai-pei countryside was carried out by young intellectuals. Indeed, the first local party branch constituted in Shou County, Anhwei, was simply a reorganization of the former students' union in the area. The group gained public attention in December 1927 by its demonstrations against Christian missions in northern Anhwei. Although the offensive succeeded in attracting to its cause a number of young people, the movement collapsed in the face of government suppression.[1]

In the spring of 1928, the CCP initiative was resumed with the proclamation of a northern Anhwei soviet by some thirty thousand supporters in Fu-yang County. The leader of this experiment, Wei Yeh-ch'ou, was a party member from Shensi with considerable experience in youth work and mass mobilization. In three months of intensive activity, Wei oversaw the establishment of party branches in numerous northern Anhwei villages, even managing to infiltrate the government army with several undercover Communist agents. Peasant associations were set up which conducted struggles against landlords. Before designs for land redistribution could advance, however, a Kuomintang backlash soundly quashed the fledgling soviet, killing Wei Yeh-ch'ou and dispersing his followers.[2] Thus, at the end of 1928 CCP peasant movement leaders described the development of peasant associations in Anhwei as regrettably backward, compared to that in other provinces. Only Su could claim a county-level peasant association, and even there the organization was deemed superficial at best.[3]

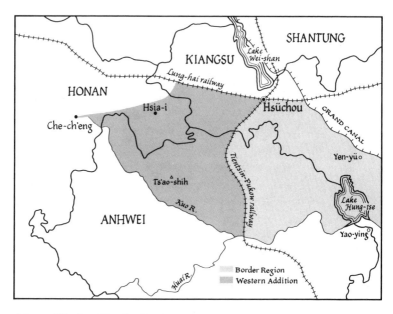

Map 4. Huai-pei Border Region

In the early 1930s, Communist attention in Huai-pei shifted to the tax riots then erupting across northern Anhwei and Kiangsu. In Su-tung County, for example, cadres mobilized thousands of peasants for a two-month revolt against the unpopular opium tax.[4] However, despite the lasting impression that such incidents may have made upon the local inhabitants, the activities continued to be suppressed by overwhelming Kuomintang opposition. Not until the War of Resistance against Japan did CCP involvement demonstrate sustained results. The war occasioned an important escalation of Communist activity in Huai-pei. Patriotic youths continued to compose the main source of recruits during the early months of the war, when mobilization efforts focused upon urban intellectuals. With the fall of Hsüchou to the Japanese in May 1938, however, CCP concern began to turn away from the cities to the rural villages.[5] An experienced work team was sent to northwest Anhwei from the Tapieh mountains and the peasant movement started to gain a modicum of momentum.*

With the military backing of the New Fourth Army, the Communists were able between 1939 and 1941 to open a large base area that spanned eastern Honan, northern Anhwei, and northern Kiangsu. However, after the New Fourth Army incident in January 1941, Kuomintang retaliation forced the CCP to retreat to a more confined area straddling the Anhwei-Kiangsu border. On August 23, 1941, the Huai-pei border government was officially proclaimed, with Liu Jui-lung and Liu Yü-chu as chairman and vice-chairman respectively. Its jurisdiction included roughly all the area north of the Huai River, east of the Tientsin-Pukow railway, south of the Lung-hai railway, and west of the Grand Canal (see Map 4). In 1942, about 60 percent of this territory, containing a population of nearly two million, was under nominal Communist control.[6]

---

*Liu Jui-lung, 1944a, p. 4. Before the loss of Hsüchou, mass work had been under the jurisdiction of two groups: the Anhwei provincial mobilization committee and the Hsüchou battle zone mobilization committee. Both groups had centered their activities on urban intellectuals.

Only in 1943, with the relative relaxation of Japanese pressure, were the Communists able to devote much time and money to constructive enterprises. That year, some 3,700 square miles of additional territory, populated by more than half a million people, was incorporated within the border region. Mass mobilization efforts were stepped up dramatically. Peasant associations were formed in nearly four hundred *hsiang*, representing about 80 percent of the territory of the designated border region. In terms of population, however, fewer than 23 percent of the households had been mobilized to join the new organizations.[7]

In 1944, a major Japanese military offensive against the KMT, known as the Ichigo campaign, created new opportunities for the Communists. The enemy advance resulted in the evacuation of Kuomintang forces from Huai-pei, thereby allowing the New Fourth Army to move in and retrieve its former bases west of the Tientsin-Pukow railway. Relying on cavalry that had been developed in the years of confinement along the Kiangsu-Anhwei border, the New Fourth Army was able to mount a rapid western advance that succeeded in retaking hundreds of fortified communities (*yü-chai*) in northwest Anhwei and eastern Honan. An area that included some two and a half million people and stretched a hundred miles from east to west and seventy miles from north to south was now constituted as the western flank of the Huai-pei border region.[8]

Mass mobilization came less easily than military victory, however. Although a rent reduction campaign was carried out which affected more than 3,000 landlords and 18,000 tenant families in the western area, at the end of 1944 only 5 percent of the populace had been organized into mass associations. By the close of the war, the Huai-pei region had grown to include twenty-four counties and a population of 6 million. Despite this impressive achievement, the secretary of the Huai-pei Party Committee, Liu Tzu-chiu, confessed that not a single model village, model party branch, or model battalion had been established in the area.[9] Liu modestly attributed the failure to incorrect attitudes and work style on the part of the cadres, but it is clear that preexisting conditions in the area itself bore more than a little responsibility for the difficulties the Communists encountered. Actually, Huai-pei was recognized by CCP authorities as one of the more socially complex regions of the country. As a major Communist leader summarized the climate: "Feudal associations [secret societies] such as the *san-fan*, Green and Red Gangs, Sword Society, and *shen-hsien-tao* abound. . . . As for brigands, it is common knowledge that the areas around Lakes T'ai, Ch'ao, Kao-yü, and Hung-tse . . . rank among China's most infamous bandit lairs. Even today many villages in northern Kiangsu and eastern Anhwei are protected by moats, stone walls, and watch towers."[10] In short, the predatory and protective cycle continued. And, as we would expect, these traditional patterns exerted a powerful influence on the style and success of Communist efforts to mobilize the local populace.

Initial Encounter: The Peasant Movement Period

When the Chinese Communists turned their attention toward the North China peasantry in the mid-1920s, they were attracted by the massive rural movement that had developed there as an indigenous means of community defense: the Red Spear Society. Eager to extend the establishment of peasant associations to the North China Plain, the CCP viewed the rebellious Red Spears as a promising entrée. Thus, as early as 1925, trained peasant movement personnel were dispatched to Honan, charged with infiltrating and reorganizing the Red Spear Society. Technically, the mobilization initiative was conducted under the auspices of the Kuomintang's Peasant Bureau, founded in January 1924, and its subordinate Honan Provincial Peasant Committee, established in April 1925. Despite the united-front label, the effort was in fact a wholly Communist operation, carried out in accordance with Comintern advice. Based on enthusiastic reports by members of the Soviet embassy staff in China, who considered the Red Spears the harbinger of an imminent peasant revolution, the Comintern had instructed the CCP to assume direction of the burgeoning movement.[11]

Initial overtures made few inroads. On September 17, 1925, after several months of intensive efforts, the Communist cadres convened a meeting of thirty-five delegates from Red Spear chapters in twelve locations in Honan, Kiangsu, Anhwei, and southern Shantung. The number of places represented was very small relative to the total number of extant chapters, and the majority of delegates who attended were in fact Communist Party members assigned to Red Spear work.[12]

Despite the lack of immediate success, CCP interest in the Red Spears grew. This attention was reflected in a series of articles about the society written by prominent activists in 1926 and 1927. In March 1926, the CCP journal *Guide Weekly* published a piece calling for special consideration to the Red Spears, who were said to compose a formidable force of several million armed peasant members. To be sure, the assessment of this growing rural organization was not unmixed. Although the Red Spears had originated as a self-defense movement intended to resist oppression, the article pointed out that ambitious and unprincipled leaders had in some instances undermined its purely defensive stance. Lacking a clear political program, the Red Spears constituted a pivotal force in the North China balance of power. Whether they would swing to the side of revolution would depend upon CCP organizational efforts.[13]

A less cautious appraisal of the Red Spears appeared in the same journal less than three months later. The author of this enthusiastic piece was none other than Ch'en Tu-hsiu, cofounder of the Chinese Communist Party. Ch'en likened the Red Spears to the Taiping and Boxer rebellions, declaring them the latest episode in a glorious two-thousand-year history of Chinese peasant uprisings. Although tainted with a "backward and superstitious ideology," the Red Spears—opposed as they were to warlords, bad officials, and taxes—were viewed as an extremely important form of resistance to the ruling class. Unlike the time of the Taipings, concluded Ch'en, the present time had produced a revolutionary party and army that could unite with peasant power to supersede the shortcomings of traditional rebellions.[14]

This optimistic perspective gained an even stronger endorsement from the other founder of the CCP, Li Ta-chao, in an article on the Red Spears published in the summer of 1926. Li triumphantly pronounced the Red Spears "proof that the Chinese peasantry has awakened!" Although acknowledging certain "backward" aspects of the movement, Li held that these limitations, if properly redirected by Communist leadership, could be transformed into strengths. The localism of the Red Spears he interpreted as a kind of nascent class consciousness. Ascribing xenophobia to the movement, Li claimed to detect a primitive form of anti-imperialism. Messianic yearnings were but a desire for order, and the invulnerability cult would disappear once effective weaponry was placed in their hands. Li concluded his analysis with a plea to village activists to turn their crop-watching societies into democratic peasant associations and their Red Spear chapters into modern self-defense leagues.[15]

Subsequent articles appearing in CCP journals during the fall of 1926 and on into the following year presented more extensive analyses of the Red Spears, discussing in some detail their social composition, organizational structure, rituals, and involvement in antiwarlord struggles. Although the picture presented was a complicated one that admitted the movement's dangerous potential for unbridled violence, the overriding message was a call to Communist cadres to provide the necessary discipline and leadership to transform the Red Spears into a truly revolutionary force.[16]

Official policy was thus reasonably clear on the general direction recommended for Communist mobilization endeavors in North China. Entering an unfamiliar territory plagued with a chaotic military and political situation, the Communists sought to extend the rural strategies developed during several years of experience in South China to their new field of operations as well. The existence in the North of a peasantry already to a large degree organized, armed, and engaged in violent struggle seemed to promise a hospitable starting point.

At a meeting of the Central Committee of the Communist Party in Shanghai in July 1926, a resolution was passed dealing specifically with the Red Spears. Describing the society as a "primitive organization for the self-defense of the middle and poor peasantry," the party resolved to "guide this force and see that it is not utilized by the militarists and local bullies." Specifically, the Red Spears were judged a useful steppingstone to the establishment of peasant associations in North China. Moreover, once peasant associations were developed, the Red Spears would not be eliminated, but would be transformed into the armed force of the peasant associations. For the present, two organizational steps were proposed. First, the various independent Red Spear groups should be persuaded to form a united communications bureau for exchanging information and arranging for mutual assistance. Second, a conference of Red Spear leaders should be convened to draw up a common political platform which would express opposition to bandits, undisciplined troops, corrupt officials, oppressive taxes, forced military and labor conscription, and circulation of warlord currency. With respect to the question of religious beliefs, it was deemed "unnecessary actively to oppose the superstitious dogmas of the Red Spears, because they are the essential factor in bringing these people together. . . . We only want their activities to benefit the development of the revolution."[17]

Despite this rather mild policy, the Red Spears proved less approachable than anticipated. In March 1927, the main CCP emissary to the Red Spears, Yü Shu-teh, reported to Wuhan that the Communists had succeeded in gaining the support of fewer than one-third of the Honan Red Spears. To deal with the problem, Yü requested an increase in money and personnel. Wuhan responded generously, instructing Mao Tse-tung's Peasant Training Institute to admit two hundred more students from Honan in order to augment the number of cadres working among the Red Spears.[18]

In April, as part of the Northern Expedition, forty Honanese students trained at the institute were sent home to assist in the mobilization effort. Their arrival met with less than a warm welcome. A report in July 1927 by cadre Teng Liang-sheng detailed the disillusionment of the returned students:

According to all we had heard, the Honanese peasantry was very revolutionary. So when we went to Honan we were prepared to lead the peasants to participate in revolutionary work. Our hopes were very high. However, when we arrived in Honan we saw that conditions were completely different from our expectations. . . . Because the peasants' conservatism was so strong and their feudalist thought so pronounced, we had great difficulty in propaganda work, finding that all the handbills and slogans we had brought with us were inappropriate. We were forced to change our strategy, writing in official government style and affixing seals in order to gain their trust. . . . The Red Spear Society is not a revolutionary organization, but simply a kind of feudal association. They follow the orders of the landlords absolutely. Whereas we wanted to strike down the landlords to carry out rural revolution, the Red Spears were protecting the landlords. . . . Their thinking is very backward and they easily believe the slander of the reactionaries who accuse the KMT of advocating "communal property, communal wives" [kung-ch'an kung-ch'i]. Once when our political bureau distributed a poster in the name of peasants, soldiers, and *women*, this was seen as proof of the "communal wives" accusation. Because their thinking is immature, they accept the reactionary propaganda and refuse to trust the KMT. Furthermore, our cadres are too few and lack experience. Most are from South Honan and, because of language difficulties, cannot work effectively in the north.[19]

Established explicitly for the purpose of protecting their holdings against the demands of outsiders, the Red Spears were predictably resistant to these attempts by young intellectuals to reorganize them into "modern" peasant associations. The Communists' slogan of "Down with oppressive landlords" did not find wide appeal among a peasantry of whom some 80 percent owned land. The slogan "Down with rotten gentry" alienated a Red Spear Society whose leadership *was* the local elite.

In May 1927, when the Communists executed twenty-four "local bullies and rotten gentry" in Hsin-yang County, the Red Spears responded to the challenge by mobilizing a force of more than a thousand that killed two peasant movement workers, nine political bureau officials, and four party members. They also managed to cut the Peking-Hankow railway in three places, thereby severing communications between the Northern Expeditionary Army and Wuhan.[20] In response, on May 30 the left wing of the KMT called a temporary halt to the mass movement work in Honan.*

Interest in the Red Spears, we remember, had focused on the possibility of converting these societies into full-fledged peasant associations. The work of organizing peasant associations in Honan began in August 1925. Just one year later, according to central Peasant Bureau statistics, Honan had the second highest number of peasant association members in the country. Although the statistics themselves suggested an impressive organizational achievement, the reality was quite different. In the summer of 1927, just after the split in the United Front, Chu Ch'i-hua, a professional Communist organizer, traveled to Honan and discovered the situation there to be considerably less under control than official reports had indicated. What the inflated figures in fact represented was the number of Red Spear members whose leaders had allegedly expressed some nominal allegiance to the Communists. The groups were by no means genuine peasant associations in the sense intended by Party Central. Very few of them observed any party direction at all; most were, on the contrary, actively hostile to leftist propaganda.[21]

According to Chu Ch'i-hua's investigation, the existence of the Red Spears rendered the peasant movement in Honan qualitatively different from that in the South. Whereas peasant associations in the southern provinces were based primarily on the poor peasantry in opposition to the militia of the landlords and gentry, the northern Red Spears were themselves under the leadership of the landlord-gentry class. Because warlord control

*Chiang Yung-ching, 1963, pp. 376–78. This decision was apparently not endorsed by the Comintern. At the eighth meeting of the Third International in Moscow in June 1927, a resolution was passed stressing the need to pay greater attention to the Red Spears, who were given credit for destroying warlord power in North China (STSP, July 7, 1927, p. 3).

in the North oppressed rich and poor alike, the inhabitants were united in opposition. The superior status of the landlords and literati had allowed them to assume leadership of the movement, thereby presenting a major obstacle to Communist efforts at mobilization.[22]

Cognizant of shortcomings in their work to date, the Honan Provincial Committee on August 1–5, 1927, called together ten cadres working with Red Spears throughout the province to analyze and improve their methods. The KMT's bloody betrayal that spring had probably left Communist organizers feeling less optimistic about the possibility of any alliance with members of the local elite. In any case, the outcome of the August meeting was an admission that the Red Spear movement was controlled by "local bullies and bad gentry," and a pledge to try to stimulate dissension between leaders and the rank and file. The report issued from the field on August 30 estimated that the Red Spears accounted for 90 percent of the peasant activism in Honan and expressed an interest in creating several independent Red Spear chapters under Communist direction. "Our sole work in Honan from now on," it declared, "is to seize the hegemony of the Red Spear movement."[23] On September 2, Party Central responded to the field report. Applauding the decision to undertake sustained efforts at mass mobilization, the Center nevertheless cautioned its representatives in Honan against an erroneous tendency to equate the Red Spears with the peasant movement as a whole. Insisted Party Central, "We are not assimilating the peasant association work into the Red Spear Association work but, on the contrary, we want to assimilate the Red Spears into the peasant associations."[24]

On September 4, the Honan Provincial Committee issued another report criticizing its former methods of work among the Red Spears. Sobered by the experiences of the past two years, the Provincial Committee admitted to "no foundation among the peasants" and declared that "the peasant work must start anew." The overall strength of the Red Spears was predicted to be on the decline, and they were characterized as a force organized to smash the genuinely revolutionary groups of impoverished peasants. "Most of the poor peasants," it was now said, "realizing the senseless sacrifice and little benefit they are gaining for themselves, tend to disassociate themselves from the Red Spears." Nevertheless, rather than abandon entirely the attempt to organize them, the committee encouraged its cadres to infiltrate the society and even attempt to attain the esteemed status of religious teacher so as to redirect the focus of the movement. Despite their counterrevolutionary tendencies, it was still felt that Red Spear–type societies constituted an essential vehicle for mass mobilization in the area:

In the present political situation of Honan, names like the peasant association and the peasant headquarters cannot be used in organizing the peasant masses. Since the culture of peasants in Honan is particularly backward, it is not easy for them to accept this kind of organization. They still ask the Red Spear Association to send men to organize them. In order for the peasant movement to reach the peasantry, it is necessary at this time to utilize their superstitious psychology by employing for independent activity a special organization similar to the Red Spear Association.[25]

This latter segment of the report from the field elicited strong criticism from party headquarters. On September 24 a reply to the Honan Provincial Committee noted that:

Central considers your independent organization of the Red Spears inappropriate. The style of your "independent organization of the Red Spears" bears as yet no great difference from the old one, and it is still a superstitious and clannish organization. . . . The Central considers that the Red Spear movement should assimilate the Red Spears into the peasant association through struggle—in the course of uprisings for land revolution we should on the one hand remould the political ideas of the rank and file of the Red Spears and change them from being defensive and conservative into aggressive and revolutionary, and we should on the other hand alienate the rank and file Red Spears from their reactionary leaders and return them to the banner of the peasant association.[26]

Such instructions from Party Central expressed a strain of wishful thinking not easily translated into effective action by cadres in the field.

The Red Spears were not about to submit to the designs of alien revolutionaries without a struggle. The resulting animosity was well demonstrated in the case of Hsin-yang County. A center of opposition to the Communists, Hsin-yang was also, we recall, the scene of intense local conflict between the Red Spears and the Bare Egg Society (*kuang-tan-hui*), a predatory association of unemployed people who made a living by robbery, often at the expense of Red Spear leaders. The Red Spears in Hsin-yang had formed in 1925 in defense against marauding troops stationed in the area. Over the next several years, the society staged attacks on warlord and Northern Expeditionary forces alike. Their adamant opposition to intrusion of any sort made the Red Spears unreceptive to Communist propaganda efforts. As a result, the cadres began to turn their attention to the rival Bare Eggs. By the summer of 1927, the Bare Eggs had established themselves on a mountain some thirty miles southwest of the Hsin-yang county seat, near the Honan-Hupeh border. From the peak of the mountain, a good view could be had of the four contiguous counties; hence its name, Four View Mountain. On the mountain lived some six hundred families, all in dire poverty.[27] When Communist cadres reported the existence of this organized predatory force, Party Central responded enthusiastically:

We should send military personnel to organize and train them. Right now they may be in the style of Liang-shan-po [mountain lair of the bandit heroes of *Water Margin*], recruiting soldiers and purchasing horses in the locality, looting the rich to relieve the poor, raiding trains and seizing rifles. We can use the name "Honan Subcommittee of the Revolutionary Committee of China" to issue bulletins . . . to organize peasant associations, to execute confiscation of the land in adjacent areas.[28]

Under the leadership of cadres Wang Po-lu and Chang Li-shan, the Communists set up a soviet government among the Bare Eggs on Four View Mountain. In reaction, in the winter of 1927, a new official militia was instituted at Hsin-yang for the purpose of rooting out the Communist base. A series of offensives against the mountain ended in failure, however. On December 3, the Communist-led Bare Eggs attacked the Hsin-yang railway station, capturing and killing the leader of the new militia. In late January 1928, they staged an assault on the town of Ch'ang-t'ai-kuan in which several dozen gentry and local security force personnel were killed. A branch headquarters was set up and posters calling for the defeat of landlords, confiscation of property, and institution of communism were issued. On January 30, the group launched a destructive attack against a Red Spear chapter on the eastern shores of the Huai River.[29] These offensives resulted in retaliation by a combined militia and Red Spear force which finally succeeded in taking Four View Mountain in February 1928. Deprived of their home base, the Bare Eggs moved into mobile warfare. On March 14, more than two thousand roving members of the group were held responsible for an attack on a Catholic church.[30]

The importance of the Bare Egg Society in mobilizing the poor peasantry was not limited to Hsin-yang. In Anhwei's Ssu County, the Bare Eggs were also the major vehicle of Communist organizational efforts. Located on a mountain hideaway north of the county seat, the Ssu group had popularized a folk song about their activities:

> Enter the Bare Egg Society;
> You'll never be blamed.
> Defeat the Northern Hegemon,
> Everyone will have food and clothing.

The Northern Hegemon was a landlord by the name of Hsü Hua-t'ing who owned several hundred *mou* of land in the area. A degree holder, Hsü was also director of the local militia. In addition to rents amounting to 60 percent of the harvest, Hsü demanded of his tenants fees for maintaining the militia. In 1930, after having just paid the better part of their wheat crop to Hsü, several tenant farmers and hired laborers got together and decided to form a Bare Egg Society, as was happening in nearby villages. In the space of two days, more than a thousand peasants—armed with farm and kitchen implements—had joined the group. The Bare Eggs stormed the militia arsenal and seized twelve guns; they then proceeded to Hsü's home to open the granary. The group agreed to submit to Communist leadership, sending two hundred of its members to the Red Army and coordinating a series of uprisings with other Communist-led Bare Eggs in the area.[31]

In their early effort to penetrate North China, the Communist cadres in the field thus found the predatory Bare Egg Society a more receptive ally than the Red Spears in whom they had once placed such hopes. Led by landlords and rich peasants, the Red Spears were generally hostile to outside intrusion and to redistributive ideology in particular.* The Communist message at this time thus met with greater enthusiasm among impoverished predators such as the Bare Eggs. Attracted by the radical policies espoused by the CCP in its initial approach to the countryside, the land-hungry and unemployed constituted ready recruits. As a September 1927 party directive outlining the work plan for Anhwei acknowledged:

The present targets of the peasant movement should be the hired hands, tenant peasants, as well as the unemployed peasants as the core; that is, the landless as the center because in the present rural revolution—the land revolution—only they can be the main force. . . . Bandits and lumpens are all jobless peasants, and are the ones who actively participate in the land revolution. We should regard them as our brothers and go out to lead them to take part in the land revolution. The peasant associations should accept organized bandit groups. Our party should also accept revolutionary bandit elements.[32]

Although Party Central continued to advocate mobilization of the Red Spears, using the rationale that "though they are the

*Certainly there were some exceptions. One member of the Red Army has described how in October 1928 a Red Spear group of which his father was a member was converted wholesale into a Red Army unit. Those who had acted as Red Spear leaders assumed leadership positions in the new Red Army division as well. This particular Red Spear group was unusual, however, inasmuch as its previous activities had centered on attacking local landlords. (HCPP, vol. 3, pp. 39–44.)

armed forces of the landlords, the Red Spears are the poverty-stricken peasants carrying the red shafts," the urgings were to little avail.[33] It was true that the Red Spear rank and file were far from affluent, but patron-client and community bonds with their leaders inhibited horizontal class identity. Communist dreams of mobilizing the rebellious Red Spears were dashed by the harsh reality of encounter with an entrenched protective movement anxious to defend its parochial interests against all forms of outside intervention.

The experience was not unique to Huai-pei. In this period, protective groups in other parts of the country demonstrated a similar hostility to Communist organizational efforts. In western Kwangtung, for example, the Divine Strike Corps (*shen-ta-t'uan*), a village defense league that also relied on an invulnerability cult to oppose both bandits and soldiers, proved a major enemy to Communist-led peasant associations.[34]

The hostile response was partly a reflection of the CCP's emphasis on land reform, a program that threatened the social order that such protective groups were established to defend. In addition to their revolutionary platform, the Communists' mobilization of men and materiel was itself a challenge to the local power structure. Among predators, however, the cadres found a more receptive audience. As we know, bandit outfits constituted an important base of support for the growth of soviets in China at this time.[35] The Red Army was the home of many a former brigand, attracted both by the stable income and by the promise of social change.

The Tables Turn: The War of Resistance

Although bandits proved relatively friendly allies in the initial Communist encounter with the countryside, the picture would change in time. Except for sporadic tax riots, the early 1930s saw a reduction in CCP activity in Huai-pei. Ready recruits though such groups as the Bare Eggs might be, they apparently did not form the foundation for the construction of stable base areas. That accomplishment would have to wait for some years, until the Japanese invasion highlighted the strategic importance of the region. And, as the battle for the Huai-pei countryside got underway, it became clear that the Communists would look beyond the confines of predatory bands in their search for comrades-in-arms.

In 1937, New Fourth Army general Ch'en I, in an important article on rural mobilization, highlighted the special tasks for the CCP occasioned by the war. The main purpose of mass mobilization, Ch'en emphasized, was to oppose Japanese imperialism. "Our aim in going to the villages," he explained, "is to organize the peasants into resisting the enemy; it is not to instruct them to divide the land." In keeping with this policy, local village notables were to be contacted and encouraged to cooperate in establishing defense arrangements. Traditional methods of security such as the *pao-chia* system were to be retained, and groups like the Red Spears were to be encouraged to transform themselves into guerrilla units that would carry out resistance against the Japanese.[36]

In Huai-pei, implementation of new resistance policies was complicated by the fact that the region remained rife with banditry. The area surrounding Lake Hung-tse was completely bandit-controlled, and a mobile brigand outfit dubbing itself the "Ninth Route Army" harassed the Communists with KMT approval.[37] The question of how to deal with such elements was a major problem for CCP strategists. As Liu Shao-ch'i, secretary of the party's North China Bureau, summarized the dilemma in 1938: "Some bandit groups are sincerely interested in resisting Japan, but most raise the banner of resistance only to camouflage their true intentions of plunder. Others actually fight on the side of the enemy."[38] Liu advocated cooperation with all groups willing to oppose the Japanese. Bandits committed to an anti-Japanese position were no exception. The problem, however, was that the political allegiance of bandit groups was often open to question. A few outfits were indeed successfully incorporated into the Communist forces, but others resisted cooperation, sometimes inflicting heavy losses in the process. A variable policy was thus proposed. In Communist base areas—where political and military control had been established—Liu advocated harsh treatment. Bandits must either submit to reorganization under CCP direction or else leave the base area to carry out disruptive activities in enemy zones. Those who refused either option were subject to liquidation. In Japanese-controlled territory, by contrast, those bandits not under enemy direction were regarded as useful agents for disrupting order. In these zones, cadres were encouraged to ally with bandit elements, seeking to reform them gradually in the process of joint struggles against the enemy. All independent bandits who truly wished to resist Japanese intrusion were welcomed, so long as they agreed to expel their "impure elements," undergo political education, cease actions disruptive to the Communist cause, and obey instructions.[39]

That same year, the report of a Communist student working in Kuan County, Shantung, demonstrated the possibility, albeit difficult, of successfully incorporating these independent bandit outfits. The Kuan bandits, known as "local sticks" (*t'u-kan*), operated across an area of two or three counties. Numbering more than four thousand, they were almost all former peasants whose livelihood had been destroyed by successive years of floods and marauding troops. When the Japanese occupied the Kuan county seat, Communist students moved into the countryside in an effort to arouse rural resistance. There they faced two enemies: bandits and local defense forces. Concluding that the bandits were more amenable to rectification, the students decided to surrender to the brigands with the secret intention of eventually reforming them. As conditions for their surrender, the Communists required that they be permitted to operate as a unit and to recruit new members. Although the bandits were suspicious of the students' motives, they were in desperate enough straits to welcome the additional manpower despite the accompanying conditions. To gain trust, the students participated enthusiastically in the bandits' offensives against the local defense forces. Gradually they convinced the brigands to accept instruction in methods of organization, leading them to tighten their chain of command. Finally, after three months of agitation, the bandits were persuaded to surrender to Communist leadership. Their decision was prompted by the assurance that they would be guaranteed enough to eat and perhaps at some later time the possibility of earning official rank.[40]

The case of Kuan County constituted a rare instance of the type of success story the Communists hoped to bring about more generally. As P'eng Teh-huai, deputy commander of the Eighth Route Army, noted in 1942, bandits in enemy-occupied zones should be encouraged to steal Japanese goods, develop special guerrilla forces, and protect Communist transport routes. P'eng stressed that patient mobilization work would permit the conversion of such bandit outfits into regular anti-Japanese guerrilla units. Only those bandits under enemy control would have to be destroyed.[41] At the same time, it was recognized that there were definite limits on the degree to which bandits could realistically be expected to reform. Li Ta-chang, Red Army chief of staff in the Chin-ch'a-chi region, warned that the bandit mentality was "very suspicious and belligerent." Having no sense of nationalism, bandits were basically interested in "harming others to benefit themselves." They could be used to carry out anti-Japanese operations and urged to accept political education, but they could not be forced to reorganize under Communist leadership. Li cautioned that cadres who worked among bandits must show great patience and a respect for brigand life-styles.[42]

Often, however, patience and respect proved of little avail. More than a few bandit groups chose to fight under the Japanese or Kuomintang flags, since in so doing they could continue their pillage while at the same time acquiring official rank. Such terms were far more tempting than the stringent Communist requirements, which demanded that bandits join the New Fourth Army as individuals rather than as units, and that they refrain from plunder and submit to political reeducation.

To meet the threat posed by recalcitrant gangs, the CCP began to adopt an increasingly antagonistic position. As the war continued, military campaigns were launched against many of the more formidable bandit outfits. In the spring of 1941, two New Fourth Army brigades succeeded in liquidating the large group of brigands at Lake Hung-tse. To the north, Communist attacks managed to subdue the bandit army led by the infamous chieftain Liu Hei-ch'i. Ruler of many lairs across southern Shantung, Liu had risen from bandit to army commander to collaborator with the Japanese to official in the Kuomintang's Kiangsu-Shantung military region. At the time of his demise, he simultaneously held titles from both the Japanese and the Kuomintang—rewards for having killed countless Communist cadres in the area.[43] Although official CCP policy was to limit executions to bandit chieftains, offering the possibility of reform to their followers, the differential treatment was hard to maintain in practice.

In addition to deploying troops, the Communists adopted a companion method for dealing with hostile predators. Local communities were encouraged to reactivate indigenous protective responses to provide for their own defense. As Liu Jui-lung, chairman of the new Huai-pei border government, proclaimed, "We are perpetuating the ancient pattern in Chinese history whereby the people spontaneously establish military defenses to protect their country and their native villages."[44]

Strategy had come full circle. As changed circumstances relegated the land revolution to second place behind the more pressing concern with the wartime effort, the Communists began to find their priorities more akin to those of protectors than to those of predators in Huai-pei. Now that the consolidation of stable base areas replaced the formation of peasant associations as the top item on the CCP agenda, protective impulses assumed renewed importance. The same groups that had once constituted such an obstacle to CCP designs for land revolution became a means of furnishing protection in a hostile environment.

It was Liu Shao-ch'i who formulated the initial CCP policy for dealing with local defense forces during the War of Resistance.

Liu noted that associations such as the Red Spears were spontaneous, yet long-lasting, groups that had revived under the impact of disturbances by Japanese, bandits, and disbanded soldiers. Although led for the most part by "gentry," the groups were described as politically neutral—approaching all matters from the standpoint of personal interest and resisting anyone who interfered with their welfare. Their base of support was parochial and their membership forceful in safeguarding local interests. In dealing with these groups, Communist cadres and soldiers would have to demonstrate strict discipline and a respect for the societies' beliefs and practices. In times of Japanese attack, the Communists should aid the local groups in resisting, while at the same time carrying out education to inspire a sense of nationalism. Sometimes, conceded Liu, myth could actually prove a useful weapon in dealing with the sects. Noting that in certain places rumor held that Red Army commander Chu Teh was a descendant of the imperial Ming line, Liu explained that in those areas Communist relations with secret societies were especially amiable.[45]

In the early years of the resistance war, this rather lenient policy seems to have enjoyed a certain success. In 1938, for example, there were several cases of joint Communist and Red Spear offensives against Japanese forces in Shantung.[46] In 1940, the New Fourth Army in Anhwei was reported to have carried out a highly effective campaign among Red Spears, Big Swords, and *lien-chuang-hui*. Having instructed their forces not to insult such groups, the Communists gained the consent of many local leaders to absorb their followers into the New Fourth Army. By 1940, 75 percent of the *lien-chuang-hui*, 43 percent of the Big Swords, and numerous Red Spears were said to have enlisted on the Communist side. Thousands of Red Spears in northern Anhwei, having been reorganized into the ranks of the New Fourth Army, constituted a front line in the anti-Japanese struggle.[47]

Militarily speaking, the wartime base areas were intended to provide an oasis of order within an otherwise chaotic situation. According to Chairman Mao Tse-tung's earthy metaphor, they were the "buttocks of the revolution." Just as a person without buttocks—having no means of sitting down—would soon tire, so the revolution required a spot to rest and regain the strength needed to continue the struggle.[48] Building a restful base area in Huai-pei was far from an easy order, however. Occupying a strategic position between North and South China, the region was the scene of fierce battles for control of its rivers and railways. To develop secure resistance bases in this critical locale would require the support of age-old methods of rural defense.

The case of the Ssu-ling-sui guerrilla base, located in the heart of Huai-pei on the Kiangsu-Anhwei border, illustrates the way in which traditional forms of community defense played an important transitional role in the growth and consolidation of the base area. Wrested from the Kuomintang in 1941, Ssu-ling-sui had more than twenty different protective religious sects in operation. The area was also known as bandit territory, with groups of brigands numbering in the hundreds. To counter the threat of enemy and bandit attack alike, the Communists successfully allied with local sects and defense organizations, despite the fact that they were generally led by landlords and rich peasants.[49] Likewise, to undertake mass work within the villages of Ssu-ling-sui, CCP cadres found it necessary to come to an understanding with a variety of local power holders. The heads of the village security apparatus (pao-chia-chang), because of their capacity to inspire fear in the peasants, were especially important to the initial stages of mass work. Once appeased, they could be used to summon people to meetings, disseminate propaganda, and explain government directives. School teachers, educated youths, and secret-society members constituted other key contacts in this regard.[50]

Although cadres working in the Huai-pei field were compelled to forge pragmatic alliances with a variety of local protective groups, official policy toward secret societies remained somewhat ambiguous. According to a directive issued by P'eng Teh-huai in May 1942, the Communist position was to be flexible, adapted to the different locations and allegiances of the various groups. In enemy-occupied zones, an effort should be made to infiltrate the sects for long-term work, gradually augmenting their sense of nationalism in hopes of converting them into a mass association against the Japanese. Outside the enemy zones, secret societies were to be discouraged by issuing proclamations informing the public that religious sects abetted the Japanese. Already established societies in these areas, if unsympathetic to the national cause, were to be suppressed and eliminated as the opportunity presented itself.[51]

In December 1942, Li Ta-chang prepared a more detailed position paper outlining CCP policies toward local protectors. Three types of groups were singled out for consideration: puppet units, sects, and gangs. The puppet units (*wei-t'uan*) were groups established after the start of the war by local notables. Although many of them had formally submitted to Japanese direction, in reality the localistic orientation of the groups placed significant restrictions on their loyalty to the Japanese. For this reason, Li advocated a policy of persuasion rather than force in dealing with them. He suggested that the CCP attempt to conclude agreements with such groups, recognizing their legitimacy in return for a pledge of friendship and protection. Only the most resolutely intractable units should be attacked. The sects (*hui-men*) were defined by Li as "feudal organizations" which included Red Spears, White Spears, Green Spears, Yellow Spears, Yellow Sands, Big Swords, Long-haired Way, and *lien-chuang-hui*. Although frequently controlled by landlords and often enjoying connections with the Japanese, these groups nevertheless retained an essential spontaneity and localism. As mass organizations that cut across class lines in providing for community defense, the sects were said to constitute a critical ally in the anti-Japanese struggle. Li proposed that Communist cadres join the groups and patiently carry out long-term educational work among them. Both open and clandestine cadres were admonished to respect the "feudal superstitions, practices, and leaders" of the sects. Elements within the *hui-men* who were adamantly opposed to the CCP should be attacked, but in such a way as to make clear that the object of struggle was not the sect itself. The third form of indigenous protective association, the gang (*pang-k'ou*), Li described as a "remnant of feudalism" whose organization was based upon slogans of nativism, chivalry, and public interest. Of the two types of gangs prevalent in North China, the *hung-pang* was said to be more active in rural villages, especially along mountain transport routes, whereas the *ch'ing-pang* was concentrated in cities and along water routes. Since the war, the Kuomintang had been making strenuous efforts to win over these groups, using the *ch'ing-pang* to undermine the CCP's workers' movement and the *hung-pang* to destroy the peasant movement. Li encouraged the Communists to compete for the allegiance of the gangs, training a special contingent of cadres to infiltrate and remold the groups into a pro-CCP force. In the liberated zones, he predicted, they would automatically lose their feudal character as they came to participate in the mass movement. In Kuomintang areas, they would have to be approached more indirectly. Cadres were enjoined to adopt subtle tactics such as changing traditional gang slogans of "Oppose the Ch'ing; restore the Ming" into a more contemporary refrain: "Oppose the Japanese; oppose Manchukuo."[52]

In practice, Li's distinction of three types of protective association was difficult to draw precisely. All were led by local notables for the primary aim of community defense, all cut across class lines, and all subscribed to a brand of ideology deemed "feudal" by the Communists. As powerful forces in the countryside—the Red Spears alone were said to include half a million followers in Huai-pei at this time—the groups would have to be approached in hopes of converting them to the resistance cause. Thus on April 1, 1942, the CCP in Huai-pei issued a classified document listing procedures for secret-society members to join the party. Although expecting eventually to supplant the local forces, in the meantime the Communists would have to reach an accommodation with them.[53]

The decision to admit sectarians to the CCP, while facilitating party expansion, also entailed serious problems for party purity.

A report on the state of the party delivered to a Huai-pei border region work conference on July 1, 1945, showed graphically how party growth had taken place at the expense of quality. Of the 281 cadres at the administrative village (*hsiang*) level in four key Huai-pei counties (*hsien*), about 70 percent were said to have participated in "feudal associations." Possibly as a result of these activities, 60 to 70 percent of the cadres were described as "politically unstable," and corruption was suspected to have tainted up to 98 percent of them. Despite the fact that nearly half the cadres were of poor peasant or hired laborer background and that a series of three rectification campaigns had been conducted between 1941 and 1944, the political and moral reliability of party leaders was in serious doubt.[54]

Part of the problem with leadership quality may have been the result of tension between outside and local cadres. In 1941, a report issued by the Political Department of the New Fourth Army noted that both the Communist Party and the army were "guests" (*k'e*) in the Huai-pei area. The peasant movement developed under their direction thus evidenced a "local-guest contradiction" (*t'u-k'e mao-tun*) between the native peasantry and the cadres from outside. Peasant participation in groups such as the Red Spears was cited as evidence of the strength of Huai-pei localism, an obstacle to Communist mobilization that could be overcome only by cultivating more indigenous cadres.[55] Two years later, in 1943, Liu Tzu-chiu still pointed to the lack of politically reliable local cadres as one of the greatest weaknesses in Huai-pei party work. Relatively few locals had been assigned important responsibilities, and those who had, often proved a disappointment—either so tied to their home connections that they were guilty of "tailism," or else so heady from their new rise in status that they took on airs. Liu advocated gradual promotion of locals, giving them increasing responsibilities yet ensuring that they remain tied to their home communities for their livelihood.[56]

Some headway in localization was subsequently made. In early 1944, the program to recruit local administrative cadres resulted in the replacement by indigenous personnel of six *hsiang* chairmen and vice-chairmen, twenty-six district (*ch'ü*) chairmen and vice-chairmen, and forty-nine lower-level cadres.[57] Unfortunately, the reports do not tell us whether it was these newly recruited cadres who were responsible for the sorry statistics mentioned earlier which claimed that the majority of *hsiang*-level cadres suffered from secret-society ties, political unreliability, and corruption. The inference seems plausible, however. In the search for local cadres, the party was naturally drawn to villagers with organizational experience and wide contacts among the native populace. Members of sectarian associations met these criteria. Yet although it was clear that the CCP had to reach out to such groups if the revolution was to take root among the villagers of Huai-pei, the problems entailed in an accommodation with these parochially oriented outfits were considerable.

A PLAGUE ON BOTH YOUR HOUSES!

As the Huai-pei border government was able to consolidate its position in the aftermath of the Ichigo campaign of 1944, it grew increasingly impatient with predatory and protective groups alike. Although the early years of the war had seen a pragmatic encouragement of local defense institutions in order to reduce the threat of bandit betrayal, the predatory menace had not been entirely eliminated. To be sure, indigenous defense measures were given major credit for exterminating some seventy-five bandit chiefs, several of whom had hundreds of followers, in the three years from 1940 through 1942. Nevertheless, the problem persisted. In 1943 more than thirty cases of banditry were brought before the Huai-pei Public Security Bureau. In late 1944, Huai-pei's Ssu-ling-sui guerrilla base still harbored numerous active bandit groups, the larger of which counted some five or six hundred members. Many of the brigands farmed by day and robbed by night, continuing the familiar pattern of supplementing an inadequate agricultural income with plunder from adjacent areas.[58]

The fostering of protective societies had proved an inadequate antidote to bandit activity. Moreover, just as bandits demonstrated an unwillingness to adhere to the discipline demanded by the revolutionary movement, protective units also posed certain difficulties. The conservative mentality of the groups undermined Communist innovations. From the perspective of protectors, alliances with the CCP were prompted by much the same motivation that had generated Red Spear conversion to official Kuomintang defense leagues a decade before. As long as the governing authorities showed a commitment to public order and a willingness to forgo tampering with extant social structures, protective societies were amenable to cooperation. Demands for change, however, met with a less enthusiastic reception. As CCP authorities discovered, sectarians were not reliable candidates for leadership roles in the new revolutionary movement.

To neutralize the deleterious influences of both forms of traditional organized violence in Huai-pei, the Communists began in 1944 to adopt a new style of mass mobilization. Under the auspices of the "Weed out traitors campaign" (ch'u-chien yün-tung), secret-society members were subject to the same reprisals as bandits. In some villages, security measures reminiscent of the traditional pao-chia were reintroduced, now under firm CCP control, for the purpose of clarifying and purifying the allegiance of local residents. Households within a village were requested to group together in units of five. The groupings were voluntary, but households within a group were required to guarantee the good behavior of their fellow group members.

When this security system was introduced into the community of Chu-hu, Anhwei, a total of twenty-three people were unable to find guarantors.[59] Of this total, six were denied protection because they had had dealings with the Japanese, six because of bandit connections, three because they were outsiders not well known in the community, two because they belonged to secret societies, two for illicit sexual conduct, two because they had traveled to enemy zones for unknown reasons,

236 The Communist Movement

Table 11. Self-Confessed Crimes in Chu-hu, 1944

Crime	No. of culprits
Member of *san-fan-tzu* (a local secret society)	35
Sworn brotherhood	26
Joined KMT army	18
Sworn sisterhood	12
Member of *yen-kuang-hui* (a local secret society)	11
Banditry	8
Member of incense society	3
Refused to increase laborer's wages	2
Refused to reduce tenant's rent; corruption; sold opium; sold son; Catholic; Protestant; connections with bandits; stole wheat; stole cow; stole salt; stole piglet	1 each
TOTAL	126

one because he had deserted the army, and one for some unstated reason. An example of those who failed to gain a guarantor was Chu Ch'ang-hsien, a bandit known as "top tiger" who had trafficked with the Japanese and engaged in opium smuggling. Refused sponsorship, Chu was denied access to foodstuffs by his home community, a powerful inducement for reform. After having established the lines of the guarantee system, cadres urged all persons—within and outside the system—to acknowledge any past crime or participation in secret associations. To encourage others, party members and activists who themselves had engaged in such improprieties first carried out public confessions. Soon others were persuaded to come forward to proclaim their misdoings. At three public meetings, a total of 126 self-confessions were volunteered. The offenses admitted are shown in Table 11. In addition to these openly confessed crimes, further investigation revealed a number of unacknowledged offenses, as shown in Table 12.

Offenders who pledged to make amends were subject only to the punishment of public humiliation, but the Communists had nevertheless turned from a policy of cooperation with secret societies to one of active opposition. The shift was the reflection

Table 12. Unacknowledged Crimes in Chu-hu, 1944

Crime	No. of culprits
Fictive kinship (*jen kan-lao-tzu*)	32
Sworn brotherhood	30
Joined KMT army	29
Member of *san-fan-tzu*	17
Member of *yen-kuang-hui*	13
Banditry	13
Member of "Monkey Society" (*hou-tzu-hui*)	6
Member of "Heavenly Immortal Way" (*t'ien-hsien-tao*)	4
Member of incense society	3
Spied for Japanese	1
TOTAL	148

both of increasing CCP power in rural Huai-pei and of a growing distrust of local sects. As the border government gained strength and confidence, it felt less wedded to an alliance with groups whose composition and creeds were so at odds with its own. In the breathing period following the abeyance of the Japanese "mop-up" campaigns, the Communists thus began to assume a more hostile stance toward unreliable elements.

The unreliability of the sectarian groups was becoming increasingly evident. A striking example occurred on January 24, 1945, when a secret society in Li-ch'eng, Shantung, succeeded in staging simultaneous uprisings in sixty-nine villages. Although the area was ostensibly under Communist control, party headquarters had received no advance warning of the outbreak. The leader of the uprising was in fact the Communist-appointed *hsiang* self-defense force commander who, under the pretext of carrying out rent reduction, had actually been proselytizing for his secret society. Landlords, ex-cadres, and others who had been subjected to mass struggles were the main proponents of the revolt, but the party branch secretary, peasant association chairman, and several village heads and militia captains also participated. The uprisings began with incense-burning, feasting, and the distribution of white turbans to all participants.

Under slogans calling for cooperation with the KMT in opposition to both the Japanese and Communists, the rioters managed to capture seven CCP cadres and kill some thirty activists. Although the insurgency was quickly quelled by superior Communist forces, it left the party shaken and thoroughly disillusioned about the possibility of cooperation with secret societies.[60]

With the close of the War of Resistance, as the CCP began to expand from the rural areas into the cities of Huai-pei, the problems posed by sectarian societies grew even more acute. During the war, urban sects had forged close relationships with the Japanese and/or Kuomintang. They thus constituted strong pockets of resistance to the CCP's postwar advance. The case of Su-ch'ien city was probably fairly typical.[61] When the Communists entered Su-ch'ien shortly after the end of the war, they found a city whose total population of 24,130 included at least 1,000 *san-fan-tzu* adherents, more than 300 members of the *i-kuan-tao*, more than 200 Red Swastika members, 100 followers of the Morality Society (*wan-kuo tao-teh-hui*), numerous *hsien-t'ien-tao* and *san-chiao-t'ang* members, as well as 240 fervent Buddhists, 100 devotees of *li-chiao,* 300 Catholics, and 200 Protestants. None of the groups evidenced any pleasure at the CCP's arrival.

The Red Swastika Society was a kind of umbrella association to which the important members of all the other groups belonged. Its leader having previously served as president of the city's chamber of commerce, the Red Swastika Society had been pro-Kuomintang before the war, but had collaborated with the Japanese after enemy occupation of the city. The Morality Society was especially favored by the Japanese and included among its ranks many former Green Gang members. Both the Red Swastikas and the Morality Society were composed predominantly of businessmen and bureaucrat-landlords who were resolutely opposed to the Communist take-over of the city. In addition, just outside the city limits were Small Sword and Big Sword Societies whose combined force numbered about ten thousand people. Although staffed by peasants, the groups were bastions of Kuomintang support. Faced with such determined opposition, the CCP decided to take a firm stand against all these "feudal associations." Rather than attempt to conclude some sort of mutual understanding, as had been common during the war, the Communists no longer felt it prudent or necessary to brook competition from sectarian groups. The strategy was now an all-out effort to undermine the sects by calling mass struggle meetings to attack their leadership.

MOBILIZATION, COMMUNIST STYLE

It was the border government's gradual success in building up committed support among sizable numbers of local inhabitants that had permitted it eventually to reach beyond strategic alliances with predatory and protective groups. What set the Communists so apart from earlier rebel movements in Huai-pei was, of course, their program to restructure local society. As we have seen, entrenched patterns of rural life in this area, conditioned by the realities of the natural environment, were not accidental. Nevertheless, they were also not immutable. As the painstaking work of Communist cadres in Huai-pei would demonstrate, group action to overcome—rather than reflect—prior conditions was also within the range of human possibility. Campaigns to reduce land rents and interest on loans, to provide job security and higher wages for hired laborers, and—most significantly—to develop new forms of mutual aid among rural inhabitants, created a milieu in which traditional forms of collective violence became less adaptive.

The rent and interest reduction policy, which took effect in early 1942, marked the first concerted effort of the Huai-pei border government to carry out mass mobilization. Although the policy was ostensibly moderate, stipulating that rents and interest were to be paid in kind and reduced by approximately 25 percent, implementation had revolutionary results. The real significance of the campaign lay less in its stated aims than in its stress on popular participation. The movement was conducted by a style of mass agitation known as "big sword–expansive axe" (*ta-tao k'uo-fu*), intended to involve large numbers of peasants in the practice of mass struggle for economic reform. The campaign was initiated by teams of cadres sent in from outside the Huai-pei area, who selected certain key villages for intensive work. Cadres visited peasants in the chosen villages, sought out potential activists among them, and organized small groups to investigate local conditions and direct the progress of the campaign in their home communities. Mass struggle sessions were then convened to convince reluctant landlords and creditors to comply with the new policy. When the campaign had been successfully introduced in two or three villages, the cadres would move up the administrative hierarchy to organize groups at progressively higher levels. In this fashion, district and county committees for implementing the campaign were also established. The cadres' work was known as "putting up the scaffold" (*ta-chia-tzu*), providing a new organizational framework for mass action. Local activists were charged with "laying the foundation" (*ta-chi-ch'u*), going door to door to contact all inhabitants and then moving out to neighboring communities to spread the message.[62]

In practice, of course, the campaign evidenced great variation in form as it was introduced in different places. Villages with high tenancy rates required a different approach than freeholding villages, and both of these were distinct from the more complicated market towns. In communities where landholding was severely concentrated, the struggle for rent reduction had to proceed cautiously, so as to prevent its being snuffed out prematurely by harsh landlord reprisals. In villages where tenants were few or nonexistent, the main focus was on interest reduction and improvements for hired agricultural laborers. Here cadres had less to fear from local power holders, but they still needed to avoid antagonizing the more affluent of the owner-cultivators. Market towns, which were often bases of militia and secret-society organization, as well as centers for the limited commercial activities of Huai-pei, proved most challenging for the implementation of both rent and interest reduction.[63] An instance of the first type of situation, a landlord-tenant community, was the village of Yao-ying, located along the Anhwei-Kiangsu border just south of Lake Hung-tse. The largest landlord in the community, Yao Chieh-chin, owned thirty-six *ch'ing* of land, part of which he rented out to eleven tenants. His relative, Yao Hai-chou, who owned fifteen *ch'ing* and employed seven tenants, was the head of the local self-defense force. Although the landlords extracted 50 percent of the harvest in the form of rent, five visits to the village by outside cadres proved fruitless in stimulating tenant struggle. The difficulty in initiating the campaign stemmed largely from the fact that Yao Chieh-chin's nephew Yao Hei-tzu, who was both tenant and rent collector for his uncle, had convinced other tenants to refrain from participating in the campaign. Long discussions between the cadres and Yao Hei-tzu finally convinced the nephew to cease blocking the movement. Two activists were then chosen from among the other tenants, and a mass struggle session was convened at which it was decided to change the terms of rent so that 65 percent of the crop would go to the tenant, with only 35 percent ending up in landlord hands.[64]

An example of the freeholding situation was Yen-yü, in northern Kiangsu's Ssu-yang County. Yen-yü had experienced a series of floods in the early 1940s which forced many of its owner-cultivators into banditry or debt. Cadres were able to appoint several activists as the core of interest reduction committees, but investigation work proceeded slowly since many debtors were afraid that revelation of their debts would jeopardize chances for future loans. In the many instances where the creditors were also kinsmen, family loyalties inhibited participation in the interest reduction campaign. Only when cadres explained that those who declined to comply would be denied access to government granaries and bank loans were large numbers persuaded to register their debts. Once registration had been completed, methods of repayment were determined by small groups of local inhabitants.[65]

Concomitant with the effort to reduce interest payments was the campaign to improve the lot of hired laborers. Groups of agricultural workers were organized to decide upon a fair wage scale and to press for annual, rather than seasonal, employment. Although opportunities for hired labor continued to fluctuate with harvest conditions, the campaign did result in a general increase in wages and length of tenure.[66]

A more complicated setting for the implementation of rent and interest reduction was, of course, the market town. An instructive example of CCP efforts in this arena was the case of Ts'ao-shih, largest market in the northwest Anhwei area. Ts'ao-shih, we may recall, had in the 1850s been the home of a famous local militia, known as the "Niu Family Army." Probably a branch of the Old Cow Society, the militia had achieved official recognition for its success in combating the Nien. Almost a century later, in January 1945, nine CCP cadres arrived in Ts'ao-shih to carry out mass mobilization. The Niu family was still a major power in the town, its members having served as army commanders and county magistrates for generations. Their descendant, Niu Hsi-p'eng, was currently a Kuomintang judge in the county court of Fu-yang. In the past, the town had been a Red Spear headquarters; now it was a major center of the *san-fan-tzu* secret society. After several investigation meetings to determine the structure of power, the cadres decided to initiate rent reduction with a struggle against Niu Hsüeh-feng, largest landlord in Ts'ao-shih. Hsüeh-feng had already fled town, and his wife was prepared to comply with CCP guidelines. Then the campaign shifted to Niu Pao-k'un, clan leader and head of the town militia, who rented his vast landholdings to thirteen tenants, one of whom was his nephew and rent collector. As in the case of Yao-ying, it was necessary to persuade the nephew to refrain from taking his uncle's side. Once this had been accomplished, a struggle meeting was conducted at which the powerful Niu

Pao-k'un agreed to the demanded reduction. After this crucial victory, other landlords felt compelled to follow suit in reducing rents.[67]

Although rent decreases directly affected only a minority of peasants in Huai-pei, success in certain key towns and villages was a dramatic stimulus to further mass involvement. The campaign to lower rents was usually followed by the implementation of interest reduction, the effects of which touched a large proportion of owner-cultivators as well. After a critical mass of popular support had been developed through these pioneer efforts, it was possible to proceed to the establishment of mutual aid arrangements.

The growth of mutual aid represented a genuine breakthrough in the pattern of social action in Huai-pei. In an area where tenancy was relatively unpronounced, yet where group competition among owner-cultivators flourished, the development of new forms of cooperation outweighed rent reduction in its significance for rural transformation. The introduction of mutual aid teams in Huai-pei, like the initiation of rent and interest reduction, occurred at the prompting of outside cadres. A small group of amenable villagers—usually some twenty to thirty people—would be organized to pool their labor and to share draft animals and tools. In contrast to the rent and interest reduction campaign, however, mobilization for mutual aid did not follow the rapid *ta-tao k'uo-fu* method. Rather than involve as many people as quickly as possible, the emphasis in mutual aid development was upon the formation of durable organizations that would yield lasting results. Only after the initial small group had demonstrated visible economic accomplishments was it encouraged to expand to encompass an entire village.

Mutual aid groups were not instituted without considerable problems. Villagers in different economic circumstances regarded the program with varying degrees of ambivalence. Rich peasants with a surplus of land welcomed the formalized labor exchange inasmuch as it spared them the trouble of hiring laborers. At the same time, however, they were reluctant to contribute their animals and tools, fearful that these possessions would suffer from communal use. Poor peasants who owned no farming implements saw the mutual aid group as a means of overcoming their lack of equipment. However, such people had a surplus of labor power which they had in the past applied in short-term work to increase their income, an option that disappeared as cooperative farming absorbed more of their time. Those "middle" peasants who enjoyed a desirable balance among land, labor power, and equipment also had reservations about becoming involved in a time-consuming venture that seemed irrelevant to their economic interests.[68]

In order to overcome these difficulties and provide an incentive for peasants at all economic levels to participate, mutual aid groups in Huai-pei put great emphasis on the development of low-capital sideline economic pursuits: manufacturing oil, bean curd, and noodles, raising hogs, spinning, producing straw bags and capes, and the like. The activities, which varied in accordance with local conditions and availability of capital, were managed entirely by the mutual aid group members themselves, who divided up the work and profits. Such sideline pursuits were explicitly intended to absorb the seasonal surplus labor so evident in the villages of Huai-pei, putting it to a productive use that would augment income for all participants. In places where there was too little surplus capital to initiate manufacturing ventures, mutual aid groups mobilized their members in labor-intensive campaigns such as digging ditches and repairing dikes for flood control.[69]

For a group to work effectively, its members had not only to share complementary economic interests, but also to enjoy a sense of trust and community. Frequently party members and their kinsmen constituted the initial core of mutual aid members.[70] Thus kinship proved a two-edged sword in CCP mobilization efforts. On the one hand, family ties had created difficulties in the implementation of rent and interest reduction, with tenants and debtors reluctant to struggle against their relatives. On the other hand, for the formation of mutual aid, kinship connections were an important starting point. To cooperate successfully, members had to share certain emotional bonds (*kanch'ing*) most commonly found among kinsmen. Often the first mutual aid groups were formed by converting preexisting loan societies to a new purpose. When a group was able to demonstrate concrete results, however, other households might be inclined to apply for admission. An effort was always made to include the most experienced and productive laborers, so that others might learn from their example.

Once the group had shown a capacity for raising agricultural output, it was encouraged to innovate in cropping patterns as well. In late 1944, mutual aid groups in some Huai-pei villages were instrumental in converting part of their farmland to cotton cultivation. The switch provided extra work for domestic textile manufacturers and allowed the villages to become self-sufficient in clothing. Since the price of cotton had risen with the wartime disruption of marketing, local production of clothing permitted a significant saving for participating villages. The program was conducted at the initiative of the border region government, which provided technical advice to groups willing to undertake the innovation.[71]

Although the implementation of mutual aid was a slow, painstaking process, its small but significant successes gradually established the feasibility of cooperative productive effort. Just as competition for scarce resources had engendered persisting patterns of violence in Huai-pei, so cooperation in the development of new resources would reduce the appeal of such traditional behavior.

CONCLUSION

The Communist way was the way of neither the bandit nor the sectarian. Unlike many previous peasant uprisings in Huai-pei, this revolution was no parochial response to scarcity and insecurity that assumed national proportions almost by historical accident. To the extent that the Communists transformed peasant protest from its vicious predatory-protective cycle into a positive articulation of new social arrangements, their success cannot be explained as the ability to assimilate an ongoing secret-society network or as a simple continuation or culmination of earlier patterns of revolt. In fact, as it turned out, some of the thorniest problems for Communist cadres involved the stubborn persistence of age-old forms of collective violence.

To be sure, both predatory and protective strategies provided crucial assistance to the CCP at different critical periods. In the peasant movement era, the Communists—thwarted in the attempt to convert large numbers of Red Spears to their cause—turned successfully to predatory groups like the Bare Eggs. During the War of Resistance, however, the revolutionaries grew disenchanted with their predatory allies. Although sometimes bandits could be converted into guerrilla outfits assigned to harass enemy zones, seldom could they be fully disciplined into a revolutionary army. As the brigands proved receptive to competing offers from the Japanese and Kuomintang, they came to constitute a threat to the development of stable base areas in Huai-pei. Thus the war saw a rapprochement between the CCP and a host of protective groups who offered aid in opposing bandits and enemy forces alike. So long as the revolutionaries emphasized security, they elicited the support of protectors anxious to defend their property. Once the Communists gained the upper hand in Huai-pei, however, they were able to move from a policy of reconciliation to one of confrontation with predatory and protective strategies alike.*[72]

Precisely because these modes of collective violence were *strategies*, whose form and level of activity corresponded to ecological and political circumstances, they became less attractive as the CCP proved capable of changing the ground rules. Ultimately, peasants were less committed to a strategy per se than to the need to secure a livelihood. When new policies pointed

*See note 72 for further discussion of changing CCP relations with local groups.

the way to a more efficient method of group survival, it was possible to transform peasant behavior.

In carrying out social change, the CCP was by no means acting in isolation from preexisting rural conditions. Although broader motives may have prompted the outside cadres to enter Huai-pei in the first place, their eventual success in overcoming traditional patterns of collective violence was based upon their investigation and amelioration of local socioeconomic problems. Only as the party demonstrated a willingness and capacity to solve ongoing dilemmas by alleviating the burdens of tax and rent and providing opportunities for the productive investment of labor and capital, was it able to alter the structure of collective action.

7. Conclusion

The revolutionary entrance of the peasantry onto the stage of world history has prompted many a social science theory intended to explain why peasants revolt. Anthropologists, historians, sociologists, and political scientists alike have recently formulated answers to this critical question.[1] Although the approaches have varied according to the discipline and predilections of the particular theorist, they share a nearly universal emphasis upon the *novelty* of the peasant's participation in revolution, locating the cause of this new behavior in the unprecedented expansion of world capitalism. The intrusion of the international market, we are told, opens the village to outside forces, thereby undermining traditional rural culture, disrupting patron-client ties between landlord and tenant, and "freeing" the peasant to engage in protest activity.[2]

There is much merit in this explanation; certainly the sudden emergence of rural revolutions worldwide is closely linked to the incorporation of agrarian sectors into an international capitalist system. Yet preoccupation with peasant *revolution* offers little help to the study of traditional precapitalist *rebellion*. If contemporary peasant revolt is a product of new capitalist relations, how are we to account for the multitude of uprisings that occurred for centuries prior to the penetration of the global market? More than a few scholars have expressly linked the existence of a rebel tradition to the likelihood of subsequent agrarian revolution.[3] Even if we accept that the latter phenomenon was in large measure generated by the impact of the world economy, however, where do we seek the roots of the far more numerous and persistent earlier uprisings?

This book has attempted to answer precisely that question—a question central to the understanding of peasant revolution, yet largely overlooked by theorists of the subject. The answer is tentative. Based on one century in but a single geographical region, the findings are of course subject to amendment and elaboration by further research. Nevertheless, the case of Huai-pei does suggest that the study of traditional peasant rebellion may call for an approach somewhat different in emphasis from that developed for the analysis of agrarian revolution.

More specifically, this book has tried to demonstrate the importance of the local environment in inducing and patterning a tradition of rural unrest.[4] Certain types of agrarian bureaucracies may well have engendered chronic peasant protest as a matter of course, but such protest was not evenly distributed throughout these societies. Only in particular regions did rebellion recur consistently. To explain the recurrence, one is thus well advised to look carefully at the local setting in which it developed.

Local environments are of course a combination of natural and social features. As ecologists have brought to our attention, it is precisely the interaction between physical and societal structures that constitutes a particular human ecosystem.[5] This configuration, in turn, defines certain patterns of resource availability, distribution, and conflict. Chronic rebellion, I have suggested, was a rational extension of ongoing modes of resource competition, shaped by the natural and social composition of the area. Although the redirection of violence into rebellion against the state required the intervention of precipitating historical events, the preconditions of recurring rebellion can be sought in more lasting adaptive processes. To be sure, the style of adaptation itself underwent changes over time, as new circumstances and past experiences altered the forms of human activity. Nevertheless, as long as society proved unable to shackle the forces of nature, an essential continuity prevailed.

As Emmanuel Le Roy Ladurie has demonstrated in his masterly work, *The Peasants of Languedoc,* the technological stagnation of traditional agrarian society generated cycles of population-resource interaction, punctuated by repeated peasant insurrection.[6] In Huai-pei, as well, one can trace a certain cyclical pattern in the ecological history of the past several centuries. This study, however, has not been primarily concerned with rural unrest as a function of macrosocietal demographic fluctuations. Rather, I have tried to penetrate beneath the broad contours to discover how peasant adaptation actually operated during one exceptionally rebellious century. And there we find that the composition of local society played a critical role in determining the form of peasant unrest. Although rural violence may have been fundamentally a response to environmental uncertainty, it was translated into action only through the mediation of social structure. Just as divisions of class, clan, and settlement shaped the distribution of resources within Huai-pei, so these same groupings constituted vehicles through which the struggle for redistribution of resources was conducted. In short, we have had to search beyond any purely Malthusian explanation of peasant violence in order to make sense of the fashion in which such violence was carried out.

Although a theory of demographic imbalance proves inadequate for our purposes, so also does an approach that isolates for consideration only discrete elements of the local environment. To focus on single variables—be they tenancy, cropping, or years of Protestant missionary effort—and attempt to correlate these with levels of insurgency is to deny the ecological method.[7] As Clifford Geertz has explained, the ecological mode of analysis "is of a sort which trains attention on the pervasive properties of systems *qua* systems . . . rather than on the point-to-point relationships between paired variables."[8] The challenge to the ecologist is to decipher a set of underlying dynamic interactions among natural conditions, social formations, and human behavior.

In emphasizing the mediation of social structure, we have dispensed with any notion of a uniform peasant mentality capable of explaining rural rebellion. Some peasants are likely to operate by a calculus of risk minimization, but others will move more boldly to enhance their own positions. The variation is attributable in part to natural environment, in part to socioeconomic position, and in part of course to personality differences. Under conditions of endemic uncertainty, we would expect the relatively well-off to move defensively, concerned above all to retain their precarious advantage. By contrast, the destitute, having little to defend, may be persuaded to undertake a desperate gamble at "profit maximization." Yet even when a residual factor of personality is added to this equation, a difficulty remains. For peasants—like most political actors—decide upon a course of behavior not as isolated individuals, but as members of preexisting socioeconomic groups.*

Attention to rural social structure forms a major theme in recent theories of agrarian revolution. Arguments have revolved around which rural classes are most likely to revolt. Some theorists, emphasizing objective economic interest, identify the tenant or poor peasant as most prone to engage in revolution.[9] Others, focusing on power as well as interest, see the "middle" or "free" peasant as having the greatest scope for protest.[10] Still others point to combinations of rural class relations as most liable to generate certain varieties of agrarian revolt.[11]

Theories based on class structure are a salutary antidote to previous speculation about a generalized peasant mentality, presumed to hold true for all sectors of the peasantry. Groups of peasants should indeed be expected to differ in their propensity for rebellion, depending upon their position in the social structure. This book is also grounded in an appreciation of the importance of class differences. The very notions of predation and protection make sense only in a context where material resources are unequally distributed. It is in this situation that

*For this reason I am a little uneasy with Popkin's *Rational Peasant*. Although Popkin is correct in beginning his analysis with a focus on individual decision-making, one must also recognize that social groups, once constituted, exert a powerful influence of their own. Kinship, for example, may have an irresistible pull even in cases where group benefits contradict the particular interests of individual kinsmen.

people without means for creating wealth are prompted to seize goods from the relatively affluent, whereas those with material wherewithal devise ways of protecting their advantage. As we have discovered in the case of Huai-pei, an explosive natural environment could render such resource competition a veritable way of life for rural inhabitants. When disasters removed the possibility of gaining a living by productive means, social conflict was a logical response. However, we have also seen that such conflict, though rooted in class distinctions, was frequently organized along lines that transcended strict class boundaries. A predatory band often was as much a group of kinsmen as it was a poor peasant outfit. Sometimes class and clan were mutually reinforcing identities, but in cases where they conflicted it was not uncommon for blood to constitute the primary basis of organization. By the same token, protective groups were typically established along settlement lines. Ecologically more secure villages might find it in the interest of all inhabitants to mount a defense against the threat of aggression by less well-endowed neighbors. And even where such cooperation seemed to contradict the objective interests of poorer residents, obedience to the will of a powerful overlord could exert an irresistible pull toward participation. Kinship and community had developed into effective vehicles for meeting the challenges of survival in a hostile environment. As such, they were often the media through which predatory and protective activities were conducted. Although the roots of agrarian struggle were planted deeply in the soil of inequality, the class content of that inequality could be obscured by other cross-cutting allegiances.

Just as we have found it difficult to identify any single class or combination of classes as exceptionally volatile, so we have offered few clues on the timing of a particular uprising. Individual rebellions were sparked by peculiar concatenations of natural disaster, government ineptitude, local leadership, and outside allies. The elements of both blind accident and human will inherent in such a combination fit uneasily into a theory that stresses constancy and replication. Nevertheless, the aim here has not been to devise a neat formula for predicting an outbreak of peasant rebellion, but to plumb the deeper causes of repeated uprisings. For that purpose, an ecological perspective serves well. It allows us to see that although the occurrence of a rebellion reflected certain idiosyncrasies, the preconditions for such collective action can be located in more enduring features. Furthermore, the predatory-protective dichotomy suggests a basis for systematic variation among particular rebellions. As part of an ongoing competitive process, each strategy, we may hypothesize, tended to be stronger in certain geographical areas, to be expressed through different organizations, to articulate distinct goals, to suffer different limitations, and the like. Naturally the interesting question is not the taxonomical one, but the matter of links between structures and action. In the case of Huai-pei, I have proposed that these tended to form regularities which had evolved as adaptive strategies tailored to the local environment. By identifying certain basic constancies, one constructs a more solid frame upon which to assess the role of changing historical circumstances.

Theorists of peasant revolution have emphasized the coming of the capitalist market as a foreign threat that stimulated defensive peasant reaction, but it is important to remember that outside threats were nothing new to many rural inhabitants. In certain areas, unwelcome intrusion in the form of armies, natural disasters, or government demands had long worked to upset any inward-oriented equilibrium of village life. Indeed, the very definition of peasants as members of a state society should alert us to the reality that well before the advent of capitalism, peasants were subject to the penetration of outside forces. And because such threats were a familiar, if intermittent, presence in the countryside, their appearance served less to undermine traditional rural institutions than to activate them. Peasants responded to crises, not as atomized individuals set suddenly adrift from the anchor of ancient securities, but rather as participants in organized survival strategies that antedated and outlasted any particular crisis.

Still, although the modes of local response remained essentially stable, the political implications of such activities changed with evolving historical circumstances. In our study of Huai-pei, we have found during the mid-nineteenth century that representatives of the predatory strategy were "rebels," whereas in the context of Republican China those of a protective persuasion assumed the antigovernment role. The impact of the state and of other outside allies and enemies proved crucial in deciding whether one or another strategy would turn to open revolt.

As ways of dealing with local competitors in a situation of scarcity, the predatory and protective strategies in and of themselves implied neither allegiance nor hostility to central authority. If one approaches Chinese society from the perspective of the elite, there is a tendency to categorize rural organizations as variously "orthodox" or "heterodox," depending upon their acceptance or rejection of established legitimacy. Looked at from the peasant side, however, such a distinction is less helpful. Most villagers joined bandit gangs or defense forces for the eminently practical aim of seizing or securing a livelihood. Although both strategies had wider political potential, there was nothing inherently rebellious about either.

Conventional scholarship on Chinese peasant rebellions, to the extent it has gone beyond discrete case studies to attempt some broader generalizations, has typically centered upon the secret society as the reputed vehicle of antigovernment activity by the oppressed. As Maurice Freedman has summarized the burden of scholarly opinion, "the secret societies were essentially movements which, while they may have found some of their leaders among members of officialdom and the gentry, expressed an opposition to the state characteristic of the poor and the peasantry."[12] The un-Confucian precepts of the secret society, we are told, imbued its struggling members with a revolutionary antagonism to government authority.[13]

This study, though not denying the special importance of secret societies, has portrayed them as one of many organizations through which villagers mounted collective solutions to mundane problems. The visionary—even millenarian—ideology of many secret societies did not necessarily place them on the side of the poor. To the contrary, in the case of both the Old Cows and the Red Spear Society, we have seen sects directed by members of the privileged rural elite, striving to defend their property against assault. Sectarian groups were important as both an organizational reservoir and a source of ideological inspiration, but the example of Huai-pei cautions against identifying them as the key to a general theory of Chinese peasant rebellion.

The focus here has been upon survival strategies that were, paradoxically, at once more materially based and yet less class-specific than the secret societies as portrayed in much of the literature. As methods of controlling resources in a restricted and inequitable economic order, predatory and protective competition evidenced the *logic* of class struggle, but often via a social composition forged along communal rather than class lines. Both strategies were rational ways of meeting natural and social scarcity, and both offered genuine material benefits to participants. But neither, in even its most rebellious manifestation, undertook—or so much as articulated an interest in undertaking—a rearrangement of local society. Because survival strategies were firmly embedded in preexisting communal ties, rebellions born of such ancestry were unlikely to tamper with social givens. Neither bandit gangs led by village aspirants nor militia under the direction of an entrenched elite expressed the class interests of the majority of impoverished freeholding peasants in Huai-pei. True, some predators were social bandits who plundered the rich to succor the poor; and some protectors launched tax resistance movements that benefited all landowners, poor owner-cultivators included. Still, we do not detect in these undertakings an effort to alter the basic economic or political structures themselves. Redesigning the fabric of Huai-pei society would have to await the advent of revolutionaries sufficiently free from the fetters of local connections that they could offer a recipe for true renovation.

In stressing the discontinuity between rebellion and revolution, this book again parts company with those who would look to the secret society as a bridge spanning "traditional" and "modern" styles of peasant protest. The contention that the sectarian was a "primitive revolutionary" whose actions were "necessary for a transition to more 'developed' or 'advanced' revolutionary organizations"[14] seems, in the case of Huai-pei, at variance with the historical record. The examination of a century of traditional peasant unrest in Huai-pei has not uncovered any linear progression in the forms of peasant violence that prepared the way for revolution. Although we have focused on the Nien—an outgrowth of predatory behavior—in the late nineteenth century, and on the Red Spears—a secret-society extension of the protective strategy—in the early twentieth century, this does not establish an evolution in the pattern of collective action. Each movement arose out of a particular ecologically based strategy for survival. Contemporary with, and intimately linked to, each of the rebellions was the opposing strategy. Parallel to the predatory aggression of the Nien emerged a variety of community defense measures. Similarly, the Red Spears were a protective response elicited by the rampant banditry of warlord China. Thus the two modes persisted as alternative and interdependent strategies of survival and collective action.

The Chinese Communists, who did introduce a new style and content to peasant protest in Huai-pei, were initially outsiders bearing a method of liberation conceived and developed elsewhere. Although success depended upon adapting to meet the concrete needs of the local peasantry, the new approach showed little in common with earlier rebel traditions. The support of bandits and secret societies would be elicited as necessary, but the alliances proved fragile and often counterproductive. As ecologically induced actions, both modes, despite their endurance, were severely limited in political aims and capacity.

Because parochial styles of collective action had benefited the individuals and groups involved, they had been consciously transmitted from generation to generation. It has often been pointed out, however, that processes which develop as highly adaptive responses to certain environmental conditions may actually impede a population's ability to adjust to changed circumstances.[15] As Marshall Sahlins once wrote, "To adapt then is not to do perfectly from some objective standpoint, or even necessarily to improve performance: it is to do as well as possible under the circumstances, which may not turn out very well at all."[16] Indeed, when Communist cadres moved in to alter the societal arrangements, "primitive rebels" proved resistant to the changed conditions. Just as Eric Hobsbawm has pointed out with respect to bandits and secret societies in other settings, parochial limitations made it "almost impossible for them to adapt to or be absorbed by modern social movements."[17]

Well-established mechanisms for coping with an insecure environment may dilute a population's initial hospitality to a revolutionary approach.[18] In Huai-pei, commonly characterized as one of the most "rebellious" areas of China, closer examination has ruled out any simple positive relationship between a history of rural insurrection and the success of modern revolution. This is not to contend that there was no connection between the Chinese legacy of peasant rebellion and the rise of communism.* Most of the early revolutionaries came, after all, from South China and were quite likely influenced in varying ways and degrees by the experience of their forebears. The point, of course, is that there was no single legacy of traditional Chinese rebellion, but many such legacies, each adapted to the particular ecological exigencies under which it evolved and each differing perhaps in its suitability to the service of modern revolution.

A concern with local traditions of rural unrest promises new insight, not only into the course of the revolutionary struggle, but also into the character of these same local areas even after

---

*Clearly, the drain of national resources diverted to the suppression of the mid-nineteenth-century uprisings was of great importance in undermining the economic foundations of the ancien régime, just as the localization of power which followed these rebellions deprived the state of much of its political initiative. Furthermore, the record of Chinese rural rebellion undoubtedly inspired Communist revolutionaries in their determination to mobilize the peasantry.

the consolidation of revolutionary power. In Huai-pei, despite painstaking efforts to dilute traditional rural conflict in favor of cooperation under party leadership, there is evidence that age-old forms of peasant violence were not easily supplanted. A major test of the new regime's hold came in the summer of 1950, nine months after the establishment of the People's Republic, when torrential rains drenched the Huai-pei plain. Some forty-three million *mou* were inundated, 60 percent of northern Anhwei's fields rendered unusable, and 40 percent of its population turned into disaster victims.[19] To coordinate a relief effort, the party called upon peasants in the area to turn over any surplus grain to government storehouses. In northern Anhwei's Meng-ch'eng County, people known to be harboring extra supplies who proved unwilling to comply with the directive were imprisoned in a district jail south of the county seat. The incident incited a quick reaction. Several hundred members of the underground Red Spear Society responded by burning down the district offices and assassinating the district chief. With the lower ranks of the local militia also largely composed of rebel sympathizers, by mid-July the county had fallen under Red Spear rule. A government security force dispatched from Fu-yang County to suppress the revolt was ambushed by more than a thousand Red Spears camouflaged behind the dense sorghum growing along the highway. After this setback, a larger government force was mustered. Meng-ch'eng was retaken after a month's rebellion, and contingents of Red Spear reinforcements advancing from southern Shantung and eastern Honan were dispersed. Most of the local Meng-ch'eng Red Spears attempted unsuccessfully to defy government firepower; their leader, Li Pao-kuo, is said to have committed suicide with his own spear.[20]

Once again the combination of natural disaster and government demands had prompted a protective response from people reluctant to part with their personal margins of security. Perhaps it was concern about this continued pattern that helped convince Chairman Mao Tse-tung on October 14, 1950, to issue his famous decree to harness the Huai River. Within eight months, three million peasants had been mobilized to shift 185 million cubic meters of earth, two and a half times the amount moved in building the Suez Canal. Dikes were strengthened, reservoirs and sluices built, rivers dredged, and ponds, pump wells, and canals constructed. Although the monumental engineering project had a clear economic purpose, it was also intended to revolutionize the attitudes of the local peasantry. As Wang Feng-wu, commissioner of northern Anhwei's Sui County, expressed the hope of the project:

You can see a peasant's outlook changing from day to day. . . . He comes to the river work at first to earn some relief grain to feed himself and send some back to his family. At most he has accepted the idea that he is working to stop floods on his own land or land that will be his after land reform. He expects to mark out a piece of ground, dig it out, and carry it away as an individual, measuring to the last cubic centimeter how much he has cut. Instead of that, he finds it is more convenient to work as a team. . . . Step by step, by his own experiences on the river site, he begins to think of the village instead of his farm, the district instead of his village, the county and region, and eventually he grasps the conception of China. . . . So you see, we are not only changing nature, but we are changing the outlook of our peasants at the same time.[21]

The new regime had come to appreciate that ecological transformation would be required in order to replace centuries-old forms of competition with new patterns of cooperation. To what extent the Huai River project actually succeeded in accomplishing this ambitious aim remains to be studied. Without question, however, local environmental realities had continued to impose constraints on rural activity in Huai-pei even after the political victory of the revolution.

For one local area, then, an ecological approach has sensitized us to the persistence of traditional behavior and its implications for the revolutionary and postrevolutionary scenes. Even granting its utility in this particular case study, however, we will want to ask whether the general approach is of wider comparative application. Can a similar perspective illuminate patterns for regions other than Huai-pei?

Looking at China as a whole, one is struck by distinct variations in natural setting, cropping patterns, social structure, and rebel traditions. The most apparent distinction is that between North and South, with the Huai River forming a demarcation between the two. According to a stimulating article by Yamamoto Hideo, the two areas constituted quite separate ecosystems. From late Ming times, one finds in the North an insecure natural environment, dryland wheat farming, low tenancy, and large-scale peasant wars arising from banditry and tax resistance. The South, by contrast, was the home of more intensive wet rice cultivation, pronounced tenancy, and relatively small-scale rent resistance struggles. Although Chinese peasant movements have often been characterized as "southern" or "northern," distinguished by Triad or White Lotus secret-society links, Yamamoto favors the terms *progressive* and *backward*. The "backward" uprisings of North China, he explains, were based on dry grain cultivation which yielded low agricultural output. The "progressive" South China movements grew out of rice paddy culture which enjoyed a higher productivity thanks to its absorption of large inputs of labor. The extensive dry-cropping of the North had generated a preponderance of freeholders and agricultural laborers, while the intensive wet rice cultivation of the South had given rise to tenancy as the norm. The two landholding systems, in turn, fostered distinct types of peasant uprisings. Whereas northern rebellions were usually directed against the tax-levying state, in the South rebellions tended to pit tenants against landlords in a class struggle to redefine the terms of rent. Yamamoto suggests that these two ecologically differentiated varieties of rural rebellion, which persisted from late Ming through the early twentieth century, posed distinct sorts of problems and possibilities for the Chinese Communists.[22]

While Yamamoto offers an insightful overview of China as

comprising two broad regional systems, a more refined systems approach has recently been proposed by G. William Skinner. For Skinner, the Chinese empire consisted of nine "macroregions," each with an inner core where resources of all kinds were concentrated and an outer periphery marked by the dilution of resources. Core areas were generally situated along river valley lowlands, favored by higher agricultural productivity and better transportation. Peripheral areas (with the notable exception of Huai-pei, rendered peripheral by its unstable natural environment) typically followed the lines of mountain ranges. The peripheries constituted relatively depressed economic units—low in agricultural output, commercialization, and population density.[23]

It is tempting, based on our study of Huai-pei, to suggest that peripheral zones may have been especially prone to enduring traditions of rural unrest. Defined by inhospitable ecological circumstances, peripheral areas could well have set the stage for violent forms of peasant adaptation. Indeed, there is scattered evidence to support such a hypothesis. The northern Shensi border area—noted, like Huai-pei, for its harsh and variable natural setting—was also a peripheral zone that produced generations of peasant rebels.[24] The hills of Kiangsi constituted still another peripheral area in which rural insurgents had thrived for centuries.[25] Although the general form of these struggles seems to have varied in accordance with the cropping systems and landholding patterns described by Yamamoto, their location seems associated with Skinner's peripheral zones.

In other parts of the world as well, there is some indication that ecologically unstable areas were especially likely to engender rural protest.[26] In Vietnam and Thailand, those regions where nature subjects peasants to the greatest fluctuations in yield have long been known as centers of resistance and rebellion.[27] In Brazil, the freeholding peasantry on insecure marginal lands proved particularly likely to join rebellions, especially when prompted by natural disaster.[28] The Mafia and bandit gangs of Sicily operated in an environment where the threat of catastrophe was ever present.[29] In the Middle East, traditions of raiding quite similar to those of Huai-pei predators have been explained as adaptations to extreme fluctuations in natural conditions.[30]

Again, we must stress that the relationship between environment and peasant action was by no means direct or inevitable. The challenge to the scholar is to supply the contingent connecting links, to discover the social mechanisms through which collective violence emerged as an adaptive solution. This book has endeavored to perform that task for but one local area; let us hope that others will be persuaded to take up the challenge for additional regions.

Reference Matter

Appendix A
Confession of Chang Lo-hsing
(*From Ma Jung-heng and Liu Shou-i*, 1962, p. 4)

I am 53 years of age, from Old Chang Village, east of Po County and north of Chih-ho-chi, about 100 *li* from [Meng-]ch'eng. My family includes a brother, Chang Min-hsing, a wife surnamed Ma, a son, and an adopted son.

I farmed the land to make a living, but have also engaged in salt smuggling. In 1851–1852, we fought with the Old Cows in Honan's Yung-ch'eng and Shang-ch'iu.

In 1853, the Taipings attacked the Po area. After the city fell, bandits arose all around. Only then did I, together with Kung-hsia-tzu, Wang Kuan-san, Su T'ien-fu, and Han Lang-tzu, establish banners and take to plunder to make a living. I set up the yellow banner and called myself "Everlasting King of the Han."

In 1855, Magistrate Lu of Ying Prefecture led a local militia to Miao-erh-chi to attack us. Not long after, he retreated. Our numbers increased and we gathered in Honan to attack Ma-mu-chi in Shang-ch'iu. We returned and surrounded Po for thirteen days. But due to the strong defense of the government forces, we were unable to break through. We received word that troops from Honan were attacking our old home near Chih-ho-chi, so we started for home but before we got there the troops had already burned down our village.

In 1857, I led an attack on Huai-yüan, which we held for several months.

In 1858, because provisions were exhausted, we went to Ting-yüan to join the Long Hairs from Kwangsi. They subsequently honored me with the title of "Accomplishing Heavenly Righteousness" and gave me an official seal. I lived with them for several years. But because their treatment was not good, I returned to my old village.

In December 1861, Ma Yung-ho, a subordinate of the Taiping "Brave King" Four-eyed dog [Ch'en Yü-ch'eng] requested us to help him blockade the city of Ying. I went with Chiang T'ai-lu. In March 1862 the government troops arrived and the blockade was broken. We returned to the Po area.

After repeated losses to the government forces, we fled south. Again we were routed by the Ch'ing forces and our soldiers scattered. We fled northeastward. When we reached Hsi-yang-chi in Meng-ch'eng I was captured and turned over to the authorities.

In these past few years I have plundered too many places to remember all of them clearly. My wife has been chased off by government troops and I do not know where she is. My son and adopted son have both been captured together with me. My brother, Chang Min-hsing, leading several thousand men, has taken off for the Southwest and I do not know his whereabouts. As for Kung, Su, Wang, and Han, they have all been killed by the government troops. What I report is the truth.

Appendix B
Red Spear Code

(From Suemitsu Takayoshi, 1932, pp. 124–29)

1. The goal of this society is to use military force to effect popular self-rule and self-defense in order that everyone may attain a peaceful existence.
2. Members of this society must observe the following rules:
   a. Respect parents and elders
   b. Love their country and native village
   c. Be trustworthy
   d. Suffer hardship together
   e. Obey laws and have a sense of civic responsibility
   f. Refrain from acting recklessly.
3. To eliminate any obstacles to self-rule and self-defense, the society must carry out the following duties:
   a. Suppress bandits
   b. Eliminate reckless soldiers
   c. Resist unfair taxes, surcharges, and corvée labor
   d. Punish all bad officials and staff, bandits, and lawless persons.
4. All Chinese above eighteen years of age with a certain amount of property and a regular occupation, introduced by two or more members of the society, who swear to the initiation oath and pay an initiation fee of one yüan may be admitted.
5. Members of this society must observe the following military system:
   a. Five members compose a *wu*, with its leader known as *wu-chang*
   b. Five *wu* compose a *tui*, whose 25 members have a leader known as *tui-chang*
   c. Five *tui* compose a *she*, whose 125 members have a leader known as *she-chang*
   d. Five *she* compose a *hsiang*, whose 625 members have a leader known as *hsiang-chang*
   e. Five *hsiang* compose a *t'ing*, whose 3,125 members have a leader known as *t'ing-chang*
   f. Five *t'ing* compose a *chün*, whose 15,625 members have a leader known as *chün-chang*
   g. Five *chün* compose a *lu*, whose 78,125 members have a leader known as *lu-chang*
   h. Five *lu* compose a *chen*, whose 390,625 members have a leader known as *chen-chang*

    i. Five *chen* compose a *tu*, whose 1,953,125 members have a leader known as *tu-chang*

    j. Five *tu* compose a *fang*, whose 9,765,625 members have a leader known as *fang-chang*

    k. Five *fang* compose a *t'ung*, whose 48,828,125 members have a leader known as *t'ung-chang*. The *t'ung-chang* is chosen from the five *fang-chang* to serve concurrently in this higher post. The *fang-chang* is chosen from among the five *tu-chang* and so on down the line.

6. Members must be obedient to their superiors.

7. All rewards and punishments in this society are administered according to martial law.

8. Members of this society, in addition to burning incense, swallowing charms, and reciting incantations, must undergo military and political training.

9. In times of trouble, members will assemble and serve as soldiers. In times of quiet, they will disperse and return to farming. They must be settled in regular employment and cannot be used by ambitious persons.

10. Members shall organize units to carry out local self-rule in accord with previously established or new regulations.

11. All other societies (e.g., Yellow Spears, Tasseled Spears, etc.) which share our goals of self-defense and self-rule shall be treated as friends.

12. All friendly societies must organize a liaison office in an appropriate place to unite administrative work and improve friendly relations to permit genuine cooperation.

13. In an emergency, members must assemble at appointed places and follow their superior's instructions.

14. In the event of a foreign invasion, this society and its friends will plan jointly to protect the country and resist the foreigners.

15. Funds for the society come from contributions of members, the amount varying according to the size of their property. Someone who donates a lump sum of ten yüan or more is made an honorary chairman of the society.

16. Nonmembers who donate ten yüan or more can be recommended as honorary patrons.

17. Any member who violates a society rule shall be made by his leader to stand trial.

18. Judgment of the offender may be by martial or civil law.

19. Other societies which have the same regulations as these are our friends in times of adversity.

20. These rules take effect from the day of their public proclamation; if there are inappropriate parts, they may be revised as necessary.

Appendix C
North China Protective Societies
Contemporary with the Red Spears

Name(s)	Location	Source(s)
Black Flags (hei-ch'i-hui)	S. Shantung	Shina no dōran, 1930, p. 118.
Green Flags (lü-ch'i-hui)	S. Shantung	Ibid.
Limitless Way (wu-chi-tao)	S. Shantung	Ibid., p. 119; Nagano Akira, 1931, p. 257.
Yellow Gates (huang-men)	Tsinan, Shantung	Nagano Akira, 1931, p. 254.
Red Gates (hung-men)	Tsinan, Shantung	Ibid.
Black Rifles (hei-ch'iang-hui)	Tsinan, Shantung	NCS, May 12, 1926, p. 5.
Way of the Sages (sheng-hsien-tao)/ Bitches (mu-kou-hui)	Shantung	Nagano Akira, 1931, p. 257.
Yellow Flags (huang-ch'i-hui)	W. and s.w. Shantung	Shina no dōran, 1930, p. 118.
Green Spears (lü-ch'-iang-hui)	Shantung; Honan	Chang Chen-chih, 1929, p. 134; Hsiang Yün-lung, 1927, p. 36.
Red Sands (hung-sha-hui)	Shantung; Honan	Shina no dōran, 1930, p. 119.
Feather Baskets (mao-lan-hui)/	Shantung; Feng-ch'iu & Yang-wu,	Hsiang Yün-lung, 1927, p. 37;

Name(s)	Location	Source(s)
Flower Baskets (hua-lan-hui)	Honan	Nagano Akira, 1931, p. 256; Shina no dōran, 1930, p. 119; Tanaka Tadao, 1930, p. 251; Wu Ping-jo, 1927, p. 54.
White Spears (pai-ch'iang-hui)	Shantung; An-yang, Honan	Chang Chen-chih, 1929, p. 134; Chen Hsin, 1927, p. 1; Hsiang Yün-lung, 1927, p. 36; Nagano Akira, 1931, p. 255.
Yellow Sands (huang-sha-hui)/ Yellow Way (huang-tao-hui)	An-yang, Honan	Nagano Akira, 1931, p. 256; 1933, pp. 237–38.
Great Immortals (ta-hsien-hui)	An-yang, Honan	Nagano Akira, 1931, p. 254.
Clear Way (ch'ing-tao-hui)	Pi-yang, Honan	Hsiang Yün-lung, 1927, p. 37.
Heavenly Spirits (t'ien-shen-hui)	K'ai-hsien, Honan	Chang Chen-chih, 1929, p. 149; Nagano Akira, 1931, p. 255.
Black Spears (hei-ch'iang-hui)	Yang-wu, Honan	Chang Chen-chih, 1929, pp. 146–47; Chen Hsin, 1927, p. 1; Nagano Akira, 1931, p. 255; Shina no dōran, 1930, p. 117; Tanaka Tadao, 1930, pp. 249–50.
Long Hairs (ch'ang-fa-hui)	Yao-shan, Honan	Hsiang Yün-lung, 1927, p. 36; Shina no dōran, 1930, p. 119.

Name(s)	Location	Source(s)
Fans (shan-tzu-hui)	Yung-ch'eng & Lu-i, Honan	Chang Chen-chih, 1929, p. 149; Nagano Akira, 1931, p. 258.
Nine Immortals (chiu-hsien-hui)	Ch'i-hsien, Honan	Hsiang Yün-lung, 1927, p. 37.
Five Dragons (wu-lung-hui)	Wu-an, Honan	Nagano Akira, 1931, p. 256.
Pinchers (nieh-tzu-hui)	Ch'en-ch'iao, Honan	Hsiang Yün-lung, 1927, p. 37.
Mourning Clothes (hsiao-i-hui, ma-i-hui)/White Heads (pai-t'ou-hui)	Honan; Ta-ming, Hopei	Hsiang Yün-lung, 1927, p. 37; Nagano Akira, 1931, p. 256; Tanaka Tadao, 1930, p. 254; Wu Ping-jo, 1927, p. 54.
Emperors (t'ien-huang-hui)	Yung-ning, Hopei	Hsiang Yün-lung, 1927, p. 36; Nagano Akira, 1931, p. 255.
True Military Way (chen-wu-tao)/ Loyal Filial Corps (chung-hsiao-t'uan)	Shun-teh, Hopei	Nagano Akira, 1931, p. 256.
Heavenly Gates (t'ien-men-hui)	Hopei	Chang Chen-chih, 1929, p. 135; Hsiang Yün-lung, 1927, p. 36; Nagano Akira, 1931, p. 255; Shan-yü, 1927, pp. 2018–19; Tanaka Tadao, 1930, p. 215; Tzu-chen, 1927, pp. 2163–64.

Name(s)	Location	Source(s)
White Tassels (pai-ying-hui)	Hsüchou, Kiangsu	Nagano Akira, 1930, p. 233.
Red Tassels (hung-ying-hui)	Hsüchou, Kiangsu	Ibid.
Small Swords (hsiao-tao-hui)	N. Kiangsu	J. L. Buck, 1927; Chang Chen-chih, 1929, p. 192; Nagano Akira, 1931, p. 274; Wu Shou-p'eng, 1930, p. 67.
Big Swords (ta-tao-hui)	S. Kiangsu	J. L. Buck, 1927; Chang Chen-chih, 1929, p. 166; Nagano Akira, 1931, pp. 274–75; Suemitsu Takayoshi, 1932, pp. 149–74.
Miao-tao-hui	Shao-lin Temple	Chang Chen-chih, 1929, p. 135.
Steel Forks (kang-ch'a-hui)	?	Nagano Akira, 1931, p. 256.
Moon Brightnesses (yüeh-ming-hui)	?	Hsiang Yün-lung, 1927, p. 37.
Blue Tassels (lan-ying-hui)	?	Nagano Akira, 1931, p. 256.
Yellow Spears (huang-ch'iang-hui)	?	Chang Chen-chih, 1929, p. 134; Chen Hsin, 1927, p. 1; Hsiang Yün-lung, 1927, p. 36; Wu Ping-jo, 1927, p. 54.
Yellow Silks (huang-ling-hui)	?	Chang Chen-chih, 1929, p. 149.

Name(s)	Location	Source(s)
Brothers (hsiung-ti-hui)	?	Chang Chen-chih, 1929, p. 149; Wu Ping-jo, 1927, p. 54.
Hummers (heng-ha-hui)	?	Nagano Akira, 1931, p. 256.
Sword Daggers (t'o-tao-hui)	?	Ibid.
K'ung-ming-hui	?	Hsiang Yün-lung, 1927, p. 37.
Descendants of 100 Spirits (sun-pai-ling-hui)	?	Nagano Akira, 1931, p. 256.

Notes

Chapter 1

1. Wolf, 1966, p. 17.
2. See, for example, Chiang Siang-tseh, 1954; Geoffrey, 1927; Hanwell, 1939; Teng Ssu-yü, 1961.
3. Wolf, 1966, p. 2.
4. Moore, 1966, pp. 201–27; Skocpol, 1979, pp. 112–54; Wolf, 1969, pp. 118–19.
5. See especially Jerome Ch'en, *Mao and the Chinese Revolution* (New York, 1967); Friedman, 1974a and 1974b; Thaxton, 1975a and 1975b.

Chapter 2

1. Li Tse-kang, 1940, p. 41. At the close of the T'ang (618–907), rebellion and banditry were also concentrated in Huai-pei. See Robert M. Somers, "The End of the T'ang," in *Cambridge History of China*, ed. D. Twitchett and J. K. Fairbank (London, 1979), vol. 3, pp. 682–779.
2. Chi Ch'ao-t'ing, 1963, p. 34.
3. Ho Ping-ti, 1959, p. 171.
4. Hu Huan-yung, 1952, p. v; Mallory, 1926, p. 23; Shen Ping, 1960, p. 23. Actually, from 1194 to 1495 the Yellow River had two channels, only one of which joined up with the Huai. In 1495, the northern route dried up and all of the Yellow River flowed into the Huai (Hu Huan-yung, 1952, p. 3).
5. Kane, 1947, p. 168.
6. See the table on following page.
7. John Meskill, *Ch'oe Pu's Diary: A Record of Drifting Across the Sea* (Tucson, 1965), bk. 2, p. 101.
8. Parsons, 1970.
9. Ch'en Ch'iao-i, 1954, p. 27.
10. Fu Kuang-tse, "An-hui-sheng t'ien-fu yen-chiu" [A study of the land tax of Anhwei Province], in *Min-kuo erh-shih nien-tai chung-kuo ta-lu t'u-ti wen-t'i tzu-liao* (Taipei, 1935; rpt. ed., 1977), p. 8211.
11. Shen Ping, 1960, p. 14; Silbert, 1915, p. 117.
12. Chang Yung-ch'uan, "Pei Huai-min" [Pitiful Huai people], in *Ch'ing-shih-tuo* (Peking, 1960), vol. 2, p. 472.
13. Mallory, 1926, p. 49.
14. *Huai-ho hsin-p'ien* [Huai River] rev. ed., Peking, 1975), p. 74.
15. Kuo Han-ming and Hung Jui-chien, 1936, p. 1.

Table for Note 6.   Natural Catastrophes in the Huai River Valley

Time period	No. of floods	No. of droughts	Time period	No. of floods	No. of droughts
256–101 B.C.	11	16	900–999	54	68
100 B.C.–1 A.D.	13	15	1000–1099	46	61
1–99	15	25	1100–1199	29	48
100–199	26	30	1200–1299	35	43
200–299	26	19	1300–1399	73	50
300–399	24	36	1400–1499	74	56
400–499	22	33	1500–1599	93	67
500–599	24	33	1600–1699	94	68
600–699	29	28	1700–1799	96	58
700–799	26	34	1800–1899	87	53
800–899	40	46	1900–1948	42	23

Source: Ch'en Ch'iao-i, 1952, p. 23.

16. Ho Ping-ti, 1976, p. 549.
17. Ch'en Ch'iao-i, 1952, p. 1; 1954, p. 26.
18. *Kuo-yang-hsien chih*, 1924, 8/12.
19. Kane, 1947, p. 22.
20. Tuan Yi-fu, 1970, p. 11.
21. Ibid., pp. 29–30.
22. Quoted in Silbert, 1915, p. 118.
23. T. H. Shen, 1951, pp. 24–28.
24. Hu Huan-yung, 1935, pp. 1–10.
25. Wu Shou-p'eng, 1930, p. 361.
26. J. L. Buck, 1964a, p. 65.
27. Ida Saburo, 1940, p. 193.
28. J. L. Buck, 1964a, p. 63.
29. Kōain, 1940, pp. 14–17.
30. *An-hui-sheng t'ung-chi*, 1934, p. 105; Hu Huan-yung, 1935, p. 62.
31. Kōain, 1940, p. 14.
32. Ida Saburo, 1940, p. 195.
33. Kōain, 1940, p. 12.
34. J. L. Buck, 1964b, pp. 314–15.
35. Kōain, 1940, pp. 14–17.
36. J. L. Buck, 1964a, pp. 224–25.
37. Ibid., p. 233.
38. *I-hsien fang-chih*, 1904, 6/3.
39. *T'ung-shan-hsien chih*, 1926, 4/32–33.
40. Wu Shou-p'eng, 1930, pp. 342–43.
41. *Nung-ts'un shih-k'uang pao-kao*, 1935.
42. J. L. Buck, 1964a, p. 57.
43. Ida Saburo, 1940, p. 202.

44. Kuo Han-ming, 1938–39, pp. 129–33.
45. *Chung-kuo nung-ts'un*, 1971, p. 56; "T'ung-shan nung-ts'un," 1931, p. 380.
46. *Nung-ts'un shih-k'uang pao-kao*, 1935.
47. Chang Chieh-hou, 1927, p. 73.
48. Hu Ch'ü-fei and Yen Hsin-nung, 1933; Powell, 1925, pp. 15–17.
49. Ibid.
50. *Chung-yang jih-pao*, May 7, 1928, p. 12.
51. Wu Shou-p'eng, 1930, p. 75.
52. *T'eng-hsien chih*, 1846, 3/2.
53. *Hsü-i-hsien chih kao*, 1873, 1/26.
54. Kōain, 1940, p. 7.
55. Wu Shou-p'eng, 1930, pp. 75–76.
56. *Po-hsien chih lüeh*, 1936, p. 15.
57. Kumagaya Yasushi, 1940, p. 28.
58. *Chi-ning-chou chih*, 1840, 3/3.
59. *Feng-t'ai-hsien chih*, 1882, 4/3–7; *Feng-yang-fu chih*, 1908, 12/4.
60. *Huai-an-fu chih*, 1884, 2/3–8.
61. Kuo Han-ming and Hung Jui-chien, 1936, p. 13; *Ssu-hsien chih lüeh*, 1936, p. 22.
62. Ch'en Han-seng, 1939; Myers, 1970, pp. 199–202.
63. *Sui-ning-hsien chih*, 1887, 3/8.
64. *Huai-an-fu chih*, 1884, 2/3–8.
65. *Nung-ts'un shih-k'uang pao-kao*, 1935.
66. *Sui-ning-hsien chih*, 1887, 3/8.
67. *Kuo-yang-hsien chih*, 1924, 8/12.
68. *Ssu-hsien chih lüeh*, 1936, p. 21.
69. *Hsü-i-hsien chih kao*, 1873, 1/26; *Huai-an-fu chih*, 1884, 2/3–8; *Tsou-hsien chih*, 1716, 3/1.
70. *Fu-yang-hsien chih*, 1829, 5/1; *Sui-ning-hsien chih*, 1887, 3/5–7.
71. Hu Ch'ü-fei and Yen Hsin-nung, 1933.
72. Kuo Han-ming, 1938–39, pp. 137, 143.
73. *Nung-ts'un shih-k'uang pao-kao*, 1935.
74. Kuo Han-ming, 1938–39, p. 137.
75. NC, vol. 1, pp. 314, 378; vol. 4, p. 28.
76. Bianco, 1973; Li Tso-chou, 1935.
77. "Shiyō no nōson," 1942, p. 115.
78. Chang Chieh-hou, 1927, p. 71.
79. Ibid., p. 116; Ida Saburo, 1940, p. 193; Kuo Han-ming and Hung Jui-chien, 1936, p. 12.
80. Chang Chieh-hou, 1927, p. 71; "Shiyō no nōson," 1942, p. 116.
81. Kuo Han-ming and Hung Jui-chien, 1936, pp. 12–13.
82. Ibid.; Chang Chieh-hou, 1927, p. 71; Ida Saburo, 1940, p. 193; "Shiyō no nōson," 1942, p. 116.
83. Chang Chieh-hou, 1927, p. 74; Ida Saburo, 1940, p. 193; "Shiyō no nōson," 1942, pp. 116–19.

84. *Nung-ts'un shih-k'uang pao-kao*, 1935; "Shiyō no nōson," 1942, p. 119.
85. Redfield, 1965.
86. Erasmus, 1968.
87. Foster, 1969.
88. Solomon, 1971, pp. 105–34.
89. Fanon, 1963.
90. Huizer, 1972.
91. *Lu-i-hsien chih*, 1896, 9/1–5.
92. *T'ung-shan-hsien chih*, 1926, 9/32–33.
93. *Feng-t'ai-hsien chih*, 1882, 4/3–7.
94. Rawski, 1972.
95. Jameson, 1912, p. 74.
96. *Chi-ning-chou chih*, 1840, 3/22–24; *Feng-t'ai-hsien chih*, 1882, 4/6–7; *Po-chou chih*, 1894, 2/28–29.
97. Wei Yüan, *Wei Yüan chi* [Collected work of Wei Yüan], vol. 1, p. 358. Quoted in Namiki Yorinaga, 1978, p. 56.
98. Vayda, 1968, pp. 88–89.

Chapter 3

1. Anthony Oberschall, *Social Conflict and Social Movements* (Englewood Cliffs, N.J., 1973); Charles Tilly, *From Mobilization to Revolution* (Reading, Mass., 1978).
2. Ho Ping-ti, 1959, pp. 58–59.
3. *Hsü-chou-fu chih*, 1874, 12/53–54, gives the figures shown in the table below. See Aird, 1968, pp. 266–67, for some of the methodological problems with sex ratio statistics for Ch'ing China.
4. *An-hui-sheng t'ung-chi nien-chien*, 1934, p. 68.
5. Chang Wei-ch'eng, 1943a, pp. 47–54; Wu Shou-p'eng, 1930, p. 61.
6. "T'ung-shan nung-ts'un," 1931, p. 387.
7. *Po-chou chih*, 1894, 2/29.

Table for Note 3. Sex Ratio Among the
Population of Hsüchou Prefecture, 1874

County	Males	Females	Males per 100 females
T'ung-shan	450,903	337,211	134
Hsiao	177,087	148,986	119
Tang-shan	170,560	170,277	100
Feng	337,536	246,992	137
P'ei	272,198	216,536	126
P'ei-chou	266,750	266,748	100
Su-ch'ien	659,330	439,554	150
Sui-ning	260,682	159,991	163

8. *Huai-an-fu chih*, 1884, 2/4.
9. NCH, October 4, 1856, p. 38.
10. KCT-TK 0008605–1, HF 001658.
11. *Feng-t'ai-hsien chih*, 1882, 4/6.
12. The following discussion is based on NC, vol. 1, pp. 13–30; *P'ei-hsien chih*, 1920, p. 16.
13. "Internal Chinese Migration," in *Agrarian China*, 1938, p. 256.
14. See Nagano Akira, 1931, 1938, for a discussion of Huai-pei's role in generating soldiers; Wu Shou-p'eng, 1930, p. 65.
15. NCH, March 5, 1927, p. 388.
16. Hsü Hung, 1972.
17. NCPC, p. 8.
18. For information on the career and policies of T'ao Chu, see Metzger, 1962.
19. NCPC, p. 6.
20. *Feng-yang-fu chih*, 1908, p. 4; *Meng-ch'eng-hsien chih*, 1915, p. 6; Mu Lien-fu, 1959, pp. 77–83.
21. *Chung-yang jih-pao*, August 30, 1928, p. 1.
22. Billingsley, 1974, pp. 118–20.
23. Ma Ch'ang-hua, 1959, pp. 22–23.
24. NCPC, p. 7.
25. Nagano Akira, 1931, p. 66; 1938, p. 199.
26. *Hsiao-hsien chih*, 1874, 4/5–6.
27. Yüan Chia-san, 1911, 5/31.
28. Examples appear in numerous articles in *Min-chien wen-hsüeh* [Folk literature] during the late 1950s and early 1960s. A general collection is contained in *Chung-kuo nung-min ch'i-i ti ku-shih* [Stories of Chinese peasant uprisings], 1952, Shanghai. Interviews with former Huai-pei residents in Taiwan reinforce the impression of a strong bandit tradition, perpetuated through oral story-telling.
29. Ho Hsi-ya, 1925, pp. 39–41, 65–76; NC, vol. 1, pp. 192–288; vol. 4, pp. 210–49; NCPC, pp. 6, 29.
30. NCPC, p. 29; WCT-TK 5/9/26.
31. Ho Hsi-ya, 1925, pp. 49–56; Tai Hsüan-chih, 1973, pp. 61–62.
32. Nagano Akira, 1931, p. 27.
33. Wang Tsung-yü, 1964, pp. 23–24.
34. *Shan-hsien chih*, 1936, p. 1.
35. Ho Hsi-ya, 1925, pp. 83–94; Nagano Akira, 1938, pp. 226–27; *Shina no dōran*, 1930, pp. 27–56.
36. Hobsbawm, 1965, pp. 13–29; 1969, pp. 34–49.
37. Jo Mu, 1959, p. 52; *Kuo-yang-hsien chih*, 1924, 15/6; *Shih-hsüeh yüeh-k'an*, no. 2 (1960): 20; Wang Fan-t'ing, 1975, p. 15.
38. Nagano Akira, 1933, p. 269.
39. *Chung-yang jih-pao*, March 7, 1928, p. 3.
40. Ho Hsi-ya, 1925, pp. 34–35; Tai Hsüan-chih, 1973, pp. 61–62.
41. Ho Hsi-ya, 1925, pp. 34–38.

42. Friedman, 1974a, pp. 151–56; Wang Tsung-yü, 1964, pp. 20–21.
43. Ho Hsi-ya, 1925, p. 9.
44. Tai Hsüan-chih, 1973, p. 61.
45. *Tung-p'ing-hsien chih*, 1935, p. 5.
46. Nagano Akira, 1933, p. 270.
47. Ibid.
48. Nagano Akira, 1938, pp. 149–54.
49. NCPC, p. 28.
50. *Feng-t'ai-hsien chih*, 1882, 4/5.
51. KCT-HF 001949.
52. KCT-TK 009663.
53. KCT-TK 010929, 00838.
54. FL 1/1–3.
55. Bianco, 1976, p. 320.
56. KCT-HF 002504.
57. WCT-TK 29/8/24.
58. *Hsiang-ch'eng-hsien chih*, 1911, 5/47; *Lu-i-hsien chih*, 1896, 9/1; *Suining-hsien chih*, 1887, 3/6.
59. *Feng-t'ai-hsien chih*, 1882, 4/5.
60. Harry J. Lamley, "Hsieh-tou: The Pathology of Violence in Southeastern China," *Ch'ing-shih wen-t'i*, 3, no. 7 (1977): 1–39. Although feuds in Huai-pei were less elaborate, there was a certain amount of ritualistic behavior. For a description, see NC, vol. 1, p. 387.
61. *Feng-t'ai-hsien chih*, 1882, 4/6.
62. *Lu-i-hsien chih*, 1896, 9/3.
63. Gamble, 1963, pp. 69–70; Smith, 1970, pp. 121–22.
64. Mills, 1873.
65. Gamble, 1954, pp. 156–57; Smith, 1970, pp. 119–24; M. C. Yang, 1945, pp. 148–49.
66. Hatada Takashi, 1973, pp. 67, 68, 174–224, 225.
67. Ibid., pp. 64, 74–76; Myers, 1970, pp. 60, 100.
68. See Kuhn, 1970, pp. 10–36, for a discussion of this point.
69. KCT-HF 007580.
70. Yokoyama Suguru, 1964, pp. 44–45.
71. NC, vol. 2, p. 177.
72. Wang Yeh-chien, 1973, p. 114.
73. Kanbe Teruo, 1972, p. 91.
74. NC, vol. 2, pp. 174–91; vol. 4, pp. 415–44.
75. For details on the evolution and organization of Anhwei local defense during this period, see Ch'iu Kuo-chen, 1940. Ch'iu distinguishes three types of defense forces: the "protect-peace corps" (*pao-an t'uan-tui*), the guerrilla forces (*yu-chi pu-tui*), and the county self-defense corps (*hsien tzu-wei-tui*). Each had a distinct origin and purpose. The "protect-peace corps" was apparently the most effective in combating banditry. See Tsou Jen-meng, 1940, for an account of their success in bandit extermination during the Republican period.

76. *Wan-pao*, February 22, 1939, p. 3.
77. Hibino Takeo, 1953, pp. 141–55.
78. Kuo Han-ming, 1938–39, p. 156.
79. *Chung-mou-hsien chih*, 1935, 2/2–4.
80. *An-hui-sheng t'ung-chi nien-chien*, 1934, pp. 153–55; *T'ung-shan-hsien chih*, 1926, 10/1–20.
81. *Kuo-yang-hsien chih*, 1924, 2/19–24.
82. Ch'en Hung-chin, 1939, pp. 86–88. Another description of a freeholding type of *yü-chai* is found in Hsia Fei-jui, "I chung-yüan Hua-ch'eng-chai" [Memories of Hua-ch'eng Fort], *Chung-yüan wen-hsien*, 6, no. 9 (1974): 32–33. This western Honan fort included one thousand households with six hundred guns. Slightly affluent households all possessed their own guns, wealthy families had several guns, and poor families cooperated in buying weapons to share.
83. Wu Shou-p'eng, 1930, p. 71.
84. Ibid., p. 72.
85. Ibid., p. 73.

Chapter 4

1. Chang Wen-ch'ing, 1953; Chiang Siang-tseh, 1954; Chiang Ti, 1956a, 1956b; Teng Ssu-yü, 1961.
2. The point that the Nien are most fruitfully approached in relation to their local setting has been made in several fine Japanese studies: Namiki Yorinaga, 1978; Ono Shinji, 1961; Ōta Hideo, 1978; Sano Manabu, 1958, vol. 4; Shimizu Minoru, 1977. The research of an investigation team at the Anhwei Institute of Modern History also emphasizes the importance of the Huai-pei environment in giving rise to the Nien Rebellion (Hsiao Liu, 1959; Ma Ch'ang-hua, 1959). The aim here is to expand upon this ecological theme, suggesting that the connection to the environment can be analyzed in terms of adaptive behavior.
3. Chesneaux, 1971, p. 94; Chiang Siang-tseh, 1954, pp. 8–15; Chiang Ti, 1959, pp. 7–13; Kuhn, 1970, p. 179; Teng Ssu-yü, 1961, p. 37. Recently Western scholarship has been moving away from this interpretation. See Kuhn, 1978, pp. 310–16; K. C. Liu, 1978, pp. 456–75.
4. *Kuo-yang-hsien chih*, 1924, 15/6; NC, vol. 1, p. 1; WCT-TK 29/8/24, TK 25/11/27. Interviews with former residents of Huai-pei also confirmed this interpretation.
5. NC, vol. 3, pp. 470, 478, 481, 498.
6. NC, vol. 1, p. 309; vol. 2, p. 289; vol. 3, p. 114; vol. 4, p. 28. For the debate among Chinese historians over the correct title for the movement, see Lo Erh-kang, 1960; Ts'ao Mu-ch'ing, 1956; and Wu Han, 1961.
7. *Chin-hsiang-hsien chih*, 1862, 10/21. Both the Annals of Shantung Military Operations (NC, vol. 4) and the Annals of the Honan Army (NC, vol. 2, pp. 157–446) also refer to the Nien from Anhwei in this fashion. That the term *nien* was not a consistent reference to one tightly knit movement is borne out by an 1851 memorial that characterized

Taiping leaders Hung Hsiu-ch'üan and Feng Yün-shan as commanding groups of *"nien"* who worshiped Jesus! (YCT-HF 1/7/2.)
8. NC, vol. 1, p. 1. This account also incorrectly locates the Nien origins in Shantung.
9. NC, vol. 1, p. 309.
10. NCPC, pp. 6, 8.
11. NC, vol. 1, p. 309.
12. SCSH-CL 254.
13. NCPC, pp. 6–8.
14. CSLC, 37/38–39; SCSH-CC 101; *Ta-ch'ing lü-li*, 23.
15. CSL-TK 41.
16. NC, vol. 1, p. 315.
17. FL 1/14–16.
18. NCPC, pp. 29–30.
19. FL 320/5; NC, vol. 1, pp. 309–10.
20. Ma Ch'ang-hua, 1959, p. 23.
21. Hsiao Liu, 1959, p. 9.
22. For descriptions of Nien warfare, see Lo Erh-kang, 1939; and Teng Ssu-yü, 1961. Lo began his research during the summer of 1938 in hopes that a study of Nien mobile warfare might prove applicable in the War of Resistance against Japan (Lo Erh-kang, 1957, p. 1).
23. Hsiao Liu, 1959, p. 9.
24. Jo Mu, 1959, p. 52; *Kuo-yang-hsien chih*, 1924, 15/6. Field investigations conducted by historians in 1954 discovered a family tree carved onto one of the stones in the Chang family graveyard, two *li* southeast of the village. For further information on various family members, see Chu Hsieh, 1954.
25. Jo Mu, 1959, p. 53.
26. WCT-TK 27/11/16.
27. FL 3/2–4, 3/10–12.
28. FL 1/7/20; NC, vol. 3, p. 15; WCT-HF 2/6/17; WCT-TK 27/11/28.
29. *Kuo-yang-hsien chih*, 1924, 15/6.
30. Ma Ch'ang-hua, 1959, pp. 25–26.
31. *An-hui t'ung-chih*, 1877, 102/24.
32. *Nien-chün ku-shih-chi*, 1962, pp. 68–80, 196–207.
33. KCT-HF 000709.
34. Ibid.
35. KCT-TK 002316.
36. CSL-HF 53/12–13; CSL-TK 167/26–28; FL 2/4–5; KCT-HF 004731.
37. FL 7/8.
38. NC, vol. 1, pp. 325–26.
39. Ibid., p. 310.
40. KCT-TK 010608.
41. FL 1/21–22; 2/86; KCT-HF 001254.
42. FL 2/6–7; 6/19, 24–26; 6/27; NC, vol. 1, p. 311.
43. NC, vol. 1, p. 323.
44. KCT-HF 005339; WCT-HF 2/6/8.

45. KCT-HF 005104.
46. KCT-HF 005322.
47. A description of these mid-nineteenth-century disasters and their effect on peasant livelihood in Huai-pei is contained in Hsiao Liu, 1959, pp. 10–12.
48. YCT-HF 3/5/2.
49. KCT-HF 004050; NC, vol. 2, p. 2.
50. Ma Jung-heng and Liu Shou-i, 1962, p. 4.
51. WCT-TK 2/6/17; YCT-HF 1/11/1.
52. FL 5/9–10, 24.
53. FL 246/16; NC, vol. 4, p. 417; vol. 6, pp. 295–96; Wang Ting-an, 1889, 16/2.
54. NCPC, pp. 87, 104–05.
55. FL 4/9–11, 18–20; 8/17–18; KCT-HF 005990, 006452.
56. NC, vol. 5, p. 168.
57. NC, vol. 1, p. 5.
58. FL 9/32, 15/21, 77/27.
59. An-hui t'ung-chih, 1877, 105/23.
60. NC, vol. 3, p. 21.
61. NC, vol. 1, pp. 399–400.
62. Shan-tung chin-tai-shih, 1957, vol. 1, pp. 35–36.
63. NC, vol. 4, p. 395; Shan-tung chin-tai-shih, 1957, vol. 1, pp. 37–43.
64. Liu Pao-kuang, 1957, pp. 262–68.
65. FL 15/1, 53/23, 147/29–30. The figure of several thousand inhabitants per fort is corroborated by other sources. Yüan Chia-san (1911: 9/30) reported that in the southern part of Su County there were a dozen Nien forts with a total of more than 10,000 people. According to the confession of Nien blue-banner leader Lu Lien-k'o, the six forts under his control had included more than 13,000 people (FL 60/8). When Ch'ing general Sheng Pao pacified eight forts to the southwest of Meng-ch'eng, he found over 17,000 women, children, and aged and 6,400 adult men in residence (FL 59/19).
66. FL 3/5; NC, vol. 2, pp. 302, 303; Yüan Chia-san, 1911, 2/46.
67. There is some controversy over the exact title Chang Lo-hsing assumed at this time. According to the Annals of Honan Military Affairs (NC, vol. 2, pp. 289 ff.), he adopted the title of "Great Han King of the Manifest Mandate" (ta-han ming-ming-wang). In Chang's confession, however, he refers to himself as "Great Han Eternal King" (ta-han yung-wang), whereas in his proclamation he terms himself "Great Han Alliance Leader" (ta-han meng-chu). See Ma Jung-heng and Liu Shou-i, 1962. Most local gazetteers suggest that Chang was referred to simply as "alliance leader" (meng-chu).
68. Kuo-yang-hsien chih, 1924, 15/9.
69. Chiang Ti, 1959, pp. 241–42.
70. Chang Shan, 1959b, pp. 32–33.
71. NC, vol. 2, pp. 301–03. A slightly different version of the list has been reprinted in Chin-tai-shih tzu-liao, no. 30 (1960): 30–36.

72. Ma Ch'ang-hua, 1959, pp. 20–21.
73. NC, vol. 1, pp. 179–83, 299–305.
74. FL 14/6; NC, vol. 1, p. 13.
75. FL 69/24, 73/15; NC, vol. 1, p. 55; Yüan Chia-san, 1911, 8/48, 19/13.
76. Liu T'ang's narrative is taken from NC, vol. 1, pp. 348–55.
77. According to one source, a full 50 percent of all loot went to the banner chiefs (NC, vol. 1, p. 311).
78. *Li-tai min-ko i-pai-shou* [One hundred folk songs from ages past] (Shanghai, 1962), p. 95. "Old Lo" was a familiar reference to Chang Lo-hsing.
79. "Ch'ing-tai ch'i-pai ming-jen chuan," p. 1121; NC, vol. 1, p. 295. An informative secondary account of Li Chao-shou's career is presented in Watanabe Atsushi, 1967.
80. Li Hsiu-ch'eng, 1955, p. 75. Detailed descriptions of military cooperation between Nien and Taipings are found in Chang Shan, 1959a, 1959b; Chiang Ti, 1958, 1963; and Ch'ien Hung, 1950. As a reward for his participation, Chang Lo-hsing was granted four Taiping leadership titles between 1857 and 1862 (*T'ai-p'ing t'ien-kuo*, 1950, vol. 2, pp. 721, 746).
81. NC, vol. 1, p. 286.
82. FL 37/28, 39/1, 41/9.
83. For an exhaustive accounting of the location of the various Nien chieftains after the 1858 split, see Chang Shan, 1959a.
84. Ma Jung-heng and Liu Shou-i, 1962, p. 4.
85. Ibid.; Li Hsiu-ch'eng, 1955, p. 97. A similar statement is found in the Po gazetteer: "The Nien . . . attached themselves to the Long Hairs [Taipings], grew out their hair, received their titles and seals, went to their court with tribute, but would not take orders from them" (*Po-chou chih*, 1894, 8/22).
86. FL 48/16; NC, vol. 1, p. 313; vol. 4, pp. 36–37.
87. *Hsiang-ch'eng-hsien chih*, 1911, 13/15.
88. Martin, 1868.
89. Hobsbawm, 1965, p. 26.
90. Blok, 1972, p. 496.
91. Laffey, 1976, p. 81.
92. Chesneaux, 1972, p. 16.
93. Davis, 1977, p. 4.
94. Chiang Siang-tseh, 1954, p. 13.

Chapter 5

1. Lu Ching-ch'i, "I-ho-t'uan yün-tung tsai Shan-tung ti pao-fa chi ch'i tou-cheng" [The explosion and struggles of the Boxer movement in Shantung], in *I-ho-t'uan yün-tung liu-shih chou-nien lun-wen-chi* (Peking, 1961), p. 69.
Even before the Sino-Japanese War of 1894–95, taxes were onerous. A telling illustration is found in a December 28, 1874, article in the news-

paper *Shen-pao*, which printed an appeal by a certain Ch'en Chen-pang who was then actively leading tax resistance. As Ch'en explained, "I was once a member of the Nien. . . . However, when I saw that bandits were wantonly destroying the villages, I captured these bandits and exerted my energies on behalf of the government. Although I thought the government would reduce land taxes, contrary to my expectation, once the fighting ceased the officials actually increased the tax burden. How could the people suffer this hardship?" Quoted in Ninomiya Ichiro, "Kōen kōryō tōsō" [Tax resistance struggles], in *Kōza Chūgoku kindaishi*, ed. Nozawa Yutaka and Tanaka Masatoshi (Tokyo, 1978), vol. 2, p. 100.

2. The exact mix of militia and sectarian strains in the origins of the Boxers has been an issue of considerable scholarly controversy. Proponents of a militia emphasis include George Nye Steiger, *China and the Occident* (New Haven, 1927), and Tai Hsüan-chih, 1963.

Those stressing sectarian origins usually base much of their argument on the 1899 report of Lao Nai-hsüan, then magistrate in Chihli, "I-ho-t'uan chiao-men yüan-liu-k'ao" [A study of the sectarian origins of the Boxers], in *I-ho-t'uan* (Peking, 1951), vol. 4, pp. 433–39. Scholars who emphasize the sectarian side include Purcell, 1963, and Chester Tan, *The Boxer Catastrophe* (New York, 1971). See also Fan Wen-lan, *Chung-kuo chin-tai-shih* [Modern Chinese history] (Peking, 1962), vol. 1, pp. 399ff.; and *I-ho-t'uan yün-tung liu-shih chou-nien lun-wen-chi* [Essays commemorating the sixtieth anniversary of the Boxer movement] (Peking, 1961).

3. See *Ho-nan nung-min*, p. 4; "Initiation Ceremonies," 1934; NCS, May 6, 1926, p. 8; January 8, 1927, p. 7; and especially Chang Chen-chih, 1929, pp. 131–32. According to Chang, the earliest name of the Red Spears was the Benevolent Society (*jen-i-hui*), once active in eastern Honan and western Shantung. The sect is said to have gone underground during the Yüan Shih-k'ai period and to have resurfaced in 1917, when it developed into the Red Spears. Chang also tells of two legends current among Red Spear members about the founder of their society. According to one legend, the founder was a man by the name of Liu I who had served as a military leader in the Taiping Rebellion. When Liu realized that the Taipings were on the decline, he went to sacred Omei Mountain in Szechuan Province, where he became a monk, practiced breath control, and attained immortality. He was said to have taken eight disciples who popularized his magical arts as a means of resistance to banditry. Another legend identified the founder of the Red Spears as Chang Lao-tao, a descendant of the Taoist master Chang Tao-lu. Lao-tao was a monk reputed to have attained physical invulnerability.

The earliest dating of the Red Spears I have come across appears in a pamphlet by Chieh Ch'en-shih. This rather suspect account states that "Red Spears" was a name adopted as early as the Yüan and Ming dynasties when White Lotus groups, suffering under official persecution, adopted the Red Spear name as a cover-up. By early Ch'ing, there were alleged to have been many Red Spear adherents, and during the Chia-ch'ing reign the group was said to have proselytized publicly in Honan and Shantung. According to this account, the Boxers were simply one offshoot of the preexisting Red Spear Society.

A more credible account is found in Chen Hsin, 1927, pp. 1–3. Chen Hsin suggests that although the name Red Spears did not actually appear until around 1920, the group was probably related to the Golden Bell Armor (chin-chung-chao) and Iron Shirts (t'ieh-pu-shan), White Lotus sects active in Honan's Lo-yang area during the Ch'ing, and to the Hard Heads (ying-t'ou-erh), a sect that appeared in western Honan in 1917–18. All these groups claimed invulnerability to weapons. The same explanation appears in "Genzai shina," 1927, pp. 59–77; and in Tanaka Tadao, 1930.

An interesting variant is presented by Hsiang Yün-lung, 1927, p. 35, who argues that the Red Spears originated in *opposition* to the Golden Bell Armor sect which, during the late Ch'ing, had been using its claim of invulnerability to demand monetary contributions and carry out other coercive actions in the villages of Honan. To resist, peasants armed themselves with red-tasseled spears. Although at this time the resistance movement had no organization, subsequently the bandit ravages of the Republican period evoked the founding of a formal Red Spear Society as a means of village defense.

4. The common militia origins of the Boxers and Red Spears are discussed at length in Tai Hsüan-chih, 1963 and 1973.

5. The 1911 date is found in Pao Chih-ching, 1939, p. 59. The 1915–16 date is given in Chieh Ch'en-shih, p. 3; Ho-nan nung-min, 1927, p. 4; and Shina no dōran, 1930, p. 91. The 1920s dating is found in a number of sources, among them Hsiang Yün-lung, 1927, p. 35; and Satomi Hajime, 1927, p. 128.

6. On the ecological conditions see Junkin, 1912, pp. 75–81. For a summary of warlord battles during this period, see Ch'i Hsi-sheng, 1976. On banditry see Nagano Akira, 1931, pp. 64–66; 1938, pp. 197–99; Tai Hsüan-chih, 1973, p. 66.

7. NCH, March 26, 1927, p. 521; Tai Hsüan-chih, 1973, pp. 61–62. On Pai Lang's career see Friedman, 1974a, pp. 144–64.

8. See Myers, 1970, p. 262, on the growth of community activities.

9. See Hatada Takashi, 1973, p. 225, on the dissolution of single-lineage settlements in North China.

10. Bianco, 1972, p. 214.

11. Nagano Akira, 1930, p. 233.

12. The following discussion is taken from Nagano Akira, 1930, p. 239; 1931, pp. 251, 297–98; Shih-pao, September 6, 13, 15, 19, 1923; and "Shina ni okeru buryoku dantai" [Military units in China], Gaiji Keisatsuhō, no. 75 (1928): 35–38.

13. T'ung-shan-hsien chih, 10/1–30.

14. Chiang-su-sheng nung-yeh tiao-ch'a-lu, 1925, p. 3.

15. Webber, 1927.
16. Billingsley, 1974, p. 43.
17. Ibid., p. 103; Tai Hsüan-chih, 1973, pp. 206–08.
18. Billingsley, 1974, p. 245; Nagano Akira, 1930, p. 240. Certainly the long-standing animosity between Shensi and Honan must also have been a factor in the assault. See Sheridan, 1966, p. 207.
19. Jen-ching, 1924, pp. 551–53.
20. NCS, August 7, 1926, p. 4.
21. For more information on Yüeh Wei-chün's exactions from the peasantry, see Mitani Takashi, 1974, pp. 238–39; and Sheridan, 1966, pp. 161–62. Mitani suggests that Yüeh was actually sympathetic to the mass movement then developing in Honan, but that his lack of independent financial resources forced him to add bandits to his army and squeeze the peasants for funds.
22. Shen-pao, January 13, 1926; Shih-pao, January 13, 1926. Background on the sending of Red Spear emissaries from Hsin-yang to other trouble spots in Honan is provided in a novel by Hsiu Hu-sheng, Hung-ch'iang-hui ch'i-hsia-chuan [Strange chivalrous tales of the Red Spear Society] (Shanghai, 1929).
23. Hsiao Hsiang, 1926, p. 1545.
24. NC, vol. 5, p. 175.
25. Chi Fan, 1927, p. 14; Hsiao Hsiang, 1926, pp. 1545–46.
26. Hsiao Hsiang, 1926, p. 1546; NCS, September 12, 1926, p. 5.
27. Hsiang Yün-lung, 1927, pp. 35–36.
28. Hsiao Hsiang, 1926, p. 1546; Shih-pao, May 27, 1926.
29. Shih-pao, June 4, 10, 1926.
30. Chiang-su-sheng nung-min pao-kao, 1926, p. 2; Slawinski, 1972, p. 202.
31. NCH, December 31, 1926, p. 97.
32. Ch'en Han-seng et al., 1934, p. 332.
33. NCH, January 16, 1926, p. 97.
34. Mitani Takashi, 1974, p. 250.
35. Nagano Akira, 1938, pp. 227–28. For other examples of "Red Spear" bandits, see Geoffrey, 1927; STSP, December 20, 1927; Wang I-k'o, 1932, p. 71.
36. STSP, January 31, 1927, p. 2; July 22, 1927, p. 2.
37. Crossett, 1946, p. 55.
38. Shen-pao, January 16, 23, 1926.
39. Tzu-chen, 1927, pp. 2163–64; Shan-yü, 1927, pp. 2018–19.
40. Chung-yang jih-pao, March 7, 1928, p. 3; Shina no dōran, 1930, p. 99.
41. NCS, September 14, 1927, p. 6; Shina no dōran, 1930, p. 99.
42. The following case is based on Yokota Minoru, 1928.
43. STSP, February 19, 1928, p. 2.
44. For details on these battles, see Chen Hsin, 1927, p. 3; Chieh Ch'en-shih, pp. 4–5; Tai Hsüan-chih, 1973, p. 230.
45. Tai Hsüan-chih, 1973, p. 230.

46. Ibid., p. 198; *Hua-hsien chih*, 1932, p. 12.
47. Quoted in Hsiang Yün-lung, 1927, pp. 39–40.
48. *Chung-yang jih-pao*, February 2, 1928, p. 4; Wu Shou-p'eng, 1930, pp. 66–67.
49. Reprinted in "Genzai Shina," 1927, p. 63.
50. Chi Ch'eng, "Shan-tung-sheng" [Shantung Province], *Tung-fang tsa-chih*, 24, no. 16 (1927): 134–36; Tanaka Tadao, 1930, p. 269.
51. Baba Takeshi, 1976, pp. 73–74; *Chiang-su-sheng nung-min pao-kao*, 1926, p. 3; Decimal File on China, 893/9774, January 26, 1927; 893.43/3, October 24, 1928; Geoffrey, 1927, p. 68; NC, vol. 4, pp. 416–17; NCS, August 11, 1927, p. 1; STSP, March 12, 1927, p. 7; Tai Hsüan-chih, 1973, pp. 179–80; Tanaka Tadao, 1930, p. 269.
52. Quoted in Li Ta-chao, 1962, p. 565.
53. NCS, December 18, 1926, p. 2
54. The exact nature of this accommodation has yet to be adequately established. Several doctoral dissertations currently in progress (Lenore Barkan, University of Washington; Stephen C. Averill, Cornell University; and Edward W. Laves, University of Chicago) promise to provide important information on this question for certain key local areas.
55. Wang I-k'o (1932, pp. 269ff.) reprints the regulations for Shantung and Honan.
56. Gamble, 1963, pp. 113–14; Tai Hsüan-chih, 1973, p. 181.
57. Billingsley, 1974, pp. 51–53; NCH, May 22, 1926, p. 343; NCS, July 24, 1926, p. 8. According to one source, peasants were even forced to pay opium taxes on land where the poppy was not cultivated. See Decimal File on China, 893/9774, January 26, 1927. A good discussion of the deleterious effects of lifting the ban on opium cultivation is found in Baba Takeshi, 1974, p. 92.
58. *Shen-pao*, August 16, 18, 1932; *Ta-kung-pao*, August 7, 15, 21, 22, 25, 1932; Tanaka Tadao, 1936, pp. 380–81.
59. Tanaka Tadao, 1936, p. 355.
60. Hanwell, 1939, p. 468; Wu Shou-p'eng, 1930, p. 60.
61. *Wan-pao*, August 26, 1938, p. 3.
62. Ibid., August 25, 1938, p. 3.
63. Ibid., August 26, 1938, p. 3.
64. Ibid., August 25, 1938; March 2, 1939, p. 3.
65. Ibid., February 22, 1939, p. 3; Belden, 1943, p. 180.
66. Kane, 1947, p. 168.
67. Hanwell, 1939, p. 465.
68. Ikegami Tomeyoshi, 1942, pp. 85–97.
69. Pao Chih-ching, 1939, p. 58.
70. *Ho-fei jih-pao*, March 14, 1948, p. 2.
71. Naquin, 1976, p. 30. Discussions of invulnerability to weapons can be found at least as early as A.D. 253–333 in the Taoist classic *Pao-p'u Tzu*.
72. *Ho-nan nung-min*, 1927, p. 5.
73. Chang Chen-chih, 1929, pp. 136–38; "Genzai Shina," 1927, p. 67.

74. I Shih, 1960, pp. 21–22.

75. "Hung-ch'iang shih-hsi-chi," p. 2; Nagano Akira, 1931, p. 292.

76. NCH, June 12, 1926, p. 480.

77. Wu Ping-jo, 1927, pp. 53–54.

78. STSP, February 10, 1927, p. 7.

79. Gamble, 1963, pp. 301–03. The Taipings were also prone to explain defeat on the battlefield as a result of a violation of religious precepts. See Michael, 1966, p. 50.

80. I Shih, 1960, p. 21.

81. Chang Chen-chih, 1929, p. 142. Baba Takeshi, 1976, p. 64, has raised the possibility that Red Spear regulations may be seen as inspiration for the Chinese Red Army's code of behavior.

82. Chieh Ch'en-shih, pp. 12–13.

83. Decimal File on China, 893.43/3, October 24, 1928; Kumagaya Yasushi, 1943, p. 167; Nagano Akira, 1930, p. 240; Tai Hsüan-chih, 1973, p. 107.

84. Li Ying-chou, 1926, p. 4.

85. NCS, September 12, 1926, p. 5.

86. NCH, May 12, 1928, p. 229.

87. Baba Takeshi, 1974, pp. 102, 140–45; 1976, pp. 60, 67–68, 79. Baba's argument is similar to that made by Peter Worsley about the role of millenarianism in overcoming divisions of village, clan, tribe, and the like, welding previously separate groups into a new unity. See Peter Worsley, *The Trumpet Shall Sound* (New York, 1968), p. 227.

88. Satomi Hajime, 1927, p. 131; Wo-yü, 1927, p. 2.

89. Hsiang Yün-lung, 1927, p. 37; Li Ying-chou, 1926, p. 4; Pao Chih-ching, 1939, p. 60.

90. Ho-nan nung-min, 1927, p. 4; "Initiation Ceremonies," 1934, p. 149; Pao Chih-ching, 1939, p. 60.

91. Chi Fan, 1927, p. 11; Ho-nan nung-min, 1927, p. 6; "Kōsōkai," 1928, p. 66.

92. Decimal File on China, 893.43, September 12, 1929; Geoffrey, 1927, p. 68; Hsiang Yün-lung, 1927, p. 37; Nagano Akira, 1931, p. 282; NCS, May 2, 1928, p. 8.

93. *Gaiji Keisatsuhō*, no. 75 (September 1928): 45–50; Hanwell, 1939, p. 466; Ho-nan nung-min, 1927, pp. 6–7.

94. Gamble, 1963, pp. 301–03; Hsiang Yün-lung, 1927, p. 37.

95. I Shih, 1960, p. 20.

96. "Kōsōkai," 1928, p. 47. Lists of major Red Spear commanders in 1927 are provided in Chen Hsin, 1927, p. 3, and Hsiang Yün-lung, 1927, p. 38. Chen Hsin lists a total of 63 commanders and 498,750 followers, averaging almost 8,000 members per allied command post.

97. Chen Hsin, 1927, pp. 1–2; "Kōsōkai," 1928, p. 47.

98. STSP, October 10, 1927, p. 3. By one account, it was Manchurian warlord Chang Tso-lin who sent Wang back to reorganize the Red Spears (Chang Chen-chih, 1929, p. 135).

99. Chieh Ch'en-shih, pp. 6–8; "Kōsōkai," 1928, pp. 65–66; Suemitsu Takayoshi, 1932, pp. 125–29.

100. Hsiang Yün-lung, 1927, p. 37; Nagano Akira, 1931, p. 256; Wu Ping-jo, 1927, p. 54.
101. *Shina no dōran*, 1930, p. 119. On the Red Lanterns, see Purcell, 1963, p. 233.
102. Nagano Akira, 1931, p. 257; *Shina no dōran*, 1930, p. 119. According to one source, when the Nationalists ordered the Red Spears to disband in 1930, although the organization made a show of compliance, some chapters simply changed their name to *wu-chi-tao* (Gamble, 1963, pp. 301–03).
103. Blok, 1974, p. 25.
104. Hobsbawm, 1965, pp. 41, 52–53.

Chapter 6

1. NCH, January 28, 1928, p. 133.
2. HCPP, vol. 5, pp. 20–27.
3. Ho Yang-ling, ed., *Nung-min yün-tung* (1928), vol. 2, sec. 4, p. 40.
4. "Su-tung ch'ün-chung," 1943, pp. 59–60.
5. Liu Yü-chu, 1943, p. 1.
6. Liu Jui-lung, 1942a, pp. 5–10; "Waihoku sokan," pp. 19–20.
7. Chao Min, 1944, pp. 36–42; Liu Jui-lung, 1944b, p. 19.
8. HCCP, vol. 9, pp. 65–75; *Huai-pei 1945 nien*, 1945.
9. *Huo-yeh shou-ts'e*, 1945, p. 4; Liu Tzu-chiu, 1946, pp. 32–33; Wu Chih-p'u, 1944, pp. 7–10.
10. Jao Shu-shih, 1942, pp. 21–22.
11. *Su-lien yin-mou*, 1928, vol. 3, pp. 18–21.
12. Ibid.
13. Shen-chou, 1926, pp. 1369–71.
14. Tu-hsiu, 1926.
15. Li Ta-chao, 1962, pp. 564–70.
16. Chi Fan, 1927, pp. 9–17; Shen Chung-teh, 1926, pp. 8–14.
17. Wilbur, 1956, pp. 303–05.
18. Chiang Yung-ching, 1963, p. 371.
19. Ibid., pp. 373–74.
20. Ibid., pp. 375–76; STSP, May 21, 1927.
21. Chu Ch'i-hua, 1932, pp. 3–9.
22. Ibid., pp. 19–32.
23. Pak, 1971, pp. 243–45.
24. Ibid., p. 248.
25. Ibid., pp. 255–60. Slight changes in wording have been made in several of the quotations from Pak to correct grammatical errors in the English translation.
26. Ibid., p. 264.
27. *Hsin-yang-hsien chih*, 1936, 8/1, 18/23–24.
28. Pak, 1971, p. 249.
29. *Hsin-yang-hsien chih*, 1936, 18/24; *Shen-pao*, February 20, 1928; *Shih-pao*, March 4, 1928. Further details of Communist battles with Red Spears at this time can be found in *Huang-Ma ch'i-i* [The Huang-Ma uprising] (Hupeh, 1978).

30. *Hsin-yang-hsien chih*, 1936, 8/1; STSP, March 19, 1928.
31. "Kuang-tan-hui," 1959, pp. 339–48.
32. Pak, 1971, pp. 228–30.
33. Ibid., p. 398.
34. Roy Hofheinz, Jr., *The Broken Wave* (Cambridge, Mass., 1977), pp. 203–05, 209.
35. Huang, 1978; Edgar Snow, *Red Star Over China* (New York, 1938), p. 170.
36. Ch'en I, 1937, pp. 1–5, 28, 116, 134.
37. Liu Jui-lung, 1942a, p. 8.
38. Liu Shao-ch'i, 1938, p. 50.
39. Ibid., p. 51.
40. Kao Ching, 1939, pp. 100–06.
41. P'eng Teh-huai, 1942, pp. 52–53.
42. Li Ta-chang, 1942, p. 126.
43. HCPP, vol. 6, pp. 215–25; Tai Hsüan-chih, 1973, p. 134.
44. Liu Jui-lung, 1944a, p. 8.
45. Liu Shao-ch'i, 1938, pp. 51–52.
46. Li Yü, 1938, p. 11.
47. Kumagaya Yasushi, 1943, p. 168; *Tang-p'ai tiao-ch'a*; Wang Yu-chuang, 1940, p. 105. A novelistic account of CCP overtures to Red Spears at this time is Li Hsiao-ming, *P'ing-yüan ch'iang-sheng* [Rifle sounds on the plain] (Peking, 1965).
48. Mao Tse-tung, 1966, pp. 21–22.
49. HCPP, vol. 9, pp. 65–75; Li Jen-chih, 1944, pp. 18–48.
50. Wang Kuang-yü and Li Jen-chih, 1943, p. 38.
51. P'eng Teh-huai, 1942, pp. 54–55.
52. Li Ta-chang, 1942, pp. 110–89.
53. "Waikaishō chūkyō jijō," 1945, pp. 74–75.
54. Hsieh Pang-chih, 1945, pp. 3–6.
55. *K'ang-jih chan-cheng*, 1941, pp. 5–27.
56. Liu Tzu-chiu, 1943, pp. 43–50.
57. "Hsia-ch'iu min-cheng," pp. 5–27.
58. Li Jen-chih, 1944, pp. 33–35; Liu Jui-lung, 1942b, appendix; 1944a, p. 33.
59. The following case is taken from Wu Chih-ch'uan, 1944, pp. 54–60.
60. "Ch'ü-tang-wei," 1945, pp. 9–17.
61. The following case is taken from Chang Wei-ch'eng, 1945, pp. 42–58.
62. Jao Shu-shih, 1942, pp. 8–10; Liu Jui-lung, 1944a, pp. 39–45.
63. The different requirements of the three types of communities are spelled out in *Lu-nan pa-ko-yüeh*, 1945.
64. Yin Hsiao-shun, "Hsü-feng-chia ssu-shih-t'ien ti ch'ün-chung kung-tso" [Ten days of mass work in Hsü-feng-chia], FH, no. 5 (1943): 35–46.
65. Chang Wei-ch'eng, 1943a, pp. 47–49.

66. Chang Wei-ch'eng, 1943b, pp. 55–58; Liu Jui-lung, 1944a, pp. 79–80.

67. Chao Min, 1945, pp. 55–77.

68. Lu Feng, 1947, pp. 160–63.

69. Ibid., pp. 168–69.

70. Wang Wen-ch'ang, 1944, pp. 1–8.

71. Wang Yün-chao and Sung Chün, 1944, pp. 34–54.

72. This changing relationship in different periods helps to explain some of the differences in scholarly interpretations of CCP relations with traditional patterns of protest. Lucien Bianco, writing about the 1921–33 period, calls attention to the *discontinuity* between traditional forms of peasant struggle and the revolution: "The essential difference between chronic peasant agitation and revolutionary action is that the latter is deliberately offensive in nature, whereas the former resembles the defensive reaction of a beleaguered organism" (1972, p. 213).

A somewhat different perspective is offered by Tetsuya Kataoka, who, writing about the War of Resistance, places more weight on the *continuity* between preexisting forms of peasant militarization and Communist mobilization. Speaking of traditional mechanisms of self-defense, Kataoka points out: "One element of the CCP's power in the rural areas stemmed from its ability to reshuffle and reintegrate this institution into its own revolutionary structure" (1974, p. 104). Communist treatment of secret societies in particular, Kataoka contends, was "marked by a degree of tenderness . . . presumably due to the inseparable tie between these heterodox organizations and peasant revolts against the imperial regime in the past. Secret societies had always been the primary source of strength and comfort for the poorer masses against the oppression of the orthodox hierarchy" (ibid., p. 107).

Although we may dispute the characterization of secret societies, at least in Huai-pei, as having traditionally acted primarily in the interests of the poor, it is certainly true that the CCP paid them special attention during the Resistance period, for the eminently practical reason that these armed and trained organizations constituted a much-needed source of defensive strength at the time.

To be sure, Bianco and Kataoka view the revolution as a dual process incorporating both party direction and mass involvement. Yet despite their balanced treatments, each author stresses a different side of the equation. The apparent contradiction disappears with the recognition that CCP relations to local protective groups changed over time as the revolutionary movement developed new strategies to meet different challenges.

Chapter 7

1. Hobsbawm, 1965, Migdal, 1974; Moore, 1966; Paige, 1975; Scott, 1976; Wolf, 1969.

2. An exception to this approach is the new book by Samuel Popkin,

1979. For Popkin, participation in both rebellion and revolution represents "investments" by individual peasants.

3. See, for example, Moore, 1966; Skocpol, 1979.

4. Jeffery Paige adopts a similar approach. See in particular his discussion of Vietnam (1975, pp. 278–333).

5. Geertz, 1971; Steward, 1955.

6. Emmanuel Le Roy Ladurie, *The Peasants of Languedoc* (Urbana, Ill., 1976). Identification of the population–land squeeze cycle as a prime cause of peasant rebellion in China is found in Hsiao I-shan, *Ch'ing-tai t'ung-shih* [General history of the Ch'ing dynasty] (Taipei, 1963), vol. 3, pp. 35–36; Hsiao Kung-ch'üan, 1960, p. 200; and Susan Mann Jones and Philip A. Kuhn, "Dynastic Decline and the Roots of Rebellion," in *Cambridge History of China*, ed. D. Twitchett and J. K. Fairbank (London, 1978), vol. 10, pp. 107–62. For a case study documenting the impact of such macrolevel demographic trends on the White Lotus Rebellion, see Suzuki Chūsei, 1952.

7. For an illustration of the futility of this approach, see Roy Hofheinz, Jr., "The Ecology of Chinese Communist Success," in *Chinese Communist Politics in Action*, ed. A. D. Barnett (Seattle, 1969), pp. 3–77; or *The Broken Wave* (Cambridge, Mass., 1977), chap. 6.

8. Geertz, 1971, p. 10.

9. See, for example, Arthur Stinchcombe, "Agricultural Enterprise and Rural Class Relations," *American Journal of Sociology*, 67 (1961): 165–76; Edward Malefakis, *Agrarian Reform and Peasant Revolution in Spain* (New Haven, 1970), pp. 93–130.

10. Wolf, 1969, pp. 291–93. Hamza Alavi, "Peasants and Revolution," *Socialist Register* (1965): 241–77, suggests that middle peasants are initially the most militant, but that they come to be replaced by the poor peasants as the movement progresses.

11. Paige, 1975.

12. Maurice Freedman, *Lineage Organization in Southeastern China* (London, 1965), p. 122. See Chesneaux, 1971, for an elaboration of this view.

13. A dissident from this conventional interpretation is James Polachek, 1973, who holds that secret societies retained the cyclical vision of the elite. Susan Naquin, 1976, also points out the varied social composition of White Lotus sectarians in the early nineteenth century.

14. Davis, 1977, pp. 176–77. Davis goes further (p. 5) in claiming that "the study of secret societies in traditional China is the study of the origins and progress of the Chinese revolution."

15. Rappaport, 1971, pp. 262–63.

16. Sahlins, 1964, p. 137.

17. Hobsbawm, 1965, p. 5.

18. Migdal, 1974, p. 252, notes that revolutionaries are likely to be more successful among peasants who find normal social patterns suddenly disrupted than among those who have had years to develop means of handling an unstable environment.

19. Hu Huan-yung, 1952, p. vi.

20. Chang Chao-feng, *Chung-kung chih-huai nei-mu* [The inside story of the Chinese Communists' conservancy work on the Huai River] (Hong Kong, 1953), pp. 5–6. The author of the account was an engineer who worked on the Huai River project for six months.

21. Quoted in Wilfred Burchett with Rewi Alley, *China: The Quality of Life* (Middlesex, 1976), pp. 213–14.

22. Yamamoto Hideo, "Nōmin kaihō tōsō no shintenkai, Chūgoku kyōsantō to nōmin sensō" [New developments in peasant liberation struggles: The CCP and peasant war], in *Kōza gendai Chūgoku*, ed. Suganuma Masahisa (Tokyo, 1969), vol. 2, pp. 129–66.

23. Skinner, 1977, pp. 275–351; idem, "Regional Systems in Late Imperial China," paper presented to the Social Science History Association, Ann Arbor, Mich., 1977.

24. Parsons, 1970, pp. 1–4; Selden, 1972, pp. 1–18.

25. Stephen G. Averill, 1978, "The Communists and Society in Kiangsi, 1926–31," paper presented to the Workshop on Chinese Communist Base Areas, Cambridge, Mass.; Huang, 1978.

26. See Michael Barkun, *Disaster and the Millennium* (New Haven, 1974), pp. 74–84, for a general discussion of the relationship between disaster-prone environments and (millenarian) rebellion.

27. Scott, 1976, pp. 197–98.

28. Huizer, 1972, pp. 1–18.

29. Blok, 1974, p. 19.

30. Louise E. Sweet, "Camel Raiding of North Arabian Bedouin: A Mechanism of Ecological Adaptation," *American Anthropologist*, 67 (1965): 1132–50; Jacob Black-Michaud, *Cohesive Force: Feud in the Mediterranean and Middle East* (New York, 1975).

Bibliography

Note: The locations and call numbers of archival materials are supplied in the bibliography of my dissertation, "From Rebels to Revolutionaries: Peasant Violence in Huai-pei, 1845–1945" (University of Michigan, 1978).

Agrarian China, 1938, Chicago.

Aird, J. S., 1968, "Population Growth," in *Economic Trends in Communist China*, ed. A. Eckstein, W. Galenson, and T. C. Liu, Chicago.

An-hui cheng-chih, 1941 [Anhwei politics], 4(7).

An-hui-sheng t'ung-chi nien-chien, 1934 [Statistical yearbook of Anhwei Province], Anhwei Provincial Government Statistics Committee.

An-hui t'ung-chih, 1877 [Gazetteer of Anhwei Province], ed. Ho Chih-chi.

Baba Takeshi, 1974, "Kōsōkai undō josetsu" [Introduction to the Red Spears], in *Chūgoku minshū hanran no sekai*, Tokyo.

———, 1976, "Kōsōkai" [Red Spears], *Shakai Keizaishi Gaku*, 42(1), pp. 59–83.

Belden, J., 1943, *Still Time to Die*, New York.

Bianco, L., 1972, "Secret Societies and Peasant Self-Defense, 1921–1933," in *Secret Societies and Popular Movements*, ed. J. Chesneaux, Stanford, pp. 213–24.

———, 1973, "The Land Tax in Republican China Until 1937," paper presented at University of Michigan Center for Chinese Studies colloquium.

———, 1976, "Peasants and Revolution," *Journal of Peasant Studies*, 2(3), pp. 313–36.

Billingsley, P. R., 1974, "Banditry in China, 1911–1928," doctoral dissertation, University of Leeds.

Blok, A., 1972, "The Peasant and the Brigand: Social Banditry Reconsidered," *Comparative Studies in Society and History*, 14(4), pp. 494–503.

———, 1974, *The Mafia of a Sicilian Village*, New York.

Buck, J. L., 1927, "The Big Swords and the Little Swords Clash," Decimal File on China, 1910–1929, microfilm #893/10239.

———, 1964a, *Land Utilization in China*, New York.

———, 1964b, *Land Utilization in China: Statistics*, Chicago.

Chang Chen-chih, 1929, *Ko-ming yü tsung-chiao* [Revolution and religion], Shanghai.

Chang Chieh-hou, 1927, "Huai-pei nung-min chih sheng-huo chuang-k'uang" [The livelihood of Huai-pei peasants], *Tung-fang tsa-chih*, 24(16), pp. 71–76.

Chang Shan, 1959a, "An-hui nien-chün kai-shu" [An overview of the Anhwei Nien Army], *An-hui shih-hsüeh t'ung-hsün*, 4–5, pp. 96–108.

———, 1959b, "Kuan-yü nien-chün ti tsu-chih wen-t'i" [On the question of the organization of the Nien Army], *An-hui shih-hsüeh t'unghsün*, 14, pp. 28–38.

Chang Wei-ch'eng, 1943a, "Yen-yü-hsiang ti chieh-tai wen-t'i shih ju-ho chieh-chüeh ti" [How the debt problem was resolved in Yenyü], FH, 5, pp. 47–54.

———, 1943b, "Shan-t'ou-hsiang erh-nien-lai ku-kung tiao-ch'a" [Investigation of hired laborers in Shan-t'ou-hsiang during the past two years], FH, 5, pp. 55–58.

———, 1945, "Su-ch'ien-shih i-ko-yüeh-lai ti ch'ün-chung yün-tung" [The mass movement in Su-ch'ien during the past month], FH, 19, pp. 42–45.

Chang Wei-shan, 1961, "Meng-ch'eng ti-ch'ü nien-chün ch'i-i tiao-ch'a pao-kao" [Report on investigations on the Nien uprising in the Meng-ch'eng area], *Kuang-ming jih-pao*, April 12, pp. 4–12.

Chang Wen-ch'ing, 1953, *Nien-tang ch'i-i* [The Nien uprising], Shanghai.

Chao Min, 1944, "I-nien-lai ti ch'ün-chung yün-tung" [The mass movement of the past year], *Huai-pei i-nien*.

———, 1945, "Kuo-yang-hsien Ts'ao-shih-hsiang Ssu-li Pen-chi liangpao shih-t'ien ti ch'ün-chung yün-tung" [Ten days of mass movement in Ssu-li and Pen-chi, two *pao* in Ts'ao-shih-hsiang, Kuo-yang County], FH, 17, pp. 55–77.

Che-ch'eng-hsien chih, 1896 [Gazetteer of Che-ch'eng County], ed. Yüan Huai.

Chen Hsin, 1927, "Ho-nan chih hung-ch'iang-hui" [The Red Spears of Honan], *Kuo-wen chou-pao* 4(24), pp. 1–3.

Ch'en Ch'iao-i, 1952, *Huai-ho liu-yü* [The Huai River basin], Shanghai.

———, 1954, *Chiang-huai liu-kuan ti An-hui-sheng* [Anhwei Province, traversed by the Yangtze and Huai Rivers], Shanghai.

Ch'en Han-seng, 1939, *Industrial Capital and Chinese Peasants*, Shanghai.

Ch'en Han-seng, Liao K'ai-sheng, Chang Fu-liang, Hsü Pien-chun, 1934, "Nan-min ti tung-pei liu-wang" [The northeastern migration of refugees], in *Chung-kuo nung-ts'un ching-chi lun*, ed. Feng Ho-fa, Shanghai.

Ch'en Hua, 1976, "Nien-luan chih yen-chiu" [A study of the Nien], master's thesis, National Taiwan University.

Ch'en Hung-chin, 1939, "Min-chung li-liang tsai yü-tung" [Mass power in eastern Honan], *K'ang-chan-Chung ti chung-kuo nung-ts'un tung-t'ai*, pp. 85–88.

Ch'en I, 1937, *Tsen-yang tung-yüan nung-min ta-chung* [How to mobilize the peasant masses], Shanghai.

Chesneaux, J., 1970, *Mouvements populaires et sociétés secrètes en Chine aux XIXᵉ et XXᵉ siècles*, Paris.

——, 1971, *Secret Societies in China*, Ann Arbor, Mich.

——, 1972, "Secret Societies in China's Historical Evolution," in *Popular Movements and Secret Societies in China, 1840–1950*, ed. Chesneaux, Stanford, pp. 1–21.

——, 1973, *Peasant Revolts in China, 1840–1949*, London.

Chi Ch'ao-ting, 1963, *Key Economic Areas in Chinese History*, New York.

Chi Fan, 1927, "Chieh-shao Ho-nan ti hung-ch'iang-hui" [Introducing the Red Spears of Honan], *Chung-kuo ch'ing-nien*, 126, pp. 9–17.

Chi-ning-chou chih, 1840 [Gazetteer of Chi-ning County], ed. Hsü Han.

Ch'i Hsi-sheng, 1976, *Warlord Politics in China, 1916–1928*, Stanford.

Chiang Siang-tseh, 1954, *The Nien Rebellion*, Seattle.

Chiang-su-sheng nung-min pao-kao, 1926 [Report on peasants in Kiangsu Province].

Chiang-su-sheng nung-yeh tiao-ch'a-lu, 1925 [Records of agricultural surveys in Kiangsu Province], Kiangsu Joint Educational-Industrial Committee.

Chiang Ti, 1956a, "Kuan-yü nien-chün-shih fen-ch'i wen-t'i" [On the question of the periodization of the Nien Army], *Kuang-ming jih-pao*, July 5, p. 3.

——, 1956b, *Nien-chün-shih ch'u-t'an* [A preliminary investigation of Nien Army history], Peking.

——, 1958, "Huai-nan shih-ch'i ti nien-chün chan-cheng (1857–1858)" [Battles of the Nien Army during the period 1857–1858 south of the Huai], *Shan-hsi shih-fan hsüeh-yüan hsüeh-pao*, 31, pp. 91–102.

——, 1959, *Ch'u-ch'i nien-chün-shih lun-ts'ung* [An essay on the early period of Nien Army history], Peking.

——, 1963, "Lun t'ai-p'ing-t'ien-kuo ho nien-chün ch'i-i ti kuan-hsi" [A discussion of connections between the Taipings and Nien], *Li-shih yen-chiu*, 3, pp. 65–86.

Chiang Yung-ching, 1963, *Pao-lo-t'ing yü Wu-han cheng-ch'üan* [Borodin and the Wuhan government], Taipei.

Chieh Ch'en-shih, n.d., *Hung-ch'iang-hui chen-hsiang* [The truth about the Red Spear Society], n.p.

Ch'ien Hung, 1950, "Nien-chün—T'ai-p'ing-t'ien-kuo shih-ch'i pei-fang ti nung-min yün-tung" [The Nien Army—a northern peasant movement during the time of the Taipings], *T'ai-p'ing t'ien-kuo ko-ming yün-tung lun-wen-chi*, Peking, pp. 120–35.

Chin-hsiang-hsien chih, 1862 [Gazetteer of Chin-hsiang County], ed. Li Lei.

"Ch'ing-tai ch'i-pai ming-jen chuan" [Biographies of 700 eminent persons of the Ch'ing dynasty], *Chin-tai chung-kuo shih-liao ts'ung-k'an*, ed. Shen Yün-lung, Taipei.

Ch'iu Kuo-chen, 1940, "Chan-shih An-hui ti-fang wu-li chih fa-tung yü cheng-li" [The development and reorganization of local military forces in Anhwei during the war], *K'ang-chien-chung chih An-hui*.

Chu Ch'i-hua, 1932, "1925–1927 nenjū Chūgoku daikakumeijū ni okeru nōmin undō" [The peasant movement during the great Chinese revolution of 1925–1927], *Mantetsu Shina Gesshi*, 9(1,2).

Chu Hsieh, 1954, "Nien-chün ling-hsiu Chang Yü-chüeh ho Chang Chung" [Nien Army leaders Chang Yü-chüeh and Chang Chung], *Li-shih chiao-hsüeh*, 10, p. 49.

"Ch'ü-tang-wei kuan-yü chi-ko hui-men shih-chien ti t'ung-pao," 1945 [The district party committee report concerning several secret-society incidents], *Kung-tso t'ung-hsin*, March 5, pp. 9–17.

Chung-kuo nung-ts'un tiao-ch'a tzu-liao, 1971 [Materials on China's rural villages], Taipei.

Chung-mou-hsien chih, 1935 [Gazetteer of Chung-mou County], ed. Hsiao Teh-hsing.

Chung Wen, 1972, "Three Provinces Unite to Control the Huai," *China Tames Her Rivers*, Peking, pp. 22–31.

Chung-yang jih-pao [Central Daily], Shanghai.

Crossett, M. E., 1946, *Harvest at the Front*, Philadelphia.

CSL (*Ta-ch'ing shih-lu*), 1964 [Veritable records of the Ch'ing], Taipei. References are given with initials for reign year periods, followed by *chuan* and page.

CSLC (*Ch'ing-shih lieh-chuan*), 1962 [Important biographies of the Ch'ing], Taipei.

Davis, F. L., 1977, *Primitive Revolutionaries of China*, Honolulu.

Decimal File on China: U.S. Department of State Archives, microfilm collection.

Durham, W. H., 1976, "Resource Competition and Human Aggression, Part I: A Review of Primitive War," *Quarterly Review of Biology*, 51, pp. 385–415.

Eberhard, W., 1965, *Conquerers and Rulers*, Leiden.

Erasmus, C., 1968, "Community Development and the Encogido Syndrome," *Human Organization*, 27(1).

Fanon, F., 1963, *The Damned*, Paris.

Feng-hsien chih, 1894 [Gazetteer of Feng County], ed. Yao Hung-shu.
Feng-t'ai-hsien chih, 1882 [Gazetteer of Feng-t'ai County], ed. Li Shih-hang.
Feng-yang-fu chih, 1908 [Gazetteer of Feng-yang District], ed. Chu K'ung-chang.
FH (*Fu-hsiao*) [Dawn], Huai-pei.
FL (*Chiao-p'ing nien-fei fang-lüeh*) [Records of the suppression of the Nien bandits], ed. Chu Hsüeh-ch'in, Taipei.
Foster, G. M., 1969, "Peasant Society and the Image of the Limited Good," in *Peasant Society: A Reader*, ed. J. M. Potter, M. N. Diaz, and G. M. Foster, Boston.
Friedman, E., 1974a, *Backward Toward Revolution*, Berkeley.
————, 1974b, "Primitive Rebel Versus Modern Revolutionary: A Case of Mistaken Identity?" Paper delivered to the Association of Asian Studies.
Fu-yang-hsien chih, 1829 [Gazetteer of Fu-yang County], ed. Li Fu-ch'ing.
Gaiji Keisatsuhō, 1928 [Foreign Affairs Police Report], Tokyo.
Gamble, S. D., 1954, *Ting Hsien, a North China Rural Community*, New York.
————, 1963, *North China Villages*, Berkeley.
Geertz, C., 1971, *Agricultural Involution*, Berkeley.
"Genzai Shina ni okeru himitsu kessha kōsōkai," 1927 [A secret society in contemporary China: The Red Spears], *Mantetsu Chōsa Jihō*, 7(10), pp. 59–77.
Geoffrey, C. C., 1927, "The Red Spears in China," *The China Weekly Review*, 40(3), p. 68.
Hanwell, N. D., 1939, "The Red Spears of China," *Asia* 39(8), pp. 465–68.
Harris, M., 1975, *Cows, Pigs, Wars and Witches*, New York.
————, 1977, *Cannibals and Kings: The Origins of Cultures*, New York.
Hatada Takashi, 1973, *Chūgoku sonraku to kyōdōtai riron* [Chinese villages and theories of cooperative systems], Tokyo.
HCPP, 1957–66 (*Hung-ch'i p'iao-p'iao*) [The red flag waves], Peking.
Hibino Takeo, 1953, "Gōson bōei to kempeki shōya" [Village defense and the policy of strengthening walls and clearing fields], *Tōhō Gakuhō*, 22, pp. 141–55.
Ho-fei jih-pao [Ho-fei Daily].
Ho Hsi-ya, 1925, *Chung-kuo tao-fei wen-t'i chih yen-chiu* [A study of the question of Chinese banditry], Shanghai.
Ho-nan nung-min chi nung-min tzu-wei-chün, 1927 [The Honan peasantry and peasant self-defense forces].
Ho-Ping-ti, 1959, *Studies on the Population of China, 1368–1953*, Cambridge.

————, 1976, "The Presidential Address: The Chinese Civilization—a Search for the Roots of Its Longevity," *Journal of Asian Studies*, 35(4), pp. 547–54.

Hobsbawm, E. J., 1965, *Primitive Rebels*, New York.

————, 1969, *Bandits*, New York.

"Hsia-ch'iu min-cheng kung-tso chüeh-ting," 1944 [Decision on summer-autumn democratic work], *Cheng-fu kung-tso t'ung-hsün*, 29.

Hsiang-ch'eng-hsien chih, 1911 [Gazetteer of Hsiang-ch'eng County], ed. Shih Ching-wu.

Hsiang Yün-lung, 1927, "Hung-ch'iang-hui ti ch'i-yüan chi ch'i shan-hou" [The origin and future of the Red Spears], *Tung-fang tsa-chih*, 24(21), pp. 35–41.

Hsiao Hsiang, 1926, "Ho-nan hung-ch'iang-hui pei Wu P'ei-fu chün-tui t'u-sha chih ts'an-chuang" [The tragedy of the slaughter of the Honan Red Spears by Wu P'ei-fu's army], *Hsiang-tao*, 158, pp. 1545–46.

Hsiao-hsien chih, 1874 [Gazetteer of Hsiao County], ed. Tuan Kuang-ying.

Hsiao I-shan, 1965, *Chin-tai mi-mi she-hui shih-liao* [Historical materials on modern secret societies], Taipei.

Hsiao Kung-ch'üan, 1960, *Rural China: Imperial Control in the Nineteenth Century*, Seattle.

Hsiao Liu, 1959, "Nien-chün ch'an-sheng ti she-hui pei-ching" [Social background to the birth of the Nien Army], *An-hui shih-hsüeh t'ung-hsün*, 14, pp. 1–12.

Hsieh Pang-chih, 1945, "Shu-li ch'iang-ku ti chien-tang ssu-hsiang" [Establish firm party thinking], FH, 18, pp. 1–13.

Hsin-yang-hsien chih, 1936 [Gazetteer of Hsin-yang County], ed. Ch'en Shan-t'ung.

Hsü-chou-fu chih, 1874 [Gazetteer of Hsüchou District], ed. Liu Hsiang.

Hsü Hung, 1972, *Ch'ing-tai liang-huai yen-ch'ang ti yen-chiu* [A study of the salt fields north and south of the Huai during the Ch'ing], Taipei.

Hsü-i-hsien chih kao, 1873 [Draft gazetteer of Hsü-i County], ed. Fu Shao-ts'eng.

Hu Ch'ü-fei and Yen Hsin-nung, 1933, *An-hui-sheng* [Anhui Province], Shanghai.

Hu Huan-yung, 1935, "An-hui chih jen-k'ou mi-tu yü nung-ch'an ch'ü-yü" [Population density and agricultural districts in Anhwei], *Ti-li hsüeh-pao*, 2(1), pp. 1–10.

————, 1952, *Huai-ho* [Huai River], Peking.

"Hua-chung fen-chü kuan-yü chin-i-pu fa-tung ch'ün-chung ti chih-shih," 1945 [Central China Branch Bureau directive concerning further mass agitation], *Ch'ün-chung kung-tso wen-chien*, pp. 4–8.

Hua-hsien chih, 1932 [Gazetteer of Hua County], ed. Wang P'u-yüan.

"Hua-tung-chü kuan-yü fang-shou fa-tung hsin chieh-fang-ch'ü ch'ün-chung ti chih-shih," 1946 [East China Bureau directive concerning bold agitation of masses in the newly liberated zones], *Ch'ün-chung kung-tso wen-chien*, pp. 1–3.

Huai-an-fu chih, 1884 [Gazetteer of Huai-an District], ed. Wu K'un-t'ien.

Huai-pei 1945-nien ti chien-she fang-hsiang, 1945 [The direction of construction in Huai-pei in 1945].

Huang, P. C. C., 1978, "Intellectuals, Lumpen-proletarians, Workers, and Peasants in the Communist Movement: The Case of Xingguo County, 1927–1934," in *Chinese Communists and Rural Society in the Jiangxi Period*, ed. P. C. C. Huang, L. S. Bell, and K. L. Walker, Berkeley, pp. 5–28.

Huizer, G., 1972, *The Revolutionary Potential of Peasants in Latin America*, Lexington, Mass.

"Hung-ch'iang shih-hsi chi," 1928 [A record of Red Spear practices], *Kuo-wen chou-pao*, 5(5), pp. 1–3.

Hung Nung, 1972, "Twenty Years Work on the Huai River," in *China Tames Her Rivers*, Peking, pp. 15–21.

Huo-yeh shou-ts'e, 1945 [Handbook of daily activities].

I-hsien fang-chih, 1904 [Gazetteer of I County], ed. Wang Chen-lu.

I Shih, 1960, "Tsai wan-pei k'ang-ti ti hung-ch'iang-hui ch'uan-ch'i" [Tales of Red Spear resistance in northern Anhwei], *Ch'un-ch'iu*, 73, pp. 20–22.

Ida Saburo, 1940, "Hōyōken Yokakōson nōgyō jijō" [Agricultural conditions in Yang-chia-kang village, Feng-yang County], *Mantetsu Chōsa Geppō*, 20(4), pp. 191–232.

Ikegami Tomeyoshi, 1942, "Kōsōkai shidō no ichi kosatsu" [A view of directing the Red Spears], *Shimmin Undō*, 3(9), pp. 85–97.

"Initiation Ceremonies of the Red Spears," 1934, *People's Tribune*, 6(3), pp. 147–51.

Inoue Kobai, 1923, *Hito* [Bandits], Shanghai.

Jameson, C. D., 1912, "River Systems of the Provinces of Anhui and Kiangsu North of the Yangtzekiang," *Chinese Recorder*, 43(1), pp. 69–75.

Jao Shu-shih, 1942, "Hua-chung ch'u-chien pao-wei kung-tso ti chi-pen tsung-chi chi chin-hou ti jen-wu" [Basic plan and future mission of the weed-out traitors and defense work in Central China], *Chen-li*, 1.

Jen-ching, 1924, "Ho-nan Lu-shih-hsien jen-min tui chün-fa chih fan-k'ang" [Resistance to the warlords by the people of Lu-shih County, Honan], *Hsiang-tao*, 69(2), pp. 551–53.

Jen Yu-wen, 1973, *The Taiping Revolutionary Movement*, New Haven.

Jenner, W. J. F., 1970, "Les Nian et le Laoniuhui: Les rebelles et leurs adversaires dans la tradition populaire," in *Mouvements populaires et sociétés secrètes en Chine*, ed. J. Chesneaux, Paris, pp. 205–18.

Jo Mu, 1959, "Chang Lo-hsing chuan" [Biography of Chang Lo-hsing], *An-hui shih-hsüeh t'ung-hsün*, 14, pp. 51–62.

Ju I, 1942, "Ta-liang tsu-chih ch'ün-chung ti chi-ko fang-shih" [Several methods of greatly organizing the masses], *Huai-hai tou-cheng*, 3, pp. 93–95.

Junkin, W. F., 1912, "Famine Conditions in North Anhui and North Kiangsu," *Chinese Recorder*, 43(2), pp. 75–81.

Kanbe Teruo, 1972, "Shindai kōki santōsho ni okeru 'danhi' to nōson mondai" [Militia bandits in Shantung during the late Ch'ing and the peasant village question], *Shirin*, 55(4), pp. 61–98.

Kane, J. H., 1947, *Twofold Growth*, China Inland Mission.

K'ang-jih chan-cheng ti nung-min yün-tung, 1941 [The peasant movement during the War of Resistance], New Fourth Army Political Bureau.

Kao Ching, 1939, "Wo-men tsen-ma-yang kai-tsao t'u-fei ti?" [How do we reform bandits?], *K'ang-chan-chung ti Chung-kuo nung-ts'un tung-t'ai*, pp. 100–06.

Kataoka Tetsuya, 1974, *Resistance and Revolution in China*, Berkeley.

KCT (Kung-chung-tang) [Palace memorials] in National Palace Museum, Taipei. Citations are given with reign year and memorial number.

Kōain, 1940, *Ankishi hokubu keizai jijō* [Economic conditions in northern Anhwei].

"Kōsōkai," 1928 [Red Spears], *Pekin Mantetsu Geppō*, 4(5), pp. 16–94.

"Kōsōkai no shōtai," 1927 [The true character of the Red Spears], *Shina Jihō*, 7(6), pp. 54–56.

"Kuang-tan-hui" [Bare Egg Society], 1959, in *An-hui ko-ming hui-i-lu* [Remembrances of the revolution in Anhwei], Ho-fei.

Kuhn, P. A., 1970, *Rebellion and Its Enemies in Late Imperial China: Militarization and Social Structure, 1796–1864*, Cambridge.

———, 1978, "The Taiping Rebellion," in *Cambridge History of China*, ed. D. Twitchett and J. K. Fairbank, London, vol. 10, pp. 264–317.

Kumagaya Yasushi, 1940, *Nisshi ryoseiryoku kosaku chitai (bofu) no keizai jijō* [Economic conditions in Peng-p'u, the region where Japanese and Chinese forces meet], Shanghai.

———, 1943, *Shina kyōchin zatsuwa* [Comments on China's villages], Dairen.

Kuo Han-ming, 1938–39, "Anki tochi chōsa nikki" [Diary of land investigations in Anhwei], *Mantetsu Chōsa Geppō*, 18(12), 19(1).

Kuo Han-ming and Hung Jui-chien, 1936, *An-hui-sheng chih t'u-ti fen-*

p'ei yü tsu-tien chih-tu [Land distribution and farm tenancy in Anhwei], Nanking.

Kuo-yang-hsien chih, 1924 [Gazetteer of Kuo-yang County], ed. Wang P'ei-chien.

Kuo-yang jih-pao [Kuo-yang Daily].

Kusano Fumio, 1944, *Shina henku no kenkyū* [A study of China's border areas], Tokyo.

Laffey, E. S., 1976, "In the Wake of the Taipings: Some Patterns of Local Revolt in Kwangsi Province, 1850–1875," *Modern Asian Studies*, 10, pp. 65–81.

Li Hsiu-ch'eng, 1955, *Chung-wang Li Hsiu-ch'eng tzu-chuan* [Autobiography of Loyal King Li Hsiu-ch'eng], ed. Lo Erh-kang, Shanghai.

Li Jen-chih, 1944, "Ssu-ling-sui yu-chi ken-chü-ti shih tsen-yang chien-li-ch'i-lai ti?" [How was the Ssu-ling-sui guerrilla base established?], FH, 14, pp. 18–48.

Li Ta-chang, 1942, *Ti-chan-ch'ü yü chieh-ti kung-tso fang-chen yü cheng-ts'e* [Plans and policies for work in enemy-occupied zones].

Li Ta-chao, 1962, "Lu-yü-shen teng-sheng ti hung-ch'iang-hui" [The Red Spears in Shantung, Honan, Shensi, and other provinces], *Li Ta-chao hsüan-chi*, Peking.

Li Tse-kang, 1940, "K'ang-chan-chung Chiang-huai min-tsu ching-shen" [National spirit in the Yangtze-Huai region during the War of Resistance], *K'ang-chien-chung chih An-hui*, Anhwei Provincial Government Secretariat.

Li Tso-chou, 1935, "Chung-chung fu-tan hsia ti Feng-yang nung-min" [The burdened peasantry of Feng-yang], *Chung-kuo nung-ts'un*, 1(9), pp. 71–74.

Li Ying-chou, 1926, "Mu-tu hung-ch'iang-hui chih ch'i-chi" [A strange record of observing the Red Spears], STSP, October 2, 1926, p. 4.

Li Yü, 1938, "Shan-tung k'ang-jih yu-chi chan-cheng ti fa-chan" [Development of Shantung's anti-Japanese guerrilla war], *Chieh-fang*, 49.

Liu Jui-lung, 1942a, *San-nien-lai ti cheng-fu kung-tso* [Government work during the last three years].

———, 1942b, *Huai-pei k'ang-jih min-chu chien-she* [Huai-pei's anti-Japanese democratic construction].

———, 1944a, *Huai-pei wu-nien-lai ch'ün-chung kung-tso tsung-chieh* [Summary of mass work in Huai-pei during the past five years].

———, 1944b, "Huai-pei cheng-ch'üan i-nien" [A year of political power in Huai-pei], *Huai-pei i-nien*, pp. 19–35.

Liu, K. C., 1978, "The Ch'ing Restoration," in *Cambridge History of China*, ed. D. Twitchett and J. K. Fairbank, London, vol. 10, pp. 409–90.

Liu Pao-kuang, 1957, "Ch'ang-ch'iang-hui-fei chi-shih" [A true report of the Long Spear bandits], *Shan-tung chin-tai-shih tzu-liao*, Tsinan, vol. 1, pp. 262–68.

Liu Po, 1929, "O-pei hung-ch'iang-hui chih chen-hsiang" [The true conditions of the Red Spears of northern Hupeh], *Ko-ming chou-pao*, September 1, p. 306.

Liu Shao-ch'i, 1938, "Chien-ch'ih hua-pei k'ang-chan-chung ti wu-chuang pu-tui" [Protect North China's armed forces in the War of Resistance], *Chieh-fang*, 43(4), pp. 49–53.

Liu Tzu-chiu, 1943, "Lun wai-lai kan-pu ti-fang-hua yü p'ei-yang t'i-pa pen-ti kan-pu" [Localization of outside cadres and cultivation and promotion of local cadres], FH, 2, pp. 43–50.

————, 1946, "Cheng-ch'üeh ti k'ou-hao, ts'o-wu ti fang-fa" [Correct slogan, mistaken method], *Chan-shih*, 3, pp. 32–33.

Liu Yü-chu, 1943, *Ch'ün-chung kung-tso ts'an-k'ao wen-chien* [Reference materials on mass work], Kiangsu.

Lo Erh-kang, 1939, *Nien-chün ti yün-tung-chan* [The mobile warfare of the Nien Army], Changsha.

————, 1957, *T'ai-p'ing-t'ien-kuo hsin-chün ti yün-tung-chan* [The mobile warfare of the New Taiping Army], Shanghai.

————, 1960, "Nien-chün cheng-ming" [The correct name of the Nien Army], *An-hui shih-hsüeh*, 1, pp. 11–29.

Lowdermilk, W. G., 1924, "Erosion and Floods Along the Yellow River," *China Weekly Review*, 29(2), pp. 38–44.

Lu Feng, 1947, *Kang-t'ieh ti tui-wu* [Army of steel], Hong Kong.

Lu-i-hsien chih, 1896 [Gazetteer of Lu-i County], ed. Chiang Shih-ch'e.

Lu-nan pa-ko-yüeh ch'ün-chung yün-tung tsung-chieh chi chin-hou kung-tso, 1945 [A summary of eight months of the mass movement in south Shantung and present and future work].

Ly, J. U., 1918, "An Economic Interpretation of the Increase of Bandits in China," *Journal of Race Development*, 8(3), pp. 366–78.

Ma Ch'ang-hua, 1959, "Nien-chün ti ch'an-sheng chi ch'i ch'u-ch'i ti huo-tung" [The birth and early activities of the Nien Army], *An-hui shih-hsüeh t'ung-hsün*, 14, pp. 13–27.

Ma Jung-heng and Liu Shou-i, 1962, "Kuan-yü nien-chün ling-hsiu Chang Lo-hsing ti tzu-shu ho hsi-wen" [On the confession and proclamations of Nien leader Chang Lo-hsing], *Kuang-ming jih-pao*, October 10, p. 4.

MacGowan, J., 1909, *Lights and Shadows of Chinese Life*, Shanghai.

MacMurray, 1929, "Red Spear Activities," in Decimal File on China, 1910–1919, microfilm #893.43.

Mallory, W. H., 1926, *China: Land of Famine*, New York.

Mao Tse-tung, 1966, *Basic Tactics*, ed. S. Schram, New York.

304 Bibliography

Martin, W. A. P., 1868, in Presbyterian Mission Archives, China Letters, Microfilm Reel #198.

Mateer, C. W., 1867, in Presbyterian Mission Archives, China Letters, Microfilm Reel #197.

Meng-ch'eng-hsien chih, 1915 [Gazetteer of Meng-ch'eng County], ed. Huang Yü-chün.

Metzger, T. A., 1962, "T'ao Chu's Reform of the Huai-pei Salt Monopoly," Papers on China, 16, pp. 1–39.

——, 1974, "Chinese Bandits: The Traditional Perception Reevaluated," Journal of Asian Studies, 33(3), pp. 445–58.

Michael, F., 1966, The Taiping Rebellion, Seattle.

Migdal, J. S., 1974, Peasants, Politics, and Revolution, Princeton.

Mills, C. R., 1873, in Presbyterian Mission Archives, China Letters, Microfilm Reel #197.

Mitani Takashi, 1973, "Kokumin kakumeiki ni okeru Chūgoku kyōsantō to kōsōkai" [The Chinese Communist Party and Red Spears in the National Revolution], Hitotsubashi Ronsō, 69(5), pp. 48–61.

——, 1974, "Kokumin kakumei jiki no hoppō nōmin bōdō" [Northern peasant uprisings during the time of the national revolution], in Chūgoku kokumin kakumeishi no kenkyū, ed. Nozawa Yutaka, Tokyo.

——, 1978, "Dentōteki nōmin tōsō no shintenkai" [New developments in traditional peasant struggles], in Kōza Chūgoku kingendaishi, ed. Nozawa Yutaka and Tanaka Masatoshi, Tokyo, vol. 5, pp. 117–44.

Moore, B., 1966, Social Origins of Dictatorship and Democracy, Boston.

Mu Lien-fu, 1959, "Niu Ping tsa yen-tien" [Niu Ping smashes the salt shop], Min-chien wen-hsüeh, 9, pp. 77–83.

Myers, R. H., 1970, The Chinese Peasant Economy, Cambridge.

Nagano Akira, 1930, Chung-kuo she-hui tsu-chih [Chinese social organization], Shanghai.

——, 1931, Tohi, guntai, kōsōkai [Bandits, army, Red Spears], Tokyo.

——, 1933, Shina nōmin undōkan [A view of the peasant movement in China], Tokyo.

——, 1938, Shinahei, tohi, kōsōkai [China's soldiers, bandits, Red Spears], Tokyo.

Namiki Yorinaga, 1978, "Shinmatsu kanhoku ni okeru nenshi ni tsuite" [The late Ch'ing Nien of northern Anhwei], Tōyō Gakuhō, 59 (3–4), pp. 25–60.

Nan-yen, 1924, "Hsiao-shih hua-ta ti An-hui fei-luan" [Little matters turn into big problems: Banditry in Anhwei], Tung-fang tsa-chih, 21 (14), pp. 3–6.

Naquin, S., 1976, Millenarian Rebellion in China: The Eight Trigrams of 1813, New Haven.

NC (Nien-chün), 1953 [The Nien Army], ed. Fan Wen-lan, Shanghai.

NCH (North China Herald), Shanghai.

NCPC (Nien-chün pieh-chi), 1958 [Collection on the Nien Army], ed. Nieh Ch'ung-ch'i, Shanghai.

NCS (North China Standard), Peking.

Nien-chün ku-shih-chi, 1962 [Collected tales from the Nien Army], Shanghai.

Nung-ts'un shih-k'uang pao-kao, 1935 [Report on village conditions].

Ono Shinji, 1961, "Nenshi to nengun: Shinmatsu nōmin sensō no ichi sokumen" [The Nien and Nien Army: An aspect of peasant wars at the end of the Ch'ing], Tōyōshi Kenkyū, 20(1).

Ōta Hideo, 1978, "Nenshi undō" [The Nien movement], in Kōza Chūgoku kingendaishi, ed. Nozawa Yutaka and Tanaka Masatoshi, Tokyo, vol. 1, pp. 205–22.

Overmyer, D. L., 1976, Folk Buddhist Religion, Cambridge.

Paige, J., 1975, Agrarian Revolution, New York.

Pak, H., 1971, Documents of the Chinese Communist Party, 1927–1930, Hong Kong.

Pao Chih-ching, 1939, "Wan-pei ti hung-ch'iang-hui" [The Red Spears of northern Anhwei], K'ang-chan-chung ti Chung-kuo nung-ts'un tung-t'ai.

Parsons, J. B., 1970, Peasant Rebellions of the Late Ming Dynasty, Tucson.

P'ei-hsien chih, 1920 [Gazetteer of P'ei County], ed. Yü Yün-shu.

P'eng Teh-huai, 1942, "Kuan-yü Chi-nan kung-tso ti i-chien" [An opinion on the work in Tsinan], Shantung.

Perkins, D. H., 1969, Agricultural Development in China, 1368–1968, Chicago.

Po-chou chih, 1894 [Gazetteer of Po County], ed. Yüan Teng-yün.

Po-hsien chih lüeh, 1936 [Annals of Po County].

Polachek, J., 1973, "Secret Societies in China and the Republican Revolution," Journal of Asian Studies, 32(3), pp. 483–87.

Popkin, S., 1979, The Rational Peasant, Berkeley.

Powell, J. B., 1925, "New Lung-Hai Railway Connects Central Asia with the Sea at Haichow," China Weekly Review, 33(1), pp. 15–22.

Purcell, V., 1963, The Boxer Uprising, Cambridge.

Rape, C. B., 1927, "Supernatural Soldiers in the Yangtze Gorges," Decimal File on China, 1910–1929, Microfilm #893/9870.

Rappaport, R. A., 1968, Pigs for the Ancestors, New Haven.

———, 1971, "Nature, Culture and Ecological Anthropology," in Man, Culture, and Society, ed. H. Shapiro, Oxford, pp. 237–67.

Rawlinson, F., 1905, "A Study of the Rebellions in China," Chinese Recorder, 36, pp. 107–17.

Rawski, E. S., 1972, Agricultural Change and the Peasant Economy of South China, Cambridge.

Redfield, R., 1965, Peasant Society and Culture, Chicago.

Sahlins, M., 1964, "Culture and Environment: The Study of Cultural Ecology," in *Horizons of Anthropology*, ed. S. Tax, Chicago, pp. 132–47.

Sano Manabu, 1958, *Sano Manabu chosakushū* [The collected works of Sano Manabu], Tokyo.

Santōsho keizai chōsa shiryō, 1936 [Materials on an investigation of the economy of Shantung Province].

Satomi Hajime, 1927, "Kōsōkai monogatari" [The story of the Red Spears], *Shina*, 18 (11), pp. 126–34.

Schram, S. R., 1964, *The Political Thought of Mao Tse-tung*, London.

———, 1966, "Mao Tse-tung and Secret Societies," *China Quarterly*, 27, pp. 1–13.

Scott, J. C., 1976, *The Moral Economy of the Peasant*, New Haven.

Scott, J. C., and B. J. Kerkvliet, 1977, "How Traditional Rural Patrons Lose Legitimacy," in *Friends, Followers, and Factions*, ed. S. W. Schmidt, J. C. Scott, C. Lande, and L. Gausti, Berkeley.

SCSH (*Shih-ch'ao sheng-hsün*) [Sacred instructions of ten reign periods], Peking.

Selden, M., 1972, *The Yenan Way in Revolutionary China*, Cambridge.

Shan-hsien chih, 1936 [Gazetteer of Shan County], ed. Han Chia-hui.

Shan-tung chin-tai-shih tzu-liao, 1957 [Materials on contemporary Shantung history], Tsinan.

Shan-yü, 1927, "Nan-chih yü-pei min-chung fan-k'ang Feng-chün ch'ing-hsing" [The condition of popular resistance to the Feng Army in south Chihli and north Honan], *Hsiang-tao*, 188, pp. 2018–19.

Shen-chou, 1926, "Kuo-min-chün ti-erh-chün chih shih-pai" [The defeat of the Second National Army], *Hsiang-tao*, 147, pp. 1369–71.

Shen Chung-teh, 1926, "Hung-ch'iang-hui yü nung-min yün-tung" [The Red Spears and the peasant movement], *Nung-min yün-tung*, 9.

Shen-pao ["The Shun Pao"], Shanghai.

Shen Ping, 1960, *Huang-ho t'ung-k'ao* [General study of the Yellow River], Taipei.

Shen, T. H., 1951, *Agricultural Resources in China*, Ithaca.

Sheridan, J. B., 1966, *Chinese Warlord: The Career of Feng Yü-hsiang*, Stanford.

Shih-pao [The eastern times], Shanghai.

Shimizu Minoru, 1977, "Nengun no hanran ni tsuite" [The Nien Army uprising], *Nagoya Daigaku Bungakubu Kenkyū Ronshū*, 24, pp. 1–20.

Shina no dōran to Santō nōson, 1930 [China's chaos and the villages of Shantung], Dairen.

Shina sobieito undō no kenkyū, 1934 [A study of the Chinese soviet movement], Tokyo.

"Shiyō no nōson," 1942–43 [A village in Ssu-yang], *Shimmin Undō*, 3 (9–12), 4 (1).

Silbert, W. L., 1915, "The Huai River Conservancy Project," *U.S. Army Corps of Engineers, Professional Memoirs*, 7(31), pp. 113–20.

Skinner, G. W., 1971, "Chinese Peasants and the Closed Community: An Open and Shut Case," *Comparative Studies in Society and History*, 13, pp. 270–381.

————, 1977, *Cities in Late Imperial China*, Stanford.

Skocpol, T., 1979, *States and Social Revolutions*, London.

Slawinski, R., 1972, "The Red Spears in the Late 1920s," in *Popular Movements and Secret Societies*, ed. J. Chesneaux, pp. 201–11.

Smith, A. H., 1970, *Village Life in China*, Boston.

Solomon, R., 1971, *Mao's Revolution and the Chinese Political Culture*, Berkeley.

Ssu-hsien chih lüeh, 1936 [Annals of Ssu County], ed. Lu Feng-chang.

Steward, J., 1955, *Theory of Culture Change*, Urbana.

STSP (*Shun-t'ien shih-pao*), Peking.

Su-huai, 1926, "Ho-nan chün-shih chuang-k'uang yü cheng-chih" [The military situation and political future of Honan], *Hsiang-tao*, 169, pp. 1713–14.

Su-lien yin-mou wen-cheng hui-pien, 1928 [Collection of documentary evidence of the Soviet conspiracy], ed. Chang Kuo-ch'en, Peking. Reprinted by the Center for Chinese Research Materials, Washington, D.C., 1974.

"Su-tung ch'ün-chung kung-tso tsung-chieh," 1943 [Summary of mass work in Su-tung], FH, 1(5), pp. 59–82.

Su-wan pien-ch'ü wei hsiao-ch'ing hsiao-ku t'u-fei lien-ho hsün-ling, 1945 [United proclamation for liquidating local bandits in the Kiangsu-Anhwei Border Region].

Suemitsu Takayoshi, 1932, *Shina no himitsu kessha to jizen kessha* [Chinese secret societies and philanthropic societies], Dairen.

Sui-ning-hsien chih, 1887 [Gazetteer of Sui-ning County], ed. Ting Hsien.

Suzuki Chūsei, 1952, *Shinchō chūkishi kenkyū* [History of the middle Ch'ing], Tokyo.

SYT (Shang-yü-tang) [Imperial edict record book] in National Palace Museum, Taipei. Citations given with reign year and date according to lunar calendar.

Ta-ch'ing lü-li hui-t'ung hsin-ts'uan, 1874 [Collection of laws during the Ch'ing], ed. Yao Yü-hsiang.

Ta-kung-pao ["L'Impartial"], Tientsin.

Tai Hsüan-chih, 1963, *I-ho-t'uan yen-chiu* [Studies of the Boxers], Taipei.

————, 1973, *Hung-ch'iang-hui* [The Red Spears], Taipei.

T'ai-p'ing t'ien-kuo, 1950 [The Taiping Rebellion], ed. Hsiang Ta, Shanghai.

Tanaka Tadao, 1929, "Chung-kuo nung-min ti li-ts'un wen-t'i" [The problem of village out-migration among Chinese peasants], in *Chung-kuo nung-min wen-t'i yü nung-min yün-tung*, ed. Wang Chung-ming, Shanghai.

————, 1930, *Kakumei shina nōson no jisshoteki kenkyū* [A definitive study of revolutionary China's villages], Tokyo.

————, 1934, *Chung-kuo nung-yeh ching-chi tzu-liao* [Materials on China's agricultural economy], Shanghai.

————, 1936, *Kindai shina nōson no hōkai to nōmin tōsō* [Peasant struggles and the destruction of contemporary Chinese villages], Tokyo.

Tang-p'ai tiao-ch'a chou-pao [Party investigation weekly], 20.

Tchekanov, N., 1960, "Kuan-yü nien-chün ch'i-i ti li-shih fen-ch'i wen-t'i" [On the question of the periodization of the history of the Nien Army uprising], *An-hui shih-hsüeh*, 2, pp. 9–23.

————, 1970, "La plate-forme ideologique du Niandang," in *Mouvements populaires et sociétés secrètes en Chine du XIXᵉ et XXᵉ siècles*, ed. J. Chesneaux, Paris, pp. 196–204.

Teng Ssu-yü, 1961, *The Nien Army and Their Guerrilla Warfare, 1851–1868*, Paris.

T'eng-hsien chih, 1846 [Gazetteer of T'eng County], ed. Wang Yung-li.

Thaxton, R., 1975a, "When Peasants Took Power: Toward a Theory of Peasant Revolution in China," doctoral dissertation, University of Wisconsin.

————, 1975b, "Tenants in Revolution: The Tenacity of Traditional Morality," *Modern China*, 1(3), pp. 323–57.

Ts'ao Mu-ch'ing, 1956, "Kuan-yü nien-chün i-ming ti chien-shih" [A brief explanation of the name "Nien Army"], *Li-shih chiao-hsüeh*, pp. 43–44.

Tsou-hsien chih, 1716 [Gazetteer of Tsou County], ed. Chou I.

Tsou Jen-meng, 1940, "An-hui pao-an t'uan-tui" [Anhwei's peace-protection corps], *K'ang-chien-chung chih An-hui*.

Tsou Wan-chi, 1934, "An-hui Hsü-i-hsien ti nung-ts'un kai-k'uang" [Overview of villages in Anhwei's Hsü-i County], in *Chung-kuo nung-ts'un ching-chi tzu-liao*, ed. Feng Ho-fa, Shanghai, pp. 86–90.

Tu-hsiu, 1926, "Hung-ch'iang-hui yü Chung-kuo ti nung-min pao-tung" [The Red Spears and Chinese peasant disturbances], *Hsiang-tao*, 158.

Tuan Yi-fu, 1970, *China*, London.

Tung-p'ing-hsien chih, 1935 [Gazetteer of Tung-p'ing County], ed. Liu Ch'ing-yu.

T'ung-shan-hsien chih, 1926 [Gazetteer of T'ung-shan County], ed. Wang Chia-hsien.

"T'ung-shan nung-ts'un ching-chi tiao-ch'a," 1931 [Investigation of the village economy of T'ung-shan], in *Chung-kuo nung-ts'un ching-chi tzu-liao*, ed. Feng Ho-fa, Shanghai, pp. 385–87.

Tzu-chen, 1927, "Fan-feng chan-cheng-chung ti yü-pei t'ien-men-hui" [The northern Honan Heavenly Gate Society during the anti-Feng war], *Hsiang-tao*, 197, pp. 2163–64.

Vayda, A. P., 1968, "Hypotheses about Functions of War," in *War: The Anthropology of Armed Conflict and Aggression*, ed. M. F. Fried, M. Harris, and R. Murphy, Garden City, N.Y.

―――, 1976, *War in Ecological Perspective*, New York.

"Waihoku sokan henku gyōsei kōsho no setchi," 1942 [Establishment of the Huai-pei Kiangsu-Anhwei border region administrative office], *Jōhō*, 60, pp. 19–22.

"Waikaishō chūkyō jijō," 1945 [CCP affairs in Huai-hai], *Jōhō*, 39.

Wakimura Takeko, 1968, "Nengun ni kansuru hitokosa" [A perspective on the Nien Army], *Chūgoku Kankei Ronsetsu Shiryō*, 10(4), pp. 174–87.

Wan-pao [Anhwei news], Hofei.

Wang Fan-t'ing, 1970, "Kuo-yang she-chih shih-mo" [The ins and outs of the construction of Kuo-yang], *An-hui wen-hsien*, 1(1), pp. 36–40.

―――, 1975, "Nien-fei yü Shan-tung Li-shih nü-tzu" [The Nien and Ms. Li of Shantung], *Chang-ku*, 41, pp. 15–20.

Wang I-k'o, 1932, *Nung-ts'un tzu-wei yen-chiu* [A study of village defense], K'ai-feng.

Wang Kuang-yü and Li Jen-chih, 1943, "Ssu-ling-sui ch'ün-chung kung-tso ti hsien-chuang yü ching-yen" [The condition and experience of mass work in Ssu-ling-sui], FH, 5, pp. 35–42.

Wang Ting-an, 1889, *Hsiang-chün chi* [Records of the Hunan Army].

Wang Tsung-yü, 1964, "Shih-lun Pai Lang ch'i-i ti hsing-chih" [A preliminary discussion of the character of the Pai Lang uprising], *Shih-hsüeh yüeh-k'an*, 12, pp. 20–24.

Wang Wen-ch'ang, 1944, "Shun-ho-ch'ü san-ko hu-chu-tsu ti chien-ch'a" [Investigation of three mutual aid teams in Shun-ho District], *Cheng-fu kung-tso t'ung-hsün*, 30, pp. 1–8.

Wang Yeh-chien, 1973, *Land Taxation in Imperial China, 1750–1911*, Cambridge.

Wang Yu-chuang, 1940, "The Organization of a Typical Guerrilla Area in South Shantung," in *The Chinese Army*, ed. E. F. Carlson, New York, pp. 104–06.

Wang Yün-chao and Sung-chün, 1944, "Ch'en-yü-hsiang ch'un-ch'i tsu-chih hu-chu ti ching-yen" [The experience of organizing mutual aid in Ch'en-yü-hsiang during the spring], FH, 17, pp. 34–54.

Wang Yung-jen, 1927, "Ta-tao-hui" [The Big Swords], *I-ching*, 25, pp. 75–77.

Watanabe Atsushi, 1967, "Shimmatsu karōkai no seiritsu, 1891-nen chōkō ryūiki kiji keikaku no haikei" [The establishment of the Elder Brothers Society in the late Ch'ing: Background on the planned 1891 uprising in the Yangtze delta], in *Kindai Chūgoku nōson shakaishi kenkyū*, pp. 109–98.

WCT (Wai-chi-tang) [Extra records] in National Palace Museum, Taipei. Citations are given with reign year followed by month and day of lunar calendar.

Webber, L., 1927, Decimal File on China, 1910–1929, Microfilm #893.43.

Wen Hui-chi, 1927, "Hung-ch'iang-hui" [Red Spears], *I-ching*, 25, p. 77.

Wilbur, C. M., 1956, *Documents on Communism, Nationalism, and Soviet Advisers in China, 1918–1927*, New York.

Wo-yü, 1927, "Hung-ch'iang-hui chih nei-jung" [The content of the Red Spears], *Kuo-wen chou-pao*, 4(28), p. 2.

Woddis, J., 1960, *Africa: The Roots of Revolt*, London.

Wolf, E. R., 1966, *Peasants*, Englewood Cliffs, N.J.

———, 1969, *Peasant Wars in the Twentieth Century*, New York.

Wu Chih-ch'uan, 1944, "Chu-hu ch'ün-chung ch'u-chien yün-tung" [The weed-out traitors campaign in Chu-hu], FH, 9, pp. 49–60.

Wu Chih-p'u, 1944, "Lu-hsi pan-nien ch'ün-chung kung-tso" [Half a year's mass work in the western areas], FH, 17, pp. 7–33.

Wu Han, 1961, "Nien yü nien-chün pi-chi" [Notes on the Nien and the Nien Army], *Min-chien wen-hsüeh*, 8, pp. 26–37.

Wu Hua-to, "Wo ken fu-ch'in tang hung-chün" [I and father joined the Red Army], HCPP, 3, pp. 39–44.

Wu Ping-jo, 1927, "Huai-ho liu-yü ti nung-min chuang-k'uang" [The condition of peasants in the Huai River valley], *Tung-fang tsa-chih*, 24(16), pp. 53–54.

Wu Shou-p'eng, 1930, "Tou-liu yü nung-ts'un ching-chi shih-tai ti Hsü-hai ko shu" [The lingering of Hsü-chou and Hai-chou in the era of village economy], *Tung-fang tsa-chih*, 27(6, 7), pp. 69–79, 59–70.

Yang Chi-hua, 1933, *Wan-pei nung-ts'un she-hui ching-chi shih-k'uang* [Socioeconomic conditions in northern Anhwei villages], Nanking.

Yang, M. C., 1945, *A Chinese Village: Taitou, Shantung Province*, New York.

YCT (Yüeh-che-tang) [Monthly memorial records] in National Palace Museum, Taipei. Citations given with reign year followed by month and day of lunar calendar.

Yokota Minoru, Clipping File of Chinese Newspapers in Tōyō Bunko. Volume 25 deals with the Red Spears.

Yokoyama Suguru, 1964, "Kenhoki, Santō no kōryō fūchō to mindan" [Shantung's wave of tax resistance and the militia during the Hsien-feng period], *Rekishi Kyōiku*, 12(9), pp. 42–50.

Yüan Chia-san, 1911, "Tuan-min-kung chi" [Collected works of Prince Tuan-min], *Hsiang-ch'eng Yüan-shih-chia chi*, Peking.

Yung-ch'eng-hsien chih, 1901 [Gazetteer of Yung-ch'eng County], ed. Hu Tsan-ts'ai.

Character List

ch'ang-fa-hui 長髮會

chen 鎮

chen-wu-tao 真武道

chieh-nien 結捻

chin 斤

chin-chung-chao 金鐘罩

ch'ing 頃

ch'ing-pang 清幫

ch'ing-shen 請神

ch'ing-tao-hui 清道會

ch'iu-chia-tzu 仇家子

chiu-hsien-hui 九仙會

ch'ü 區

ch'u-chien yün-tung 屈助奸運動

chün 郡

chung-hsiao-t'uan 忠孝團

fang 方

hei-ch'i-hui 黑旗會

hei-ch'iang-hui 黑槍會

hei-ch'iang-hui 黑鎗會

heng-ha-hui 哼哈會

hou-tzu-hui 猴子會

hsiang 鄉

hsiang-chu 箱主

hsiang-t'ang 香堂

hsiao-ch'i-chu 小旗主

hsiao-i-hui 孝衣會

hsiao-mao-hui 孝帽會

hsiao-tao-hui 小刀會

hsieh-tou 械鬥

hsien 縣

hsien-t'ien-tao 仙天道

hsiung-ti-hui	兄弟會
hsüeh-chang	學長
hu-t'uan	湖團
hua-hui	花會
hua-lan-hui	花籃會
Huai-pei	淮北
huang-ch'i-hui	黃旗會
huang-ch'iang-hui	黃槍會
huang-ling-hui	黃綾會
huang-men	黃門
huang-sha-hui	黃沙會
huang-tao-hui	黃道會
hui-chang	會長
hui-men	會門
hui-t'ang	會堂
hung-ch'i-hui	紅旗會
hung-ch'iang-hui	紅槍會
hung-hsüeh	紅學
hung-men	紅門
hung-pang	紅幫

hung-sha-hui	紅沙會
hung-ying-hui	紅纓會
i-kuan-tao	一貫道
i-tao-fei	曳刀匪
jen-i-hui	仁義會
jen kan-lao-tzu	認乾老子
kan-ch'ing	感情
k'an-ch'ing	看青
k'an-pien	看邊
kang-ch'a-hui	鋼叉會
k'e	客
k'uai-p'iao	快票
kuang-tan-hui	光蛋會
kung-ch'an kung-ch'i	共產共妻
k'ung-ming-hui	孔明會
lan-ch'ing-hui	闌青會
lan-ying-hui	藍纓會
lao-niu-hui	老牛會
lao-shih	老師
li	里

li-chiao 理教

liang 兩

Liang-shan-po 梁山泊

lien-chuang-hui 联莊會

lu 路

lü-ch'i-hui 綠旗會

lü-ch'iang-hui 綠槍會

lü-lin 綠林

ma-i-hui 麻衣會

mao-lan-hui 毛籃會

meng-chu 盟主

miao-tao-hui 妙道會 廟道會

min-t'uan 民團

mou 畝

mu-kou-hui 毋狗會

nieh-tzu-hui 捏子會

nien 捻

niu-t'ou-hui 牛頭會

pai-ch'iang-hui 白槍會

pai-i-hui 白衣會

pai-i-ts'u 白衣祠

pai-t'ou-hui 白頭會

pai-ying-hui 白纓會

pang-k'ou 幫口

pao-an t'uan-tui 保安團隊

pao-chang 保長

pao-chia 保甲

pao-chia-chang 保甲長

pao-wei-t'uan 保衛團

p'eng-min 棚民

san-chiao-t'ang 三教堂

san-fan(-tzu) 三番(子)

san pu-kuan 三不管

shan-tzu-hui 扇子會

she 社

shen-hsien-tao 神仙道

shen-ta-hui 神打會

sheng-hsien-tao 聖賢道

shun-tao-hui 順刀會

sun-pai-ling-hui 孫百靈會

ta-chi-ch'u 打基礎

ta-ch'i-chu 大旗主

ta-chia-tzu 搭架子

ta-han meng-chu 大漢盟主

ta-han ming-ming-wang 大漢明命王

ta-han yung-wang 大漢永王

ta-hsien-hui 大仙會

ta-ming 大明

ta-tao-hui 大刀會

ta-tao k'uo-fu 大刀闊斧

t'ang-chu 趟主

t'ang-chu 堂主

tao-shih 導師

t'i-t'ien hsing-tao 替天行道

t'ieh-pu-shan 鐵布衫

t'ien-hsien-tao 天仙道

t'ien-huang-hui 天皇會

t'ien-men-hui 天門會

t'ien-shen-hui 天神會

t'ing 亭

ting-ting 定釘

t'o-tao-hui 拖刀會

tsei 賊

tu 都

t'u-fei 土匪

t'u-kan 土桿

t'u-k'e mao-tun 土客矛盾

t'u-nien 土捻

tui 隊

t'ung 統

tzu-wei-tui 自衛隊

wan-fei 皖匪

wan-kuo tao-teh-hui 萬國道德會

wei-t'uan 偽團

wen 文

wu 武

wu 伍

wu-chi-tao 無極道

wu-lung-hui 五龍會

yao-hui 搖會

yeh-kuei 夜跪

yeh-tao-fei 掖刀匪

yen-kuang-hui 眼光會

yin 引

ying-ch'iang-hui 纓槍會

ying-t'ou-erh 硬頭兒

ying-t'u-tui 硬肚隊

yü-chai 圩寨

yu-chi pu-tui 游擊部隊

yu-min 游民

yu-nien 油捻

yüan 元

yüeh-ming-hui 月明會

Index

I-yang County (Honan), 166
Indebtedness, 52–53, 241–42
Infanticide, 51
Irrigation, 11–14, 19, 24f, 30, 45, 259

Japanese, 182–86, 211, 225–32 passim

K'ai-feng (city, Honan), 34, 165–66, 175
K'ai-hsien County (Honan), 270
K'an-ch'ing ("watching the green"), 81
K'an-pien ("watching the borders"), 82
Kao brothers (Nien chiefs), 111
Kaoliang (sorghum), 22–24, 37, 41
Kiangsu, 20–21, 27, 34; peasants in, 46, 52, 54–57; feuds in, 76, 171–72; forts in, 92–93; bandits in, 100, 154; Nien in, 103–4; Red Spears in, 157–58, 176, 181; CCP in, 221; protective societies in, 272. See also individual places by name
Kidnaping, 65, 108, 133–39
Kinship: and predatory strategy, 60; and banditry, 69, 106; feuds, 75–78; and protective strategy, 80; and Nien, 128, 131–32; and mutual aid teams, 244–45; and rebellion, 251n, 252
Ku-shih County (Honan), 116–17, 141
Kuan County (Shantung), 226–27
Kuei-teh County (Honan), 159n
Kung Teh (Nien chief), 124n, 131, 143
K'ung-ming-hui (society), 273
Kuomintang, 160–61, 176–86 passim, 205, 207
Kuo-yang County (Anhwei), 19, 27n, 37, 147, 182–83; salt riot in, 61–62; forts in, 90; Nien in, 124n, 151n; Red Spears in, 167

Laborers (hired agricultural), 29–30, 51–52, 81–83, 242
Landholdings, 25–33, 240
Landlords, 27, 32; hostility toward, 170, 181; and CCP, 209, 217–23 passim, 230f, 240–43
Lao Yang-jen (Old Foreigner), 66, 90, 107n, 154f
Lawsuits, 78–79
Li Chao-shou (Nien-Taiping chief), 141–42
Li-ch'eng County (Shantung), 237–38
Li Hsiu-ch'eng (Taiping leader), 142, 144

Li Kuang-yen (sect leader), 204
Li Pao-kuo (Red Spear leader), 258
Li Shih-lin (Nien chief), 115
Li Ta-chang (CCP cadre), 227, 231–32
Li Ta-chao, 215
Lien-chuang-hui (militia), 178, 179n, 180, 229, 231
Lien-shui County (Kiangsu), 176
Limitless Way Society, 204, 269
Lin-ch'eng County (Shantung), 65, 68–69, 74, 157
Lin-huai-kuan (town, Anhwei), 33
Ling-pi County (Anhwei), 107, 181
Liu E-lang (Nien chief), 142–43
Liu Hei-ch'i (bandit), 228
Liu Jui-lung (CCP cadre), 211, 228
Liu Kou (Nien chief), 145, 150n
Liu Shao-ch'i, 225f, 228–29
Liu T'ang, 133–39
Liu Teh-p'ei (militia leader), 126
Liu Tzu-chiu (CCP cadre), 212, 233
Liu Yü-chu (CCP cadre), 211
Loan associations, 53, 245
Loess, 14, 18
Long-haired Way Society, 231
Long Hair Society, 270
Long Spear Society, 126–27
Lo-ning County (Honan), 166
Lo-yang County (Honan), 179
Lou Pai-hsün (Red Spear leader), 164–66, 175
Loyal Filial Corps, 271
Lu-i County (Honan), 31n, 45, 82, 271
Lu-shih County (Honan), 161
Lung-hai Railroad, 34, 163n, 164

Ma P'i-hsien (bandit), 101
Males, surplus of, 51–52
Market system, 28, 33
Market towns, 90, 240–43
Meng-ch'eng County (Anhwei), 27n, 104, 120–29 passim, 134, 151n, 258, 282
Merchants, 34f
Messianic groups, 203
Miao P'ei-lin (militia leader), 140n, 142
Miao-tao-hui (society), 272
Migration, 54–57, 89n, 171–72
Militia: and Nien, 84–85, 122–23, 125–26; in Huai-pei, 84–88; and tax resistance, 86–87; oppose government, 87–88, 152–53; and

strategy, 59, 94–95; and feuds, 75; and communities, 80–81; organization of 80–81; crop watching, 81–84; militia, 84–88; and forts, 88–94; and Nien, 122–27; and Red Spears, 160, 165, 172, 186, 198, 201, 205–7; and CCP, 228, 246–47; and revolts, 253f, 258

Railroads, 33–34, 163f. *See also individual railroads by name*
Rebellion: defined, 2*n;* strategy for survival, 3, 255; and environment, 3–11 *passim,* 50, 249–52, 257; and peasants, 7f, 128*n,* 248–49; legacy of, 7, 256–57; and salt smuggling, 61–62, 106; and banditry, 70–72; and feuds, 75, 79–80; and Nien, 120–21; and religion, 121, 153; and army, 123–24; and secret societies, 149–50, 254–56; in Huai-pei, 149–50; and competition, 249, 252, 254; cycles of, 250; and kinship, 251*n,* 252; and social classes, 251–52; timing of, 252–53; and capitalism, 253; and protective-predatory dichotomy, 253f; and revolution, 255–56; and peripheral areas, 261
Red Army, 223*n,* 224
Red Beards, 61, 99
Red Flag Society, 157
Red Gate Society, 269
Red Lantern societies, 204
Red Sand Society, 269
Red Spears, 59; and protective strategy, 6, 160, 165, 172, 186, 198, 201, 205–7; and taxes, 40, 157–66 *passim,* 175–82 *passim,* 186; and feuds, 80, 170–72; and Old Cow societies, 110, 156, 172, 204; origins, 153–56, 284–85; and Boxers, 153–54, 157, 200; and religion, 154, 156, 170f, 176–77, 186–97, 206–7; and militia, 154–59 *passim,* 165, 178–80; and natural disasters, 154; and bandits, 154, 159, 169f, 184; and local defense, 155; and village institutionalization, 156; early activities, 157–60; oppose government, 157–69 *passim,* 174–77; and forts, 158; teachers, 158, 178, 187–200 *passim;* relations with

government, 158–59, 177–86; and warlords, 160–67, 174–77; and railroads, 163f; collect taxes, 164, 166; and foreigners, 167, 195–96; and predation, 167–69, 172; leaders, 171, 179, 196, 199–200; and Christianity, 171, 195–96; and local poor, 173–74; numbers, 174, 197, 232, 288; messianic platform of, 176–77; oppose Japanese, 182–86; claim invulnerability, 184*n,* 186, 190–97 *passim;* initiation rites, 187–89; training of, 187ff, 193; organization of, 197–205; codes, 201–2, 267–68, 288; variations among groups, 203–5; compared with Mafia, 206; and CCP, 213–25 *passim,* 229–35 *passim,* 258
Red Swastika Society, 238
Red Tassel Society, 272
Religion, 42, 110; and rebellion, 121, 153; and Red Spears, 154, 156, 170f, 176–77, 186–97, 206–7
Rent reduction campaign, 239–43
Rents, 30–32
Resources, 3*n,* 4–5, 47, 52, 59, 80
Revolution, 2*n,* 7, 255–56

Salt smuggling, 60–62, 98–108 *passim,* 115, 126
Secret societies, 6, 149–50, 204, 207, 229–37 *passim,* 254–56, 291
Seng-ko-lin-ch'in (Prince), 87, 96, 124
Sex ratio, 51–52, 277
Shang-ch'iu County (Honan), 77, 128, 150*n*
Shanghai, 54–55
Shantung: bandits in, 66, 67*n,* 154; tax revolts, 87; Nien in, 103, 107, 127; militia in, 122, 178, 180; and Boxers, 153; Red Spears in, 157, 196*n;* secret societies in, 204; protective societies in, 269–70. *See also individual places by name*
Shed people (*p'eng-min*), 56
Shou County (Anhwei), 38f, 67*n,* 76–77, 110f, 127, 129, 209
Shun-teh County (Hopei), 271
Silver, 39–40, 86
Small Red School (sect), 170
Small Sword Society, 171f, 176, 238–39, 272
Smooth Sword Society, 100